From Morality to Mayhem

For Margaret and Ray —

From Morality to Mayhem
The Fall and Rise of the English School Story

All good wishes —

Julian Lovelock

Julian Lovelock

L

The Lutterworth Press

The Lutterworth Press
P.O. Box 60
Cambridge
CB1 2NT
United Kingdom

www.lutterworth.com
publishing@lutterworth.com

ISBN: 978 0 7188 9540 2

British Library Cataloguing in Publication Data
A record is available from the British Library

First published by The Lutterworth Press, 2018

For the Pupils and Staff of
Akeley Wood School
Buckingham

1978 - 2005

Contents

Acknowledgements

The author and publisher would like to thank the following for permission to reproduce material in this book: Peters Fraser & Dunlop on behalf of the Estate of Alec Waugh (Alec Waugh, *The Loom of Youth*); Harriman House (Humphry Berkeley, *The Life and Death of Rochester Sneath*); David Higham Associates (Geoffrey Trease, *No Boats on Bannermere* and William Mayne, *A Swarm in May*); House of Stratus (Anthony Buckeridge, *Jennings Goes to School* and *Jennings at Large*); the Agency (Giles Cooper, *Unman, Wittering and Zigo*); Enid Blyton Entertainment (Enid Blyton, *The Naughtiest Girl in the School*, *The Twins at St Clare's* and *First Term at Malory Towers*); The Lutterworth Press (Anthony Buckeridge, *Rex Milligan's Busy Term*); Paper Lion Ltd (the novels of Gene Kemp); The Blair Partnership (*Harry Potter and the Philosopher's Stone*, Copyright © J.K. Rowling 1997); and Andy Mulligan and the Jane Turnbull Literary Agency (Andy Mulligan, *Ribblestrop*). While the author has made every effort to gain permission from copyright holders of other previously published material reproduced in this study, he would be pleased to hear from any he has been unable to contact.

The author would particularly like to thank Dr Hazel Sheeky for taking the trouble to read through a draft of the text and for her wise advice.

Referencing

There are so many editions (including ebooks) of the novels discussed in this study that I have thought it best to give the first publication date of each and to reference quotations by chapter and not by page. Full publication details and page numbers are given for critical and biographical works to which I have referred.

Introduction

It is often said that the stories we read when we are young are the ones that influence us the most, and school stories shaped many of our childhoods. When we revisit them now, they evoke not just a general nostalgia for school, but a more personal nostalgia for our own schooldays of which they were an important part. We remember where we were when we first read them, who our teachers and friends were, what they meant to us. We may or may not have attended schools like those in the stories, but they were still special places in our imagination, where we escaped from our parents and could associate closely with the triumphs and disasters, the comedy and the tragedy, of the heroes and heroines of those far off, or not so far off, schooldays. How did these stories come to be written? How did they speak to us then, and how do they speak to us now? How did (or do) they both reflect and shape their age? In many ways this is a book about going back: some of us go back further than others, and we go back with very different emotions.

My own earliest memory of school stories is of Enid Blyton's *Malory Towers* series (1946-51). I had devoured Blyton's *Famous Five* (1942-63) and *Secret Seven* (1949-63) novels, and this was an intriguing and exotic sequel, borrowed from a girl who lived close by. After the *Malory Towers* adventures, I read Anthony Buckeridge's larkish tales of Jennings and Darbishire, and William Mayne's enchanting and sometimes mystical tales of choir school life; but I disliked Billy Bunter and his mates at Greyfriars whose exaggerated humour was largely lost on me. During my early teens, I enjoyed some of Thomas Hughes's *Tom Brown's Schooldays* (1857) – it must have been on a compulsory reading list – William Goldings's *Lord of the Flies* (1954), and Rosalind Erskine's *The Passion Flower Hotel* (1962), disguised in a brown paper cover and giving an alternative and titillating account of what girls might get up to when lessons are over.

A little later, and much later, other school stories, written for an adult audience, crept onto my bookshelf: Evelyn Waugh's *Decline and Fall* (1925); E.R. Braithwaite's *To Sir With Love* (1959); Muriel Spark's *The Prime of Miss Jean Brodie* (1961); Humphry Berkeley's incomparable *The Life and Death of Rochester Sneath* (1963), which is more proof, if it is needed, that real life (here, real headmasters) can outdo in pomposity and stupidity anything an author imagines; and Zoë Heller's disturbing *Notes on a Scandal* (2003). Plays and films lie largely outside the scope of the present study, but in the theatre few are unmoved by Terence Rattigan's *The Browning Version* (1948), Alan Bennett's *Forty Years On* (1968) and *The History Boys* (2004) display Bennett's familiar and idiosyncratic nostalgia, and the various incarnations of *St Trinian's* are an anarchic antidote to the prim girls' schools stories that they satirise.

*

It is generally accepted that the first school story – and the first novel written specifically for children – is Sarah Fielding's *The Governess, or The Little Female Academy* (1749).[1] It describes ten days in the life of Mrs Teachum's 'little Female Academy' for nine girls, aged from eight to fourteen. In the eighteenth century, very few children would have gone to school, but like the generations of children who followed, they could still go there in their imagination and enjoy vicariously its friendships, adventures and disasters. Notice how 'entertainment' ranks alongside 'instruction' as an aim for the Academy: the Academy is 'calculated for the entertainment and instruction of young ladies in their education', and is clearly influenced by the belief of John Locke (1632-1704) that learning should not be regarded as work but as something to be enjoyed.[2] Locke also believed that children should learn

---

1. Sarah Fielding was the sister of the more famous Henry Fielding, author of *The History of Tom Jones* (also published in 1749); she was a member of the Blue Stocking Society, which encouraged women to discuss literature and the arts, and advocated women's education. The story was originally published anonymously.
2. John Locke, *Some Thoughts Concerning Education* (1693).

self-government through the wise teaching of a 'governor', so not only is Mrs Teachum's determination (as 'governess') that her pupils should learn as much as possible through their own discussions remarkably progressive, but the use of a child (Jenny Peace) to draw out lessons enables her to avoid the sort of patronising adult narrator that was to become horribly common.

School stories written from Victorian times until the middle of the twentieth century are usually about middle- and upper-class children in boarding schools (since there was little education for anyone else). Thus, they are about a closed world within a world, about unworldly teachers in all sorts of ways standing *in loco parentis*, about an inevitably febrile atmosphere in which tensions and passions smoulder and enflame. Charles Dickens wrote about the hidden, cruel private boarding schools in Yorkshire, while in the *Chalet School* stories (1925-1970) Elinor Brent-Dyer went as far as taking her pupils across the English Channel to set up a school in Austria. Within their world, schools build their own history. They develop their own traditions, both good and bad, which are passed down from one generation to the next; they have their own hierarchies and even their own language.

Mavis Reimer makes the useful distinction between boarding schools that are 'little worlds' – real and fictional, reflecting and intertwined with the world outside, so the one prepares its pupils for the other – and 'worlds apart', where the school isolates its pupils from the world outside so it can pursue its own agenda until the time comes for their departure.[3] I think Reimer overstates the case, and the distinction is always a matter of degree, but, that said, the majority of boys' school stories fall into the former category. Public schools, in their prime in the second part of the nineteenth century and the first part of the twentieth century, were unashamedly nurseries of the British Empire, and although in school stories the Empire remains largely as a background,[4] if indeed it is mentioned at all, there is an underlying assumption that the young heroes are being prepared to play their part in the colonial world. In *Tom Brown's Schooldays*, for example, Tom's friend East leaves to join his regiment in India; in Reed's *The Fifth Form at St Dominic's*, Loman finds some sort of redemption farming in Australia; and in Kipling's *Stalky & Co.*, Stalky goes off to subdue the natives in the Khye-Keen Hills. In the same way, in girls' school stories, fathers return from their estates and plantations in distant parts to emotional reunions with their

---

3. Mavis Reimer, 'Traditions of the School Story', in M.O. Grenby and Andrea Immel (eds), *The Cambridge Companion to Children's Literature* (Cambridge: Cambridge University Press, 2009), pp. 209-225.
4. Rudyard Kipling's *Stalky & Co.* (1899) is, of course, an exception and is discussed in chapter 4.

daughters, and Sara Crewe in Frances Hodgson Burnett's *A Little Princess* (1905) is in part an exploration of the role of girls in the Empire. However, although girls' schools today are far more outward looking than previously, most fictional girls' schools depict 'worlds apart', where their pupils learn and grow in isolation, fiercely protected from the patriarchal society beyond.

It is, I think, the otherness of boarding schools, like the otherness of island literature (such as *Robinson Crusoe,* 1719; *Swiss Family Robinson,* 1812; and *Coral Island,* 1857) and that of fantasy worlds (such as Lewis Carroll's Wonderland, C. S. Lewis's Narnia, and J.R.R. Tolkien's Middle Earth) that once made boarding school stories attractive to readers from all backgrounds. Children who attended boarding schools could enjoy a vicarious pride, both in the fictional school and in their own battle scars, and could have their own social standing endorsed; and those who did not could imagine themselves lifted into an exclusive world, putting on the uniform, and joining in the scrapes and adventures of new and privileged friends. Given that boarding schools have only ever been attended by a small proportion of the population, and hardly exist in some countries where the tales told about them have also been read avidly, the fact that they have become an element of our national identity is likely to have been caused by the literature that they inspired over a comparatively short period of time. From *Tom Brown's Schooldays* until the early twentieth century, there was a torrent of often third-rate novels about the rapidly expanding boys' public school sector, characterised by beating, fagging, sporting prowess and muscular Christianity. However, after the First World War, not only did all but a few of these novels quickly – and deservedly – lose their appeal, but little else of note was subsequently written about boys' public schools apart from the enduring and widely read accounts of *Billy Bunter* and occasional sugary and nostalgic adult novels that kept the public school myth alive – like James Hilton's *Goodbye Mr Chips* (1934) and, much later, R.F. Delderfield's *To Serve Them All My Days* (1972). Since girls' schools are newer foundations, stories about them became popular just as the boys' stories were fading. These stories also had a longer life, perhaps because girls' schools rarely had the strange and sometimes cruel excesses of boys' schools, and perhaps because they are more about 'worlds apart' and so less tied to their era.

But the cultural changes since the Second World War changed schools and the stories about them as they changed so much else. Over the past half century, with the transformed social and educational landscape, boarding schools have become less self-serving and claustrophobic, and so even less interesting to the novelist, while day school pupils now do as much growing up outside school as they do in it. As a result, the tribulations of adolescence have been confronted in that new, often issue-based genre, young adult literature, and for thirty years (1978-2008) the world of the urban comprehensive school was dramatised for young people in the popular television series *Grange Hill*. Even so, the school story has managed to survive. Novels about day schools confront the struggles of children and teenagers more honestly than before, and those about boarding schools, having lost much of their inherent excitement, are discarding the commonplace and providing the starting point for fantastic adventure.

*

Critics and historians have written perceptively about school stories, often investigating the ways in which they both reflect and influence the culture of their time. Isabel Quigly's *The Heirs of Tom Brown: The English School Story* (1982) is an insightful survey, but after considering the Victorian classics of the genre, her emphasis is on novels written with an adult audience in mind; she devotes only one chapter to girls' school stories. Similarly, Jeffrey Richards's *Happiest Days: The Public Schools in English Fiction* (1988) is an illuminating study of boys' public school stories from a historian's point of view, but again *Billy Bunter* is the only story of the past one hundred years written for schoolchildren that it singles out for particular consideration. P.W. Musgrave's *From Brown to Bunter* (1985) also concentrates on boys' school stories and their historical context up to 1945, by which time, it argues, the genre was nearly at an end. It is especially useful in its exploration of the shift in the early twentieth century towards school stories written for an adult audience.

My different aim in *From Morality to Mayhem* has been to write about school stories written primarily for the younger reader – boys and girls aged between eight and fifteen, or thereabouts – and I have included those written up to the present day. In particular, I have focused on those stories that are either milestones in the development of the school story, or that react against the development and the wider attitudes in society that were driving it. Part I is about the remarkable expansion of boys' public schools in the nineteenth century and about the array of stories that grew up around them; most of the stories are conservative, in that they endorse and even trumpet the schools in which they are set, however barbarous they appear when we look back. Part II is about the stagnation of the boys' public schools between the First and Second World Wars and the consequent decline of the stories – though their popularity was maintained for a time by their publication in comics and magazines – and by the brief flowering of the preparatory school story; here, the best stories are more enlightened, highlighting the shortcomings of the schools and advocating change. Part III is about how the rise to prominence of girls' boarding schools in the first half of the twentieth century inspired a wave of girls' school stories, just as the boys' stories were beginning to wither. However, many of these stories are fantasies, sentimentalising their subject; too often they fail to recognise and even undermine the changing attitude to women and their education. Finally, Part IV is about the often unheralded regeneration of the school story. It focuses on the novels that have emerged since the 1950s, striking out in fresh directions and injecting new life into models from the past.

Children grow up quickly and schools are constantly in flux, so school stories for young readers are, by their nature, ephemeral. Today, for a number of reasons that will become clear, they may no longer attract the attention they once did, but the best of them are more skilfully written than their predecessors and more serious in their intent. It is premature to lament their passing.

Part I

Victorian School Days

Introductory: Education, Evangelism and Empire

The Victorian era shaped the English public school system – and on the whole it made a pretty poor job of it. It was a time when the pace of educational change was largely dictated by political considerations. Demands for democracy and revolution were in the air, and education held the key to progress. The middle classes, for whom there had previously been scant educational provision since the decline of grammar schools in the eighteenth century, would no longer be held back. ('Middle class' was in Victorian times, and still is, a term that yokes together a number of disparate groups, with different aims, occupations and interests – the coming together of a meritocracy, often at odds with itself, to challenge the vested interests of political power.)

Of course, many of what are often called public schools had been founded long before and, whatever their original charitable intentions, their main purpose had soon become the education of the social and political elite.[1] The King's School, Canterbury had been teaching boys

---

1. It is hard to define a public school. They are free from state control. In the nineteenth century, many grammar and proprietary schools evolved into public schools. The Headmasters' Conference (now the Headmasters' and Headmistresses' Conference) was founded in 1869, and today the heads of 283 British public schools and fifty-four international public schools are members. HMC schools set out to offer 'academic excellence coupled with a strong emphasis on pastoral care and exceptional co-curricular opportunities' (www.hmc.org.uk) – but these

since the sixth century and a number of other Church schools followed. Winchester College, arguably the first public school, was founded in 1382 by William Wykeham and, although its purpose was to provide entrants to New College, Oxford (also endowed by Wykeham to prepare students for the priesthood), it was notable for being independent of the Church. As well as Winchester College, other important early runners in the public schools' stakes included Westminster (1179 – with royal charters in 1541 and 1560), Eton (1440), St Paul's (1509), Shrewsbury (1552), Merchant Taylors' (1561), Rugby (1567), Harrow (1572) and Charterhouse (1611).

During the eighteenth century, such schools had become seats of anything but learning, characterised by bullying, beating, and sundry other brutalities. Masters were typically lazy and either unwilling or unable to control their charges.[2] Attempts to impose discipline could be futile and, on occasion, provoked violent resistance. For example, at Rugby in 1797 there was the 'Great Rebellion' in which a posse of senior pupils blew the door off the headmaster's classroom, burned their books, and holed up on the School's moated 'Island', only giving in when the local militia arrived with pikes and muskets. But context is important. Early Victorian society was starkly divided into rich and poor, and while boys of the upper and middle classes were enjoying or enduring the dubious pleasures of school, those of the working class were often toiling in mines, mills and factories, usually in appalling conditions, or even sold into slavery as apprentice chimney sweeps. Not surprisingly, working class children do not feature much in Victorian school stories.

The first half of the nineteenth century saw some improvement in the public schools, largely through the influence of Dr Thomas Arnold (headmaster of Rugby, 1828-41). The staff-student ratio at Rugby improved from 1:63 to 1:24, resulting in better discipline and a more humane relationship between masters and boys, and there was a similar trend elsewhere. But too often the culture of bullying and beating remained (death by bullying was not unknown) and, prompted by specific complaints about the mismanagement of Eton College, the nine schools mentioned above were subjected to an examination by the Clarendon Commission (1861-64).

---

qualities didn't materialise until the second half of the twentieth century. To avoid the exclusive label, and to emphasise that they are not public at all, there has been a move towards the title 'senior independent school' – but it does not have the quite the same ring. See also footnote 5 below.

2. For an enlightening account of the state of public schools in the eighteenth and nineteenth centuries, see David Turner's *The Old Boys: The Decline and Rise of the Public School* (New Haven and London: Yale University Press, 2015).

Although the Clarendon Report exposed depressingly low academic standards, it was something of a whitewash. Its general tenor was that things were bad, but not quite as bad as they had once been. Nonetheless, as a result of the Report, the 1868 Public Schools Act made the Clarendon schools properly independent, each with its own board of governors, and allowed them to continue along almost traditional lines. Moreover, in a crucial nod to the middle classes, the schools were allowed to exchange the rights of entry of local poor children for admission based wholly on a competitive exam.[3]

Meanwhile, pressure from the middle classes for a place at the political table was bringing about the foundation of a new raft of proprietary schools that were run along the lines of the Clarendon schools, but with a more utilitarian approach (at least half of what we now term 'public schools' opened between 1840 and 1900). Ironically, since the complaint was that the public schools were an elitist 'closed shop', the proprietary schools had their own social pretensions. David Turner reports how 'At a public meeting setting up Cheltenham College, it was resolved that no one could become a shareholder of the school. . . . "who should not be moving in the circle of gentlemen. No retail trader being under any circumstances to be considered" '.[4]

Turner recounts similar attitudes at Brighton, Malvern and Rossall. Many of the proprietary schools, high and low Church, also had an evangelical purpose – bastions to hold back the advance of an increasingly secular society. For example, Lancing College (1848), Hurstpierpoint College (1849), and Ardingly College (1858) were all originally set up in Shoreham, Sussex, by Canon Nathaniel Woodard, but even they did not escape the narrow social divisions of the time: Lancing was intended for gentlemen, Hurstpierpoint for the upper-middle class, and Ardingly for the lower-middle class. One is reminded of the lyrics of C.F. Alexander's famous hymn (1848) with their dubious theology:

> The rich man in his castle,
> The poor man at his gate,
> God made them high and lowly,
> And ordered their estate.

Inevitably, since demand continued to outstrip supply, there was often an unscrupulous profit motive, which could only drive down standards. Marlborough College, established in 1843 as an affordable alternative to

---

3. As St Paul's and Merchant Taylors' were legally private schools, they were excluded from the Public Schools Act.
4. David Turner, *The Old Boys*, p. 117; M. C. Morgan, *Cheltenham College: The First Hundred Years* (The Cheltonian Society, 1968), p. 3.

the established public schools, was intended to house 200 pupils, but such was its popularity that within five years it was accommodating more than 500 boys in the most appalling conditions and under the ineffective control of fourteen teachers. It was not surprising that the boys, taking their cue from the Rugby debacle, decided to take the law into their own hands. On Guy Fawkes night, 1851, the boys launched their own rebellion by exploding a barrel of gunpowder close to the headmaster. Having failed to beat (literally) the rebels into submission, the headmaster retired and it was left to his successor (George Cotton, a protégé of Arnold) to restore some sort of order.

Subsequent to the Clarendon Commission, the whole of the remaining educational provision for the middle classes – proprietary schools, endowed grammar schools and private schools – was investigated by the Schools Inquiry or Taunton Commission (1864-67).[5] The Commission found that while the new proprietary schools were largely doing their job well, the grammar schools and many of the private schools were failing in almost every area; there was 'neither organisation, nor supervision, nor even effective tests to distinguish the incompetent from the truly successful'.[6] Moreover, there was (as there still is) an inequality of geographical provision: where you lived largely determined the quality of education you could receive – unless you were sent away to a boarding establishment. Thus, in a further sop to the middle classes, the Commission proposed a new national system of education based on social engineering rather than academic potential. The ensuing Endowed Schools Act (1869) did not adopt the proposal, but it did, like the Public Schools Act, end the automatic right of poor children to attend their local grammar school. Entry became competitive and poor children had to compete with middle-class children for the few available scholarships.

Both the Public Schools Act and the Endowed Schools Act opened the way to a broadening of the narrow and outdated classical curriculum (the original purpose of which had itself been utilitarian – the instruction of pupils in the language of the Church). There was pressure for change from the middle

---

5. Again, the classification of schools is notoriously difficult and the meaning of particular terms is in constant flux. Here, by proprietary schools I mean the glut of independent schools set up in Victorian times to serve the middle classes. By grammar schools I mean those schools that were originally set up to instruct pupils in Latin and (later) Ancient Greek. Originally these were Church schools (for example, The King's School, Canterbury, and The King's School, Rochester), since Latin was the language of the Church; but in the fifteenth and sixteenth centuries philanthropists endowed grammar schools for local children in their own towns and villages. By private schools I mean those run for profit by business-minded and often unscrupulous proprietors. See also footnote 1 above.

6. The Taunton Report, 1868.

classes, who wanted their children to learn subjects more relevant to their proposed careers, and the new proprietary schools and the day schools led the way. But many of the older foundations had little appetite for change. Two reasons for what was in part self-interested conservatism are given by Matthew Arnold (son of Thomas Arnold) in *Culture and Anarchy* (1869):

> The culture which is supposed to plume itself on a smattering of Greek and Latin is a culture which is begotten by nothing so intellectual as curiosity; it is valued either out of sheer vanity and ignorance, or else as an engine of social and class distinction, separating its holder, like a badge or title, from other people who have not got it.[7]

Yet, more than anything else, there was a simple inertia: what went on in the classroom was of little interest to a large proportion of Victorian educators.

Since the seventeenth century, when John Milton and John Locke were hugely influential in the development of education, the emphasis had been on inculcating moral values. In the nineteenth century, this philosophy remained in the ascendant, particularly among the upper classes, with character building increasingly valued over academic achievement (though as the century went on, sporting prowess became the standard by which character was judged). It is arguable that such an approach was, in its own way, utilitarian, since the real driver for the education of the ruling elite was the need to produce gentlemen and civil servants to win, defend and manage the Empire. As prefects at school, prospective soldiers, rulers and managers were given experience of leadership. They were used to hardship, and, having learnt to survive a monastic existence away from home, without its comforts, they developed a tough self-sufficiency that equipped them to endure long postings overseas.

It is worth noting for completeness that preparatory schools (preparing young boys for senior schools) first made their appearance in 1837 with the founding of Windlesham House in West Sussex; however, with the exception of Harriet Martineau's *The Crofton Boys* (see below), they did not make a significant appearance in children's fiction until well into the twentieth century.[8] In the same way, girls' education was only just beginning to be taken seriously in Victorian times, gathering pace alongside the growing feminist movement. This will be the subject of Part III.

Finally, in this brief historical outline, while the ruling class had been forced to accept the rise of the middle classes in order to maintain at least some of its political supremacy, not much was happening to the education

---

7. Matthew Arnold, *Culture and Anarchy* (1869), ed. J. Dover Wilson (Cambridge: Cambridge University Press, 1961), p. 43.
8. Preparatory school stories will feature in Part II.

of the other 90 per cent of the population – indeed, as we have seen, the working classes were being squeezed further out of the schools that had originally been set up to help them. In 1811, the Church of England established 'The National Society for Promoting the Education of the Poor in the Principles of the Established Church in England and Wales' and set up a significant number of National Schools, but this was mainly a defensive measure to stave off the increasing pressure for a secular system of state education over which it would have no control. Worse, the Church did not seem especially interested in the neediest in society.

Philanthropists weighed in with the founding of Sunday schools and ragged schools. Initially, at least, Sunday schools were targeted at the most deprived children, in the belief that education would offer them an escape from extreme poverty. Early Sunday schools were opened in Nottingham (1751) and High Wycombe (1769), but the movement really gathered momentum with the efforts of Robert Raikes. His first school (for boys) began in Gloucester in 1780, but soon he opened other schools and girls were admitted as well as boys. Fifty years later, about 1,250,000 children were attending Sunday schools across the country. Although the curriculum was largely based on the Bible and the Catechism, and pupils attended church, the schools operated on Sundays for the more practical reason that many of their children were labouring for the rest of the week. In the same vein, ragged schools set out to rescue children whose living conditions were condemning them to a life of vice and crime. The first ragged school was started in Portsmouth in 1818 and eventually there were about 350 of them across the United Kingdom. In a conference speech (1861), the Reverend Thomas Guthrie describes a typical day in an Edinburgh ragged school:

> The children come at half-past seven in the morning – and come in rags, not in the decent clothes they wear in school – that wouldn't do; the parents would soon have them in the pawn or whiskey shop. The first thing they do is to strip – not to be thrashed, but washed. We have a bath, as long as this gallery, and they march along it as slow as if they were attending a funeral; and the consequence is that they get what many people are fools not to take – a delightful bath. What comes next? Some of you are, I dare say, Scotchmen, and will understand me. They get a grand breakfast of porridge and milk. Then comes prayer; then a portion of Scripture is read; then the work of the school begins. . . . They learn to read, and to write, and to cipher; and they learn carpentering, and boxmaking, and shoemaking. . . . Then we have so many hours for play. In fact, the children were the pictures

of misery before they came to school: now there are no children happier. At half-past seven at night we take off their school dress, and give them back their rags; and they go home – and as the rags are not worth the pawning, they are allowed to keep them.[9]

But others saw education as a way of making easy money. I have already mentioned the private boarding schools, and in similar though kinder vein were the usually chaotic dame schools, run by unqualified ladies, often in the evenings. Of course, some private schools were very different, like, for example, the fictional Miss Teachum's Academy (described in the Introduction) – progenitors, perhaps, of the private boarding schools that will take centre stage in Part III. But quality was more a matter of luck than judgement, since there was no restriction on who might set up in the educational business, and most of the luck was bad. Giving evidence to the Newcastle Commission in 1859, Dr W.B. Hidgson, an Assistant Commissioner in south London, remarked:

> None are too old, too poor, too ignorant, too feeble, too sickly, too unqualified in any or every way to regard themselves, and to be regarded by others, as unfit for school keeping. Nay, there are few, if any, occupations regarded as incompatible with school-keeping, if not as simultaneous, at least as preparatory, employments. Domestic servants out of place; discharged barmaids; vendors of toys or lollipops; . . . cripples almost bedridden . . . men and women of seventy and even eighty years of age; persons who spell badly . . . who can scarcely write, and who cannot cipher at all.[10]

This absurd situation continued well into the twentieth century.

But the march of democracy did not stand still. The Trade Union movement gathered momentum and Disraeli's rumoured acceptance that 'we must educate our masters' led eventually to Forster's 1870 Education Act, passed in the face of protests from all the vested interests who saw education (in the case of the Church, state education) as a bad thing. In theory, Forster's Act made elementary education available to all, but it was not until 1891, when the state's elementary schools became free, that the Church began to lose its stranglehold. Then in 1895 the

---

9. From a speech by the Reverend Thomas Guthrie at a conference in Birmingham, 1861. Quoted in A.E. Dyson and Julian Lovelock (eds), *Education and Democracy* (London: Routledge and Kegan Paul, 1975), pp. 181-182.

10. From Dr W. B. Hodgson's evidence to the Newcastle Commission, 1859. Quoted in A. E. Dyson and Julian Lovelock (eds), *Education and Democracy* (London: Routledge and Kegan Paul, 1975), p. 152.

Bryce Report argued 'that the extension and reorganisation of Secondary Education seem entitled to a place among the first subjects with which social legislation ought to deal'. Eventually, Balfour's 1902 Education Act opened the door just a little to secondary education for the masses, but when the First World War broke out in 1914 very little progress had been made.

Spare the Child:
Charles Dickens and Charlotte Brontë

The appalling conditions in Victorian private schools were highlighted by Charles Dickens and Charlotte Brontë (among others). While the state of the public schools was bad, the state of the usually much cheaper private schools and the charity schools was often worse. In January 1838, researching *Nicholas Nickleby* (1838), Charles Dickens visited Bowes Academy, one of the notorious private schools in Yorkshire, where, for a fee of twenty pounds a year, illegitimate and other unwanted children could be quietly concealed, five to each flea-ridden bed. The one-eyed proprietor, William Shaw, had already been convicted of causing up to ten boys to go blind through beatings and negligence, and it was not uncommon for them to die at his Academy. Such were the roots of Dickens's one-eyed Wackford Squeers, headmaster of Dotheboys Hall, where poor Bolder is thrashed because his father has failed to pay all the fees and because he has warts on his hand. The nightmarish Mr and Mrs Creakle of Salem House (*David Copperfield*, 1850) are of the same ilk. Then, in the explosive opening of *Hard Times* (1854), in 'the plain, bare, monotonous vault of a school-room', the aptly named Gradgrind and M'Choakumchild epitomise the worst of utilitarian education, where, in soulless surroundings, creativity is quite squeezed out:

> Now, what I want is, Facts. Teach these boys and girls nothing but Facts. Facts alone are wanted in life. Plant nothing else, and root out everything else. You can only form the minds of reasoning animals upon Facts: nothing else will ever be of any service to them. This is the principle on which I bring up my own children, and this is the principle on which I bring up these children. Stick to Facts, sir![11]

In *Jane Eyre* (1847), Charlotte Brontë paints an equally miserable picture in her description of Mr Brocklehurst, the patron of Lowood (the charity school at which Jane has the misfortune to be a pupil):

---

11. Charles Dickens, *Hard Times* (1854), chapter 1.

> my mission is to mortify in these girls the lusts of the flesh;
> to teach them to clothe themselves with shame-facedness and
> sobriety, not with braided hair and costly apparel; and each of
> the young persons before us has a string of hair twisted in plaits
> which vanity itself might have woven: these, I repeat, must be
> cut off.[12]

Unsurprisingly, the filthy conditions at Lowood cause its own devastation by typhus fever. Mr Brocklehurst is (merely) side-lined after an inquiry and the school is transformed into 'a truly useful and noble institution'.

While day (and evening) schools were less cruel than boarding schools, they often offered nothing in return for their meagre fees. Here Charles Dickens (again) casts his eye over Mr Wopsle's great-aunt's school, which assembled in the room that was also used for her shop, sitting room and bed chamber:

> The pupils ate apples and put straws down one another's backs,
> until Mr Wopsle's great-aunt collected her energies, and made
> an indiscriminate totter at them with a birch rod. After receiving
> the charge with every mark of derision, the pupils formed in line
> and buzzingly passed a ragged book from hand to hand. The
> book had an alphabet in it, some figures and tables, and a little
> spelling – that is to say, it had had once. As soon as this volume
> began to circulate, Mr Wopsle's great-aunt fell into a state of
> coma; arising either from sleep or rheumatic paroxysm.[13]

The session continues with Biddy, the great-aunt's granddaughter, trying to supervise reading aloud from the Bible ('This part of the Course was usually lightened by several single combats between Biddy and refractory students') until the great-aunt woke up and 'staggered at a boy fortuitously, and pulled his ears', thus terminating the course and allowing the children to escape 'with shrieks of intellectual victory'.

Victorian School Stories

We sense much the same cruelty and ineptitude in the Victorian school stories written for children. Again, it is in the name of moral education and the saving of souls, but here the cruelty is often hidden under a warm glow. One of the first novels written about the Victorian boarding school was Harriet Martineau's *The Crofton Boys* (1844).[14] Set in Mr Tooke's private

---

12. Charlotte Brontë, *Jane Eyre* (1847), chapter 7.
13. Charles Dickens, *Great Expectations* (1880), chapter 10.
14. Harriet Martineau (1802-1876), a Unitarian (though she was to lose her faith

preparatory school at Crofton, it tells the story of Hugh Proctor, who, at the age of eight, is sent to Crofton to 'mend the weakness of [his] mind'.[15] Although Crofton is not the exciting place that Hugh has envisaged, he endures its minor tribulations without complaint. Mr Tooke is a benevolent figure; Mr Carnaby, a spiteful master, is dismissed; and Hugh's fellow pupils are a happy bunch. But one winter's day, when trying to escape being pelted with snowballs, Hugh is pulled from the playground wall, his leg is crushed by a falling coping stone, and his foot is amputated without fuss ('The surgeons took off his foot' – as if the loss is of no importance).[16] One might have thought that the lesson to be drawn would be the dreadful consequences of ragging and bullying, but not a bit of it. Instead, the focus of the second half of the novel is on the patient stoicism of Hugh in the face of adversity, his steadfast refusal to say who pulled him off the wall, and his destiny, in spite of everything, to perform his 'honourable duty' as a civil servant in India.[17] Says his mother:

> These misfortunes, of themselves, strengthen one's mind. They have some advantages too. You will be a better scholar for your lameness, I have no doubt. You will read more books, and have a mind richer in thoughts. You will be more beloved;—not out of mere pity; for people in general will soon leave off pitying you, when once you learn to be active again; but because you have kept faith with your schoolfellows, and shown that you can bear pain. Yes, you will be more loved by us all; and you yourself will love God more for having given you something to bear for his sake.[18]

It could be argued that Mrs Proctor is simply trying to cheer Hugh up, but nowhere does she reflect on the horror of her son's situation. At least she does better than her husband, who is too busy with his shop to worry about the trivia of a lost foot.

But it was Thomas Hughes's *Tom Brown's Schooldays* (1857), the subject of chapter 1, which caught the early Victorian thirst for education and evangelism, and was soon read by adults as well as children. Like Hugh Proctor, Tom Brown is a spirited boy who faces the initiations and bullying

---

in later life), was better known for her writing on religion, economics and social reform. She also wrote two adult novels and *The Playfellow* (1841), a collection of stories for children.

15. Harriet Martineau, *The Crofton Boys* (1844), chapter 3.
16. *The Crofton Boys*, chapter 8.
17. *The Crofton Boys*, chapter 15.
18. *The Crofton Boys*, chapter 8.

of his early years at Rugby without complaint and even with enthusiasm; he then enjoys a period of irresponsible adolescence before becoming a model citizen in the second part of the novel. A year later, F.W. Farrar's *Eric, or, Little by Little* (1852), the subject of chapter 2, took moralising to a new and extraordinary level. Eric, all innocence and enthusiasm when he arrives at Roslyn School, is (like Tom Brown) tempted into the various misdemeanours of school life and, as a direct consequence, he suffers and dies for his sins. Worryingly, Farrar was, for many years, a master at Harrow and from 1871 to 1876 was headmaster of Marlborough. However, without the efforts of *The Boy's Own Paper* and Talbot Baines Reed, the school story might have been quickly forgotten. Reed was among the first to contribute to *Boy's Own* and his *The Fifth Form at St Dominic's* (1887), the subject of chapter 3, originally ran as a 38-part serial. L.T. Meade's *A World of Girls* (1886) was the most significant Victorian girls' school story; this will be discussed in Part III.

The next thirty years or so saw the zenith of boys' school stories in volume and the nadir in quality. Harold Avery, a prolific children's author, wrote a number of jolly and lengthy novels very much in the style of Reed, based in part on his time at Eton (for example, *The Triple Alliance*, 1897, and *The Dormitory Flag*, 1899); among a host of others who have less to offer are, Walter Rhoades (for example, *The Boy from Cuba*, 1900, which reflects the racist attitudes of its time, though all turns out well) and Mrs G. Forsyth Grant (best known for *The Beresford Boys*, 1906, which has echoes of both Martineau's *The Crofton Boys* and Farrar's *Eric*). A contemporary review of Forsyth Grant's *The Boys of Penrohn* (1893) sums up why so many school stories of the age are best forgotten:

> More unreal boys than those of Mrs Forsyth Grant we never came across. It seems to be the fashion to treat boys more and more as men, and to discourse on their good looks, haughtiness, sneering manner, prettiness, gracefulness, etc. The masters, too, are either white with passion or coldly courteous, and the headmaster is ever the ideal headmaster, never appearing in class, yet seeming to know all his pupils off by heart.[19]

But F. Anstey's *Vice Versa* (1882), subtitled *A Lesson to Fathers*, is one of the early enlightened stories and turns this sort of disingenuous school story on its head. Dick Bultitude is a pupil at Dr Grimstone's Crichton House, a private school in the manner of Dotheboys Hall. With the help of a dose of magic (which was to become an occasional ingredient in later school stories), Mr Bultitude (an irascible Colonial Produce Merchant) changes

19. *The Spectator*, 9 December, 1893, p. 23.

places with Dick and discovers for a week the unpleasantness of life at Crichton House, questioning how parents can commend such suffering to their sons as the 'very happiest time of their life'.[20] The story ends with father and son back in their own bodies and with a new understanding between them. Dick leaves Crichton House and is granted his wish to go to Harrow – a 'proper' public school – instead. Sadly, if Arnold Lunn's *The Harrovians* (1913) is to be believed, the life of a small boy at Harrow would not have been much different to life at Crichton House. One of the points that both Anstey and Lunn are making is that an adult's memory of their old school somehow becomes tinged with a strange sentimentality, blotting out all the miseries that they endured.

In some ways, Rudyard Kipling's *Stalky & Co.* (1899) reverses the naïve morality of the public school story, but his heroes are bullies and it is difficult to untangle his characteristic sense of irony. Chapter 4 highlights some of the novel's complexities, and there is no doubt that as a writer Kipling far surpassed the other Victorian exponents of the school story, a form to which he gave a very different slant.

---

20. F. Anstey, *Vice Versa* (1882), chapter 2.

Chapter 1

The Doctor's Story

Thomas Hughes – *Tom Brown's Schooldays* (1857)

Most people have heard of *Tom Brown's Schooldays* (1857), but few in the last hundred years have read it in its entirety. Some young readers have enjoyed abridged editions or watched one of the many film or television adaptations; others have started out, but failed to get through the first three turgid chapters. Of those who have survived its foothills and reached the peaks beyond, some have failed entirely to associate Tom Brown's Rugby with any sort of 'real' school, while others have discovered an exciting imaginative world (the escapades of Tom and East can be great fun if you are not being roasted or caned yourself). Others still, as adults, have, with fading or rose-tinted memories, compared it nostalgically with their own experience of boarding school life.

Tom Brown's Schooldays is Thomas Hughes's first and best novel. It was followed in 1861 by *The Scouring of the White Horse* and *Tom Brown at Oxford*, but neither caught the Victorian imagination in the same way. It was written with his eight-year-old son Maurice in mind, who would one day go off to public school, and, as far as Hughes intended anything, its original audience was one of schoolboys. However, such was its immediate popularity that its readership must have been far wider than boys who went to or were destined for public schools. Indeed, it turned out to appeal equally to adults, for whom it reflected and caught the interest of the burgeoning Victorian middle classes in improvement, education, nationalism and religion.

More importantly, whatever the audience, *Tom Brown's Schooldays* laid the foundations for the thousands of school stories, especially boarding school stories, that have followed in the 150 years or so since its publication (though in part it borrows from and builds on the structure of Martineau's *The Crofton Boys*): the symbolic journey from home and the real world to the different, isolated and hierarchical other world of school; the initial bewilderment and loneliness; the often cruel and unjust treatment by masters, prefects and bullies; the making of friends, the enjoyment of various escapades, and a year or two of irresponsible adolescence (paid for by beatings and other punishments); the importance of competitive games and physical prowess (and the unimportance of academic learning); the influence of an inspirational headmaster; the learning through experience and the becoming of a force for good in the school; the final return as a leader to the real world; and often with a fair amount of religion thrown in.

Thomas Hughes and The Vale of White Horse

Tom Brown's Schooldays hovers dangerously between fiction and non-fiction, and is part autobiography and part hagiography. Though he denied it, the novel and its hero, Tom Brown, are based closely on Thomas Hughes's own experiences at Rugby School from 1834 to 1842 (from the age of eleven to the age of nineteen – a long innings by any reckoning), and on those of his older brother, George. But *Tom Brown's Schooldays* is above all 'The Doctor's Story' because it is the not-quite-accurate account of the real Dr Thomas Arnold's time at Rugby School, where he was the inspirational headmaster and hero of both Thomas Hughes and his brother, and of the fictional Tom Brown. Ironically, it became more influential in the development of the public school system than Arnold's actual beliefs and methods, which it often misrepresents, and was responsible for some of the aberrations of the vastly expanding system in the second half of the nineteenth century.

Thomas Hughes's day job was as a lawyer, but he was more influential as an educational and social reformer. He served as a Liberal MP from 1865 to 1874, losing his seat because of his support for Forster's controversial 1870 Elementary Education Act, and was a leading member of the Christian socialist movement with Charles Kingsley and F. D. Maurice among others (he was a founder of London's Working Men's College in 1857 and later became its Principal). The Christian socialists applied Christian ethics to the social problems of the Victorian age, but were never radicals, and only set out to improve the conditions of working people rather than to overturn the class system itself.

Hughes appears in *Tom Brown's Schooldays* in a number of guises: primarily as a good-natured and rumbustious narrator, who is over-familiar with the reader and ready to moralise at every opportunity, and also as Tom Brown himself (like Tom Brown, Hughes was a sportsman rather than an academic, and like Tom his career at Rugby ended with a cricket match at Lord's before he went on to study at Oxford). In spite of his liberal idealism, Hughes shared many of the conservative views of his father, who is disguised in the novel as the paternalistic Squire Brown, and he also becomes part of the persona of Thomas Arnold, whose ideals he muddles with his own.

The opening chapters describe Tom's home in The Vale of White Horse, near Farringdon in Berkshire (now Oxfordshire). It is self-indulgent (Hughes was born at Uffington in the Vale) and young readers especially may choose to accept the narrator's invitation in Part I, chapter 1: 'on this subject I must be prosy, so those that don't care for England in detail may skip the chapter'.[1] In fact it is not until chapter 5 (of eighteen) that Tom finally arrives at Rugby. But if the ponderous beginning seems to intrude from a different novel (Hughes's own *The Scouring of the White Horse*, perhaps) and is at first sight nothing to do with schooldays, it nevertheless says something important about Thomas Hughes's beliefs and Tom Brown's background, and links implicitly with Thomas Arnold's own philosophy as a headmaster.

Squire Brown

Squire Brown is associated firmly with the middle class – not the new middle class of businessmen and industrialists, but the yeomen who have long been the backbone of England, taken for granted by the ruling aristocracy. Notice the emphasis that is placed on the Browns' nationalism: much is made of their Saxon ancestry and their military service through the ages – with the implication that those in power are Norman Johnny-come-latelies.

While Part I, chapter 1, is mainly given over to descriptions of the Vale and its despoiling, chapter 2 centres on the excitements of the village 'Veast', with its 'pipe and tabor, and the drums and trumpets of the showmen shouting at the doors of their caravans, over which tremendous pictures of the wonders to be seen within hang temptingly.'[2] But all this happened when Tom Brown was a boy and the narrator reflects that twenty years on, when the novel was written, such feasts have altered for the worse – because 'gentlefolk

---

1. Thomas Hughes, *Tom Brown's Schooldays* (1857), Part I, chapter 1.
2. *Tom Brown's Schooldays*, Part I, chapter 2.

and farmers have left off joining or taking an interest in them' and because 'our sons and daughters have their hearts in London Club-life, or so-called Society, instead of in the old English home duties'.[3] In acknowledging that England may be 'in transition' and looking for a substitute for the old way of life, the reader is warned that educational reformers will have to provide something in place of the country games 'to try the muscles of men's bodies, and the endurance of their hearts, to make them rejoice in their strength'.[4] It is here we see the seed of Hughes's belief in the centrality of sport and physical prowess to character-building, which was not Arnold's philosophy, but suffuses *Tom Brown's Schooldays* and was to have marked consequences for the development of the public school. The action at Rugby is framed by 'Rugby and Football' (Part I, chapter 5) and 'Tom Brown's Last Match' (Part II, chapter 8), and includes such episodes as Tom's stoicism in blanket-tossing and roasting, and his fights with both Flashman and Slogger Williams. Significantly, Squire Brown places Tom's early education in the hands of 'Old Benjie', an elderly gamester, backswordsman and wrestler, who teaches him to fish, instructs him in the mysteries of horsemanship, and stands 'chuckling outside the door of the girls' school, when Tom rode his little Shetland into the cottage and round the table, where the old dame and her pupils were seated at their work'.[5]

Squire Brown's conservatism also leads to his suspicion of the dangers of capitalism and he laments 'the further separation of classes consequent of twenty years of buying cheap and selling dear'. Thus, reflecting Hughes's Christian socialism, the Squire encourages Tom to play with the village boys and there is great sadness when he eventually leaves the village. Rugby School itself is presented as a classless society, but in fact it only opened its doors to boys from the higher echelons of society. Although Arnold famously turned away those who would be happier among the toffs at Eton, the sons of tradesmen were not made welcome either. By 1878, Rugby's popularity as a boarding school meant that boys who lived in 'Rugby and Brownsover', the intended beneficiaries of the School's founder, had been squeezed out and as a result the Lawrence Sherriff Grammar School was opened nearby, offering the sort of commercial education that local parents demanded for their sons. Ironically, for all Hughes's lofty beliefs, once Tom is a Rugby boy, his village friends are never mentioned again.

The time comes when Tom leaves home and is sent to board at a private school. The narrator complains of the practice of the masters only 'hearing' the boys' lessons, while their supervision out of school is given over to poorly

---

3. *Tom Brown's Schooldays*, Part I, chapter 2.
4. *Tom Brown's Schooldays*, Part I, chapter 2.
5. *Tom Brown's Schooldays*, Part I, chapter 2.

educated ushers. The ushers make their own lives easier by encouraging tale-telling (a cardinal sin in public school morality) and favouring the bigger boys who become tyrants and bullies. Such supervision, the reader is told, should be the work of the headmaster, since 'The object of all schools is not to ram Latin and Greek into boys, but to make them good English boys, good future citizens; and by far the most important part of that work must be done, or not done, out of school hours.'[6] However, it is not long before the private school is closed because of sickness and Tom's dream of going to Rugby is fulfilled early. As Squire Brown ponders the parting advice he should give to his son, Hughes's own views on education are crystallised further: 'I don't care a straw for Greek articles, or the digamma, no more does his mother. . . . If he'll only turn out a brave, helpful, truth-telling Englishman, and a gentleman, and a Christian, that's all I want.'[7]

Tom Brown

So Tom clambers onto the Tally-ho coach to Rugby – the distancing journey from home to the different world of school will become a feature of the school story. Says the coachman, Rugby is a 'Werry out-o'-the-way place, sir . . . off the main road you see – only three coaches a day.'[8] He arrives on the day of the School-house match, heroically helping to prevent the scoring of a try and beginning at once to build his reputation ('Well, he's a plucky youngster, and will make a player'): as with every exciting set-piece in the novel, the narrator slips into the historic present tense to add immediacy to the description of the game.[9] After the match, Tom takes the initiation ceremony of singing a solo in the School-house hall in good part and allows himself to be tossed in a blanket by Flashman and his cronies; then the last few weeks of term pass uneventfully, except when Tom, East and Tadpole get lost playing Hare-and-hounds and have to explain themselves to an unexpectedly sympathetic Dr Arnold.

But when Tom returns to Rugby after Christmas and moves into the lower-fourth, things begin to change. He falls out with masters and, having started a rebellion of fags, is disliked by the senior boys in the house as well. After he refuses to part with a promising sweepstake ticket, Flashman and the fifth-form boys roast him in front of an open fire until he collapses with pain. Tom's spirit is nearly broken, but he declines to tell the matron

---

6. *Tom Brown's Schooldays*, Part I, chapter 3.
7. *Tom Brown's Schooldays*, Part I, chapter 4.
8. *Tom Brown's Schooldays*, Part I, chapter 4. In the 1830s, Rugby was a small, rural market town, with a population of about 2,500.
9. *Tom Brown's Schooldays*, Part I, chapter 5.

who has caused his injuries, and eventually he and East beat Flashman in a fight and are never troubled again. However, Tom's year in the lower-fourth is characterised not by heroism but by a repeated breaking of bounds and rules. He and East, still full of boyishness and without a jot of self-discipline, indulge in such things as fishing on private land, mountaineering on the school roofs, and visiting the forbidden town fair. In itself it is harmless stuff and skated over in half a chapter, but frequent punishments do nothing to curb Tom's behaviour and Part I ends with Arnold warning him that he is on the brink of expulsion.

In Part II, the mood changes from a rollicking tale of boyish excess to a moral *bildungsroman*. Tom is asked to look after a timid new boy, George Arthur, a scholar rather than a sportsman, with whom he has nothing in common; the superficially weak, often effeminate, young boy, like Arthur, was to become another common figure in the boys' school story. Though reluctant at first, Tom takes his responsibilities seriously, standing up for Arthur against the ragging and the bullying that he encounters. So Tom and Arthur become firm friends: Tom's own behaviour is transformed by Arthur and, in turn, as the novel draws to a close, East's behaviour is transformed by Tom. On the first night of term, Tom puts an end to the teasing Arthur endures when he kneels to say his prayers, and then follows Arthur's example; later, when Slogger Williams seeks revenge on Arthur for having to translate aloud in the Latin class, Tom fights him and is on the point of winning when Arnold approaches the mêlée. Two years pass and a deadly fever sweeps through the School; at one point Arthur hovers between life and death, but he survives and makes Tom promise to give up cribbing in his lessons. Another two years pass and Tom's time at Rugby is all but over. Tom, now a changed person, is captain of the cricket team, which only just loses to the M.C.C.,[10] possibly because Tom has selected Arthur and puts him in to bat before the more experienced Winter: ' "Well, I'm not quite sure that he ought to be in for his play," said Tom, "but I couldn't help putting him in. It will do him so much good, and you can't think what I owe him." '[11] The next day Tom returns (by train) to the real world, 'no longer a school-boy, and divided in his thoughts between hero-worship, honest regrets over the long stage of his life which was now slipping out of sight behind him, and hopes and resolves for the next stage, upon which he was entering'.[12]

---

10. The M.C.C. is the Marylebone Cricket Club.
11. *Tom Brown's Schooldays*, Part II, chapter 8.
12. *Tom Brown's Schooldays*, Part II, chapter 8. Hughes's belief in the importance of hero worship reflects Thomas Carlyle's influential *On Heroes, Hero-Worship, and The Heroic in History* (1841).

As Tom learns to control his 'excess of boyishness',[13] Part II is slower in pace and more reflective than Part I, and more full of good deeds and Godliness – so much so that P. G. Wodehouse suggested, only half in jest, that it was written by a different hand (namely the committee of 'The Secret Society For Putting Wholesome Literature Within the Reach of Every Boy, And Seeing That He Gets It').[14] Clearly other readers thought the same, since in a preface to the sixth edition, Thomas Hughes refutes their criticism:

> My sole object in writing was to preach to boys: if ever I write again it will be to preach to some other age. I can't see that a man has any business to write at all unless he has something that he thoroughly believes and wants to preach about. If he has this, and the chance of delivering himself of it, let him by all means put it in the shape in which it is most likely to get a hearing; but let him never be so carried away as to forget that preaching is his object.[15]

Thus in the final lines of *Tom Brown's Schooldays*, as Tom sits in the chapel at Rugby mourning the death of Thomas Arnold, the moral is made explicit, and his hero-worship of the Doctor, who has transformed his life, is seen as a stage of the Christian journey for 'all young and brave souls, who must win their way through hero-worship, to the worship of Him who is the King and Lord of heroes'.[16]

Thomas Arnold (1795-1842)

Tom's hero-worship of Arnold is the third strand of *Tom Brown's Schooldays*, and it is Hughes's hero-worship too, although it is laced with misunderstandings. Born on the Isle of Wight, Arnold was educated at Winchester College and Corpus Christi College, Oxford, and was ordained deacon in 1818. In theology he was a liberal and an implacable opponent of the high-church Oxford Movement. Before his appointment to Rugby, he lived at Laleham (on the banks of the Thames in Middlesex), where he prepared students for university entrance. It is wrong to say that Arnold had no interest in education, but for him it was the means to an end. His ambition was not just to change a school but to change

13. *Tom Brown's Schooldays*, Part I, chapter 7.
14. P. G. Wodehouse, 'The Tom Brown Question', in *The Public School Magazine*, December 1901.
15. Thomas Hughes, *Tom Brown's Schooldays*, Preface to the sixth edition (London: Macmillan, 1858).
16. *Tom Brown's Schooldays*, Part II, 'Finis'.

society by returning God to its centre, and though his charisma, fierce intelligence and writings made him into a national figure, he would have been disappointed that he was more successful in the former than the latter.

When Arnold, still in his early thirties, moved into School House at Rugby in 1827 to take charge of 260 pupils, he would have found the 'petty tyranny and thoughtless cruelty . . . which used indeed to be thought inseparable from the life of a public school'[17] – a state of affairs that he set about improving.[18] For him, education was chiefly a path to Godliness. Unusually, he took on the role of chaplain himself, and, as described in *Tom Brown's Schooldays*, 'wearily and little by little' his rousing sermons and his personal example 'won his way to the hearts of the great mass of those on whom he left his mark, and made them believe first in him, and then in his Master'.[19] However, any suggestion that he was uninterested in teaching and learning are misleading, and the fact that the classroom features so little in *Tom Brown's Schooldays* is Hughes's choice, not Arnold's. Arnold's famous dictum of 'First, religious and moral principles; secondly, gentlemanly conduct; thirdly, intellectual ability' is not a belittling of the intellectual, but a re-statement of his own ambition to reshape society through Christian living and a belief that Godliness and good manners are the blocks on which intellectual pursuits can properly be built. All the evidence is that Arnold was most at home teaching and debating with a small circle of sixth-form pupils. He added Mathematics, History and Modern Languages to Rugby's classical curriculum, but drew the line at the teaching of Science, which for him added nothing to an understanding of society and so (in a new age of democracy) to the ability to cast a vote wisely.

Arnold is often credited with inventing the prefect system in order to maintain discipline, but this was not the case – one of the worst aspects of the public school system in the early nineteenth century was the uncontrolled brutality of the older boys. What he did, however, was develop the system so that prefects (at Rugby, *praepostors*) were responsible to him personally and their duties and powers were more clearly defined; above all, he respected them and treated them as gentlemen. At the same time, he abolished the dame's houses and expected masters to live in school and take an interest in the welfare of

---

17. Clarendon Report, 16 February, 1864, describing conditions a quarter of a century earlier.
18. Pupil numbers from Rugby School's website: https://www.rugbyschool.co.uk/about/history/
19. *Tom Brown's Schooldays*, Part I, chapter 7.

the boys – it was the beginning of what we now call pastoral care. But corporal punishment remained the usual corrective for misdemeanours, and Arnold was quick to expel boys who were untrustworthy or a bad influence on others.[20]

Arnold is also credited with the dominant role that sport came to play in the Victorian public school, but it was in fact low on his list of priorities. In chapter 5, he takes a passing interest in the football match, but in the penultimate chapter, which is devoted to the cricket match against the M.C.C., he leaves for his summer holiday before it begins and it is left to the 'young Master', speaking for Hughes more than Arnold, to express the value of the game: 'The discipline and reliance on one another which it teaches is so invaluable. . . . It merges the individual in the eleven; he doesn't play that he may win, but that his side may.'[21] So, almost without their meaning it, Arnold's Godliness became traduced by Hughes and the Christian socialists, and from the 1850s the alternative belief in 'muscular Christianity' took hold: fitness and toughness of body became inextricably linked with moral fitness and toughness, further side-lining the intellectual and, ironically, the weak.[22] Likewise, sport became an essential ingredient in school stories, beginning a spiral in which fiction reflected the schools and schools reflected fiction; then it became mixed up with the values of Empire and eventually with the patriotism that inspired bravery, heroism and sacrifice in the First World War. Sport, more than God or chapel, became dominant in public school life, and the handsome and athletic 'blood' became the idol of boy-worship.[23]

---

20. Arnold expelled George Hughes, Thomas Hughes's brother, for refusing to reveal who had broken pottery. He also, of course, expelled Flashman after he had been caught returning to school 'inhumanly drunk' (Part I, chapter 9).

21. *Tom Brown's Schooldays*, Part II, chapter 8. The 'young Master' quoted here is probably modelled on George Cotton, who would later become headmaster of Marlborough College, a new foundation but already fallen into anarchy. He introduced compulsory games as a means of restoring discipline: boys were simultaneously deprived of time to get into trouble and given the opportunity to work off their aggression in a controlled way.

22. The narrator is more explicit in Thomas Hughes's *Tom Brown at Oxford* (1861), chapter 11 ('Muscular Christianity'): 'The least of the muscular Christians has hold of the old chivalrous and Christian belief, that a man's body is given him to be trained and brought into subjection, and then used for the protection of the weak, the advancement of all righteous causes, and the subduing of the earth that God has given to the children of men.' The distinction is made between 'muscular Christians' and 'musclemen' – a distinction not always clear in school stories.

23. See, for example, Horace Annesley Vachell, *The Hill: A Romance of Friendship* (1905).

It is obvious from Old Brooke's valedictory address to School House that Arnold's reforms were not always popular: 'A lot of you think and say, for I've heard you, "There's this new Doctor hasn't been here so long as some of us, and he's changing all the old customs. Rugby and the School-house are going to the dogs." '[24] But the customs were such things as 'taking the lynch-pins out of the farmers' and bagmen's gigs at the fairs' and getting rid of the 'seven mangy harriers and beagles', and the objections to their passing are, says the narrator, 'sad enough stuff to make angels, not to say headmasters, weep'.[25] Old Brooke also highlights the continuing problem of bullying in School House, as is evidenced by the activities of Flashman. Moreover, when Brooke and his contemporaries leave, it becomes clear that the effectiveness of the prefect system depends not on the system but on the people: the new *praepostors* are young and weak, discipline is undermined, bullies regain the upper hand again, and Tom and East run wild.

However, contemporary accounts suggest it was not Arnold's reforms that won him respect and pulled Rugby back from the brink, but his humanity, his fairness, and his interest in and knowledge of the pupils as individuals (when, at the end of the novel, Tom looks back on his school career with the 'young Master', he is astounded to discover that it was Arnold who took enough interest in him to arrange his mentoring of Arthur). Set against his sometimes forbidding magisterial manner are his gentleness and warmth: his kindness to Tom, East and Tadpole in the Hare-and-hounds incident; his genial manner at the start-of-term tea party with Arthur and his mother; the 'brave, and tender, and gentle things'[26] he says to inspire Arthur when he is critically ill with fever; and how 'kind and gentle' he is with the troubled East and how 'he sat down by me and stroked my head'.[27] Even his stirring sermons are delivered in 'the warm living voice of one who was fighting for us and by our sides'.[28]

Arnold left Rugby in a much better state than he found it, and its improved reputation meant that numbers had grown to around 360, but since success was achieved mainly through his own force of personality, it slipped back under his successor, Archibald Tait.[29] Nonetheless, a myth had grown up around Arnold, and it was this, together with the fact

---

24. *Tom Brown's Schooldays*, Part I, chapter 6.
25. *Tom Brown's Schooldays*, Part I, chapter 6.
26. *Tom Brown's Schooldays*, Part II, chapter 7.
27. *Tom Brown's Schooldays*, Part II, chapter 7.
28. *Tom Brown's Schooldays*, Part I, chapter 7.
29. Pupil numbers from Rugby School's website: https://www.rugbyschool.co.uk/about/history/

that a large number of Rugby's masters and (later) alumni were soon to become headmasters themselves, that contributed to change throughout the public school system.[30] However, it is ironic that some of Hughes's inventions in *Tom Brown's Schooldays*, which were later copied by other schools, were never part of Rugby School itself. Arnold would have been horrified by the way the games field, rather than the chapel or the classroom was to become the focal point of public school life, by the way Godliness was to be replaced by a dangerous 'muscular Christianity', and by the way that the individual became subservient to the team or the community.

Other great Victorian and Edwardian headmasters would make their mark in different ways – men like Cotton of Marlborough, Thring of Uppingham, Walker of Manchester Grammar and St Paul's – but it was not until J. F. Roxburgh became the founding headmaster of Stowe in 1923 that Arnold's ideals were at last seen working in practice. At Roxburgh's Stowe, the intellectual and the artist were as important as the sportsman, respect for the individual (the new boy as much as the sixth-former) was the first duty of the teacher, and (won after unseemly and unpleasant struggles with the board of governors) the purpose of the school was 'to produce men who shall be Christian in character and in faith'.[31] It is just a pity that Hughes's attempt in *Tom Brown's Schooldays* to immortalise Thomas Arnold became muddled with his own different agenda and helped to shape public schools in a way that his hero never intended.

---

30. Between 1842 and 1899, twenty-three of Arnold's assistant masters became headmasters of other public schools.
31. See Noel Annan, *Roxburgh of Stowe* (London: Longmans, Green & Co., 1965). It has to be said, however, that Roxburgh knew that to establish Stowe as a major public school he had to make it fashionable among the upper classes – a task to which he naturally warmed.

Chapter 2

The Moral Story

F.W. Farrar – *Eric, or, Little by Little* (1858)

F.W. Farrar's *Eric, or, Little by Little* (1858) appals and delights in equal measure. It is an altogether more challenging novel than *Tom Brown's Schooldays* and took the school story in a more explicitly moral and evangelical direction. Farrar (1831-1903) wrote *Eric* when, aged twenty-seven, he was an assistant master at Harrow, but it is rooted firmly in his own experiences as a pupil at King William's College, Isle of Man, which he attended for eight years from the age of eight.[1] King William's, at Castletown and overlooking the sea, opened in 1833 and was the first of the multitude of new nineteenth-century public school foundations. However, in spite of its idyllic setting, Professor E. S. Beesly, a contemporary of Farrar at King William's, speaks of the cold, the hunger, the roughness, the poor teaching, and how 'the law of the strongest prevailed'.[2] This was a pre-Arnold age.

---

1. After graduating and taking holy orders at Trinity College, Cambridge, in 1854, Farrar spent a year teaching at Marlborough College, where headmaster George Cotton was restoring order after its chaotic early years. In 1855, he joined the staff at Harrow, where he remained for fifteen years before returning to Marlborough as headmaster in 1871. From 1876, he held successively a number of senior positions in the Church of England: canon of Westminster and rector of St Margaret's, Westminster; archdeacon of Westminster Abbey; and Dean of Canterbury.
2. Quoted in Reginald Farrar's *The Life of Frederick William Farrar* (London: James Nisbet & Co), chapter 2.

Since the day of its publication, *Eric* has been variously criticised as mawkish, moralising, sensational, sentimental, cloying and pessimistic.[3] *The Saturday Review* complained that 'Everything is served up with tear sauce. The boys quote hymns, and to the infinite indignation of all English readers, occasionally kiss each other.'[4] Perhaps the main objection was best encapsulated by W. Lucas Collins: Eric himself is not 'an old hearty John Bull type', like Tom Brown, but, at least to start with, is earnest, priggish and even effeminate (more like George Arthur, in fact). Indeed, Lucas Collins goes on to suggest that Farrar's books 'look . . . as if they had been written by a lady'.[5] Certainly Farrar's Christianity is not 'muscular', but, while he was many miles away from the jocund toughness of Thomas Hughes's narrator, he was probably much closer in his thinking to Thomas Arnold himself. We have to remember, too, that both *Tom Brown's Schooldays* and *Eric* were written at a time when new Victorian ideas of manliness and the stiff upper lip of Empire were only just replacing the sentimentality that was commonplace and acceptable in the early nineteenth century. A more valid criticism of *Eric* is of the long and terrible evangelical apostrophes, warning of Eric's fall into the abyss. For example, in one of the most famous and excoriating passages (Eric is listening to a smutty conversation after lights-out):

> Good spirits guard that young boy, and give him grace in this his hour of trial! Open his eyes that he may see the fiery horses and the fiery chariots of the angels who would defend him, and the dark array of spiritual foes who throng around his bed. Point a pitying finger to the yawning abyss of shame, ruin, and despair that even now perhaps is being cleft under his feet.[6]

It was unfortunate for Farrar that such strident evangelicalism, like displays of emotion, was also beginning to go out of fashion, so *Eric* had no imitators of consequence. For all this, it was for a time a best-seller, with audiences far beyond the public schools. Before Farrar died in 1903, it was already in its 36th edition. Farrar's later school story, *St Winifred's, or, The World of School* (1862), which has much in common with *Eric*, is less ambitious

---

3. A useful summary of the various attacks on *Eric* can be found in Jeffrey Richards's *Happiest Days: The Public Schools in English Fiction* (Manchester: Manchester University Press, 1988), pp. 70-72. Richards does much to rebut the attacks and to restore the novel's reputation.

4. *Saturday Review*, 6 November, 1858, pp. 453-454.

5. In *Blackwood's Magazine*, February 1861, pp. 131-148.

6. *Eric, or, Little by Little*, (London 1858), Volume I, chapter 9.

and less strident in tone; as a result it was less popular – highlighting the essential problem of the school story, that of maintaining interest in the trivial incidents of a 'little world' without resorting to the sensational.

I have argued in the previous chapter that one of the chief problems of *Tom Brown's Schooldays* is the way in which fact and fiction are confused, and the same is true of *Eric*, though in a different way. Like *Tom Brown's Schooldays*, *Eric* is in part autobiographical: in his Preface, Farrar writes, 'To the best of my belief, the things here dealt with are not theories, but realities; not imagination, but facts.' The young Farrar came back from India with his parents, for a time attending King William's as a day-boarder, just as Eric does, and the School (renamed Roslyn) and its surroundings are described in particular detail. So the reader is again on dangerous ground and it is easy to fall into the trap of reading the novel as a true account of what happens to a real boy who yields 'little by little' to temptation in spite of myriad warnings along the way. But to think of *Eric* as no more than an overblown tale of the wages of schoolboy sin is to miss most of its point, since Farrar is also attempting a Christian allegory on a much larger scale, played out against beautifully painted landscapes and sombre seascapes, with Eric himself as an Everyman figure caught in the struggle between good and evil. In this context, *Eric*'s strengths come more clearly into focus. It is much tighter in structure than *Tom Brown's Schooldays*; the tension builds inexorably as dramatic irony takes hold and the reader can see clearly what Eric cannot; the characters he meets along his journey become not just masters and boys, but angels and devils fighting for his soul; and the vividly described schoolboy escapades are dangerous snares and battlegrounds. What remains problematic is how far a school story, written initially for children, is a suitable setting for a cosmic tug-of-war.

Volume I: Serpent in Eden

Eric opens with Eric in the care of his widowed aunt and her daughter, Fanny, who has been his tutor. Now it is time for him to go to school, but already the signposting of his fall begins as Fanny passes her sense of foreboding to the reader:

> Everything looked smiling and beautiful, and there was an almost irresistible contagion in the mirth of her young cousin, but still she could not help feeling sad. It was not merely that she would have to part with Eric, 'but that bright boy,' thought Fanny, 'what will become of him? I have heard strange things of schools; oh, if he should be spoilt and ruined, what misery it would be.'[7]

7. *Eric, or, Little by Little*, Volume I, chapter 1.

And:

> his mind seemed cast in such a mould of stainless honour, that
> he avoided most of the weaknesses to which children are prone.
> But he was far from blameless. He was proud to a fault.[8]

Eric spends six months at the local grammar school, where the boys have 'gradually unhinged' the headmaster (in one of the nice touches of the novel's humour we are told, 'an imprudent marriage had driven him to the mastership of the little country grammar school') and he eventually lands up as 'an inmate of the Brereley Lunatic Asylum'.[9]

Then Eric's parents return from India to spend his father's 'furlough' on the Isle of Man and Eric is sent to Roslyn School as a day boy. In his first lesson he is told to sit next to Barker, a bullying oaf, who is soon 'a dark background' to his life. But he is befriended by Russell (an orphan, and his especial friend), Owen, Montagu and Duncan; does well in his studies; and makes his parents proud of his achievements. He is caught passing a 'crib' to Barker, for which he is unjustly punished, and although he becomes a hero among his classmates, he senses that 'the popularity in his form would do him as much harm as the change of feeling in his master'.[10] In case we miss the significance of this, the narrator comments, 'His popularity was a fatal snare. He enjoyed and was very proud of it. . . . Russell dreaded with all his heart lest "he should follow a multitude to do evil" '.[11] And so it turns out, in a fulfilment of Fanny's premonition. Eric is persuaded to take his turn in writing out the form's crib; Barker sees to it that he is caught and punished; and Russell, who remains a friend no matter what, warns him against currying cheap favour: 'Ah, Eric . . . they will ask you to do worse things if you yield so easily'.[12] Inevitably, it is not long before Eric is in trouble again, for laughing in chapel when Llewellyn's grasshopper makes itself at home in the foliage of a stout lady's bonnet. It is a brilliantly executed scene, but after Eric has been beaten by the headmaster, and in spite of Russell's unswerving friendship, his pride is such that he is unable to pray for either help or forgiveness.

The gradual change in Eric's character is as evident at home as it is at school. He becomes impatient with his brother, Vernon; he no longer goes for walks with his parents and worries them when he stays out crabbing without their knowing. When his parents have to return to India, Eric is

---

8. *Eric, or, Little by Little*, Volume I, chapter 1.
9. *Eric, or, Little by Little*, Volume I, chapter 2.
10. *Eric, or, Little by Little*, Volume I, chapter 4.
11. *Eric, or, Little by Little*, Volume I, chapter 5.
12. *Eric, or, Little by Little*, Volume I, chapter 5.

heartbroken, repents of his behaviour and determines to do better ('Oh, I *will* be a better boy, I *will* indeed . . . I mean to do great things, and they shall have nothing but good reports of me').[13] But his good intentions are quickly forgotten, as they always will be. At Roslyn, where he is now a boarder, his new master is the saintly Mr Rose – a man who 'had come out like gold from the flame' and who worked for the boys 'with a pure spirit of human and self-sacrificing love' – and he takes a particular interest in Eric and his friends.[14] But Eric soon succumbs to the bad but more attractive influence of Upton, Russell's cousin, even though he knows that 'all his moral consciousness was fast vanishing'.[15] He takes to swearing, which amuses Upton, but a reproof from Russell brings another bout of repentance.

Chapter 9, ' "Dead Flies", Or "Ye Shall Be As Gods" ', a title that conjures up the Fall in Eden and original sin, is the turning point of the novel. In Dormitory 7, the new boy, Ball, who had 'tasted more largely of the tree of the knowledge of evil' drops into 'the too willing ears the poison of his immorality'.[16] We are never told what he says, only that it is 'ruinous, sinful, damnable' and 'the most fatal curse which could ever become rife in a public school'. Urged on by the narrator, Eric knows that he must speak out: 'Now, Eric, now or never! Life and death, ruin and salvation, corruption and purity, are perhaps in the balance together, and the scale of your destiny may hang on a single word of yours. Speak out, boy!'[17] But Eric does not, cannot speak. He has cut himself off from God: 'The darkness was not broken by the flashing of an angel's wing, the stillness was not syllabled by the sound of an angel's voice'.[18] Though the event is small, especially to a twenty-first century consciousness, we are reminded of the Godless universe that Coleridge's Ancient Mariner experiences after shooting the albatross, or Macbeth's world after the murder of Duncan, or T.S. Eliot's 'Waste Land'. The next morning Eric tries to pray, but he hears Ball's footsteps and runs away: 'so Eric did not pray'. Compare this with the Ancient Mariner:

> I looked to heaven, and tried to pray;
> But or ever a prayer had gusht,
> A wicked whisper came and made
> My heart as dry as dust.[19]

---

13. *Eric, or, Little by Little*, Volume I, chapter 6.
14. *Eric, or, Little by Little*, Volume I, chapter 8.
15. *Eric, or, Little by Little*, Volume I, chapter 8.
16. *Eric, or, Little by Little*, Volume I, chapter 9.
17. *Eric, or, Little by Little*, Volume I, chapter 9.
18. *Eric, or, Little by Little*, Volume I, chapter 9.
19. Samuel Taylor Coleridge, 'The Ancient Mariner', ll. 240-243.

The following Sunday, Eric reveals to Russell and Montagu what has happened. In a further reference to the myth of Eden, Russell tells how he has spoken out against such talk in his own dormitory: 'What I said I don't know, but I felt as if I was trampling on a slimy poisonous adder'.[20] Soon afterwards Eric is in trouble for his part (abetted by Upton) in uproarious 'theatricals' in the dormitory. As always, punishment brings out the worst in him, and his work and behaviour deteriorate further. It is not surprising that he is accused of pinning up an abusive note about Mr Gordon, a master with whom he shares a mutual contempt. He is sent to Coventry, but his friends defend him at a 'trial' and, after some effective sleuthing, prove that Barker has tried to frame him. Barker is flogged and expelled, and Eric basks dangerously in restored popularity.

Volume I draws to a close with a dramatic adventure at the Stack, an outcrop of rock on the coast near Roslyn. Eric, Montagu and Russell watch the glorious colours of the sunset, but the atmosphere is ominous. Russell recalls Rose comparing a sunset to 'a thought of death, judgment and eternity, all in one'; says Montagu, 'It'll be stormy tomorrow'.[21] Finding themselves cut off, they leap for the shore, but Russell is injured. As the tension rises with the tide, Eric returns to the Stack and nurses Russell while they wait for help. Russell is carried back to Roslyn. Alone in his room, which is nevertheless 'thronged and beautiful with angelic presences', he is delirious and rarely conscious. In a reminder of *The Crofton Boys*, his leg is amputated ('the providence of a merciful God').[22] When Eric and Montagu are allowed to visit Russell, he seems almost Christ-like as the boys kneel by the bed: 'the sick boy tenderly put his hands on their heads, and pushed his thin white fingers through their hair'.[23] As Russell's life fades, he asks Eric to pray for him, but still 'no prayer would come' and it is left for Russell to pray for them both. He begs his friends to avoid all evil and read the Bible; and Mr Rose, surely an angel, holds his hand 'as fearlessly now, yea joyously, he entered the waters of the dark river'.[24]

So it is that Eric tries yet again to repent of his failings, but it seems it is too late. That night 'the dew of blessing did not fall on him' and the struggle between good and evil is made explicit in his nightmare:

> He was wandering down a path, at the end of which Russell stood with beckoning hand inviting him there; he saw his bright ingenuous smile, and heard, as of old, his joyous words,

20. *Eric, or, Little by Little*, Volume I, chapter 11.
21. *Eric, or, Little by Little*, Volume I, chapter 13.
22. *Eric, or, Little by Little*, Volume I, chapter 14.
23. *Eric, or, Little by Little*, Volume I, chapter 14.
24. *Eric, or, Little by Little*, Volume I, chapter 14.

and he hastened to meet him; when suddenly the boy-figure disappeared, and in its place he saw the stern brow, and gleaming garments, and drawn flaming sword of the Avenger.[25]

When Eric tries to reach Russell, 'ghostly hands' and 'irresistible cords' drag him back. Although the next morning he begins to make new resolutions for the future, we half-know that he will fail and there will be no replication of the transformation of Tom in *Tom Brown's Schooldays*. And while it is easy to dismiss chapters 14 and 15 as overly sentimental, the writing is arresting and, read as allegory, it has a peculiar power – however much the reader may find the theology questionable or objectionable.

Volume II: Tested by Fire

The action of the novel resumes a year later, with Russell's death and all of Eric's good intentions both forgotten. Eric, now aged sixteen, is in the fifth form at Roslyn and captain of cricket. In a side-swipe at the culture of athleticism that was beginning to sweep through public schools (partly because of *Tom Brown's Schooldays*), the narrator comments, 'he . . . was the acknowledged leader and champion in matters requiring boldness and courage; his popularity made him giddy; favour of man led to forgetfulness of God'.[26] Eric's brother Vernon has joined the school, but, ignored by Eric, has also succumbed to evil influences, most notably in the person of Brigson – a 'fore-front fighter in the devil's battle'.[27] Eric 'takes up' with Wildney, a twelve-year-old new boy whose disregard for rules has made him a hero among his peers, and is tempted into a night-time expedition to buy beer at The Jolly Herring, where the leering landlord, Billy, is another devil-in-disguise and is to become Eric's nemesis.

It is not long before Eric is persuaded to join Wildney and his friends for an illicit and sleazy banquet at The Jolly Herring. The party is caught by masters from Roslyn, but Eric and Wildney escape through a side door. That evening, Eric is insolent to Mr Rose, who up to now has been his good angel, symbolically breaks his cane and throws the pieces into the fire. He makes an apology to Mr Rose in front of the whole school, but Brigson miscalculates in organising the humiliation of Mr Rose, who stands up to him and beats him savagely. Thus Brigson's power over Roslyn melts away and, cursing Eric, he leaves Roslyn. Still Eric and Wildney continue in their dissolute ways, smoking, drinking, cribbing, and stealing pigeons from Mr Gordon's garden for Wildney's birthday feast. By this time Eric

25. *Eric, or, Little by Little*, Volume I, chapter 15.
26. *Eric, or, Little by Little*, Volume II, chapter 1.
27. *Eric, or, Little by Little*, Volume II, chapter 1.

believes it is 'too late to repent'; he alienates his true friends (his losing fight with Montagu is reminiscent of the fight between Tom Brown and Slogger Williams); worse, he has renounced his God: 'He had long flung away the shield of prayer and the helmet of holiness, and the sword of the spirit, which is the word of God; and now, unarmed and helpless, Eric stood alone, a mark for the fiery arrows of his enemies'.[28] After the feast, Eric and Wildney turn up drunk in chapel and only escape expulsion because of the bravery Eric has displayed in caring for Russell on the Stack. At last Eric's repentance is genuine and in a moment of grace, he and Vernon 'knelt down and prayed'. As they walk together along the sands, they have 'bright hopes for future days'[29] and we assume a nicely sentimental ending.

However, the wages of sin have not yet been fully paid: 'it was God's will that he [Eric] should pass through a yet fiercer flame ere he could be purified from pride and passion and self-confidence, and led to the cross of a suffering Saviour . . . where at last he might have rest'.[30] On a holiday expedition, trying to reach a bird's nest, Vernon falls from a cliff and dies. Then Billy appears, demanding money from Eric for Brigson's unpaid bill and blackmailing him over the stolen pigeons. Eric is tempted to take the 'cricketing money', but, after a conversation with his personified Conscience, he returns the coins to the box.

Nonetheless, when the money is actually stolen, suspicion falls on Eric. Unable to escape what is Brigson's parting curse, he runs away from school and takes ship on the *Stormy Petrel*, where he is beaten almost to death by the drunken captain. Thus at last, 'he was washed, he was cleansed, he was sanctified, he was justified, he would fear no evil, for God was with him, and underneath were the everlasting arms'.[31] He finds his way back to his Aunt's and is reunited with Montagu and Wildney, who find him changed by God's fire, the image that has smouldered and leapt throughout the novel: 'Every trace of recklessness and arrogance had passed away; every stain of passion had been removed; every particle of hardness had been calcined in the flame of trial.'[32] Montagu and Wildney report that Billy has been caught stealing from Roslyn and Eric's name has been cleared. Once again we feel the story will finish here, with Eric restored to both physical and spiritual health; but the actual ending is more cloying, and, though intended to be merciful, smacks horribly of divine injustice. Eric's broken body cannot recover, and as his life ebbs away he learns that his mother,

---

28. *Eric, or, Little by Little*, Volume II, chapter 8.
29. *Eric, or, Little by Little*, Volume II, chapter 8.
30. *Eric, or, Little by Little*, Volume II, chapter 10.
31. *Eric, or, Little by Little*, Volume II, chapter 12.
32. *Eric, or, Little by Little*, Volume II, chapter 13.

discovering what has happened at Roslyn to Vernon and Eric, has been killed by grief and shame. It is more than he can bear, but he dies in the knowledge that he is forgiven and with the brightness of his smile playing over his features in a now 'lambent flame'.[33]

The final chapter of *Eric*, 'Conclusion', comes as a surprise, with the narrator, for the first time, addressing the reader informally and in a quite different register of language: 'The other day I was staying with Montagu . . .'.[34] He reveals himself as Eric's school friend who has witnessed the story's events at first-hand and has now responded to the challenge thrown out by Mr Rose in a sermon mourning Eric: 'Why do you not try and reserve some records of his life?'[35] He reports that Montagu has inherited his father's estate and is standing as a Member of Parliament; Owen has achieved a first class at Trinity College, Cambridge, and has been elected as a fellow and tutor; Duncan, Wildney and Upton have all gained commissions in the army; Brigson has become a corrupt policeman; Rose is a vicar and Rowlandson has been appointed Bishop of Roslyn. This is not the voice of the evangelical sermoniser whose sermons and apostrophes have directed our thoughts throughout the novel, but the voice of an old friend of Eric who has simply been describing 'the scenes in so many of which we were engaged together in our schoolboy days'.[36] It is a different person altogether, and what turned from a school story into an overwrought allegory of the struggle for Man's soul is brought back sharply to the trivial excitements of childhood.

*

This discussion of *Eric* has concentrated on the novel as morality, but (as 'Conclusion' reminds us) working beneath that there is still a school story struggling to get out. There is the predicament of Eric and Vernon as children of the Empire, as much orphans as Russell when their parents return to India for five years. There are the complexities of changing teenage relationships and friendships that survive the most difficult of trials. There are the dangers of older boys 'taking up' younger ones (upended when Wildney leads Eric to ruin, rather than the other way about); the quest for popularity; the bullying; the honour of never sneaking on one's peers, even one's enemies, far outweighing the honour of telling the truth; the way one disruptive influence (Brigson) can infect a whole school.

---

33. *Eric, or, Little by Little*, Volume II, chapter 13.
34. *Eric, or, Little by Little*, Volume II, chapter 14.
35. *Eric, or, Little by Little*, Volume II, chapter 14.
36. *Eric, or, Little by Little*, Volume II, chapter 14.

There are also sensible reflections (from a post-Arnold standpoint) on the prefect system ('Had the monitorial system existed, that contagion could have been effectually checked'),[37] on the dangerous new emphasis on sport, on the scorn of the intellectual and the incompetence of the teaching. And there is the unsavoury spectacle of a school dominated by corporal punishment, which in Eric provokes only hurt pride and rebellion, but by which the narrator is strangely fascinated, from the wheals on Eric's hands in chapter 4 to the account of his lashing on the *Stormy Petrel*.

Eric, or, Little by Little was Farrar's first novel and it attempts too much. It attempts to be a school story for a schoolboy audience, building on the success and model of *Tom Brown*. It also attempts to be something far grander, an evangelical epic, where the fire of God as much as the fire of Hell burns cruelly and the wages for not very great sins are the deaths of Russell, Vernon, Eric and Mrs Williams. In the end, the essential triviality of the school story and the grandeur of epic do not go hand in hand, just as the narrator's altered personality in the 'Conclusion' is unconvincing. Yet for all its excess, Farrar's writing has moments of extraordinary power. *Eric* is, I think, a failure, but a glorious failure. Its critical rehabilitation in recent years is richly deserved.

---

37. *Eric, or, Little by Little*, Volume II, chapter 2.

Chapter 3

The Popular Story

Talbot Baines Reed – *The Fifth Form at St Dominic's* (1887)

If *Tom Brown's Schooldays* and *Eric* kindled interest in the school story, it was Talbot Baines Reed who rescued it from an excess of piety and probable oblivion. Reed's stories began life as serials in *The Boy's Own Paper,* published weekly by the Religious Tract Society in which three generations of the Reed family were involved, and subsequently issued in novel form. He contributed to the first edition of *The Boy's Own Paper* in January 1879 ('My First Football Match' by An Old Boy, which was set at Parkhurst School and printed, with a half-page illustration, on the front cover). This was followed by other short stories set at Parkhurst. His first school serial was *The Adventures of a Three Guinea Watch* (1880-81), which traces the journey of a schoolboy's pocket watch from Randlebury School, through university, and to the Indian mutiny. But it was *The Fifth Form at St Dominic's* (1881-82, and published as a novel in 1887) that cemented Reed's reputation. Such are its strengths that it became the model for the wave of boarding school serials and novels that were to follow over the next thirty years. Reed's other boarding school serials were *My Friend Smith*, set (unusually for Reed) in Stonebridge House, 'a modest establishment for the "backward and troublesome" of the Do-the-boys Hall order' (1882–83),[1] *The Willoughby Captains* (1883–84), *The Master of the Shell* (1887–88),

---

1. G.A. Hutchison, Prefatory Note to Talbot Baines Reed, *My Friend Smith* (London: *The Boy's Own Paper*, 1889).

The Cock-House at Fellsgarth (1891) and *Tom, Dick and Harry* (1892–93). All were later issued as novels and many were still in print half a century later.

As well as the importance of *The Fifth Form at St Dominic's* in the development of the school story, that of The Religious Tract Society and *The Boy's Own Paper* should not be underestimated. The Society saw that with the introduction of education for all in 1870 there was little leisure reading for children apart from the frowned-on 'penny dreadfuls'. With its mix of articles on such things as sport, travel, fitness (a fit body begets a fit mind), hobbies and fiction, *The Boy's Own Paper* was a huge success and in its heyday had a print-run in excess of 500,000 copies. At first it appealed to a cross-section of society, but by the 1890s it was aimed more at a middle-class readership. The companion *The Girl's Own Paper* ran from 1880 to 1951. Not surprisingly, other weekly papers sprang up in competition, such as *Chums, The Public School Magazine, The Captain, The Gem, The Magnet*, and *The Wizard* (these were also vehicles for the popular school story), and as a result the circulation of *The Boy's Own Paper* began to decline. In 1913 it became a monthly magazine and in this format struggled on with a steadily declining readership until 1967.[2] In the context of the school story and of children's literature more widely, G.A. Hutchison, the editor of *The Boy's Own Paper* in its glory days from 1879 to 1912, was an unsung hero, resisting pressure from the Religious Tract Society to reduce the number of stories and to give more prominence to its Christian message.[3]

The Fifth Form of St Dominic's is clearly influenced by both *Tom Brown's Schooldays* and *Eric*. Like them, it includes a young hero who 'little by little' is dragged down by public school life; an initiation ceremony; a bully who gets his come-uppance; a headmaster who is a 'Doctor' and has a persuasive line in sermons; a young and enthusiastic master, who acts as a mentor and sides with the hero *contra mundum*; one or more friends who support and influence the hero through good times and bad; a cricket match; a rugby match; a fishing rod; a serious illness; a powerful narrative voice that in moments of high drama slips into the historic present; and an epilogue that revisits the characters after their schooldays are over. Similar to *Eric*, it also features an older/younger brother relationship, a leering landlord, a boat trip and a pervading dramatic irony. To the mix it adds a stolen examination

2. The Lutterworth Press, successor to the Religious Tract Society, took over publication of *The Boy's Own Paper* in 1939. From 1963 until 1967 it was published by Purnell and Sons, which, after a merger, became BPC Publishing Ltd in 1964.
3. From 1879 until 1897, James Macaulay was the supervising editor of *The Boy's Own Paper*, but it seems that Hutchison, his assistant, was its editor in all but name from the outset.

paper and a school 'newspaper' that provides an amusing commentary on
the action. But Reed is describing a school fifty years on from Hughes's
Rugby or Farrar's Roslyn, and this, combined with the fact that he was
educated at the City of London School, with a very different day-school
culture, makes St Dominic's a more civilised place and more accessible to
his wide audience. Just as importantly, he realised, with Hutchison, that
for the young reader an excess of preaching and moralising is unwelcome
and likely to produce an Eric-like spirit of rebellion. However, although
The Fifth Form at St Dominic's is mainly free from religious zeal, there
remain frequent and patronising authorial interventions and questions –
for example:

> Of course, profound reader, you have made the brilliant
> discovery by this time that Master Stephen Greenfield was a very
> green boy. So were you and I at his age; and so, after all, we are
> now. For the more we think we know, the greener we shall find
> we are; that's a fact![4]

At the start of *The Fifth Form at St Dominic's*, ten-year-old Stephen
Greenfield, a new boy at St Dominic's where his brother Oliver is a fifth-form
pupil, seems to be the conventional schoolboy hero, rather in the mould
of Tom Brown. He travels to St Dominic's by train – a similar distancing
device to Tom Brown's carriage journey to Rugby – and imagines 'all the
marvellous exploits which were to mark his career at St Dominic's. He was
to be a prodigy in his new school from the very first; in a few terms he was
to be captain of the cricket club, and meanwhile was to gain the favour of
the Sixth by helping them regularly in their lessons'.[5] He isn't troubled by
the routine initiation ceremony (a not-too-brutal walloping with a cricket
bat), becomes a fag for a sixth-form boy called Loman, is fooled by a spoof
and impossible entrance test, and is chosen as a Guinea-pig rather than a
Tadpole – random groupings of the smaller boys, whose purpose seems to
be to argue and fight pointlessly with each other. He is engaged to fight
Bramble, a troublesome Tadpole, three times a week and is at the centre of
a fags' strike (as in *Tom Brown's Schooldays*) that, after the intervention of
the headmaster, Dr Senior, fizzles out over the summer holidays. With all
the distractions, he begins to slack in class and resorts to cribbing, but Mr
Rastle takes him aside and puts him back on the right track: 'he felt that
his master had an interest in him, and that acted like magic to his soul'.[6]

---

4. Talbot Baines Reed, *The Fifth Form at St Dominic's* (London: Thames, 1887),
   chapter 3.
5. *The Fifth Form at St Dominic's*, chapter 2.
6. *The Fifth Form at St Dominic's*, chapter 10.

However, things begin to go badly wrong for Stephen when, in his naïvety, he is hoodwinked by Old Mr Cripps, the lock-keeper, into parting with his pocket money as charity, and by his son, the landlord of The Cockchafer, a low-life public house in the nearby village of Maltby. He 'buys' a cricket bat off young Cripps, who artfully refuses even to name a price, though later the bat turns out to be worthless and the price high, but Stephen, still not seeing how he is being ensnared, becomes a regular visitor to The Cockchafer. At old Mr Cripps's cottage by the weir, young Cripps and his associates try to persuade Stephen to join in with their drinking, smoking and gambling, and when he refuses they are on the point of throwing him into the river.

By chance, his brother Oliver and friends have taken a boat to escape from their studies and are able to rescue him. Knowing that Stephen has put himself on dangerous ground by visiting The Cockchafer and could be expelled if found out, Oliver tells the headmaster, Dr Senior, all that has happened. Because of Oliver's honesty, Dr Senior takes a lenient view, but, in one of the few religious passages in the novel, there is an echo of Dr Arnold in *Tom Brown's Schooldays* when later that day he preaches in chapel:

> 'Forgetting those things which are behind – reaching forth unto those things which are before' – this was the Doctor's text, and in the few simple words in which he urged his hearers to lay the past, with all its burdens, and disappointments, and shame, upon Him in whom alone forgiveness is to be found, Stephen drank in new courage and hope for the future.[7]

It is an uncharacteristic intervention, but Stephen has learned his lesson. From here on, there is still the comic relief of his involvement in the quarrels of the Guinea-pigs and Tadpoles, and his loyal support of his brother, but although he remains important structurally, as the glue that holds the various parts of the novel together, he is no longer at the centre of the action.

As the novel's title suggests, the second and central strand of the plot centres on the fifth form at St Dominic's. Public schools were, and are, especially hierarchical places, but this year the fifth form (supported by the Guinea-pigs) has more ability and more spirit than the sixth (supported by the Tadpoles), which leads to a peculiar rivalry. The situation is exacerbated by the waspish Pembury, who suggests that the *Sixth Form Magazine* is 'rubbish and unreadable' and the fifth form should produce

---

7. *The Fifth Form at St Dominic's*, chapter 22.

its own magazine, *The Dominican*, under his editorship;[8] the sixth form is an obvious target for its cynical barbs. But the leading figures in the fifth are Horace Wraysford and Oliver Greenfield. Wraysford is described as:

> handsome and jovial . . . certain to be in the School Eleven against the County, certain to win the mile race and the 'hurdles' at the Athletic Sports, and is not at all unlikely to carry off the Nightingale Scholarship next autumn, even though one of the Sixth is in it too.[9]

His best friend is Oliver Greenfield, a more complex character: 'He is quieter and more lazy, and more solemn. Some say he has a temper, and others that he is selfish; and generally he is not the most popular boy in St Dominic's.'[10] One of the features that makes the novel stand out from so many imitators is that it is Oliver, a difficult to fathom character with as many weaknesses as strengths, and not his innocent younger brother or the initially more appealing but lightweight Wraysford, who turns out to be its real hero.

For the moment, though, it is Loman, Stephen Greenfield's sixth-form fag-master, who disrupts life at the school. After he has been deputed by the sixth form to have the *Dominican* removed from the passage, he receives a mocking reception and, losing his temper, strikes Oliver Greenfield on the mouth. It is the signal for a fight, but Greenfield turns away. In doing so, he further loses the respect of the fifth form: 'For the first time in the history of their class, as far as they could recollect, a blow struck had not been returned'.[11] Greenfield offers no explanation for his behaviour and is branded a coward. Only Wraysford and Pembury stick up for him, and Loman misses no opportunity to play on Greenfield's fall from favour. But Loman has other worries. He has bought a fishing rod from young Cripps and, before he pays for it, he snaps it when practising a cast from the study window. He attempts to return the rod without acknowledging the damage on the pretext that he has been given another rod as a present. In spite of Loman's lies, the truth comes out and with it the opportunity for Cripps to blackmail him – demanding £20 on top of the exorbitant cost of the rod. As more lies follow, the debt grows and Loman's visits to The Cockchafer become more frequent.

Attention turns to the Nightingale Scholarship examination, which is where, in this skilfully constructed novel, the various strands of the plot come together. There are three candidates for the Scholarship: Greenfield,

---

8. *The Fifth Form at St Dominic's*, chapter 1.
9. *The Fifth Form at St Dominic's*, chapter 1.
10. *The Fifth Form at St Dominic's*, chapter 2.
11. *The Fifth Form at St Dominic's*, chapter 8.

Wraysford and Loman. The scholarship, worth fifty pounds, is intended for supporting the winner at university, but Loman sees it as a way of paying off his debt to Cripps. For the boys, however, the examination becomes a contest between the fifth and sixth. Greenfield and Wraysford pore over their books; Loman is going off on 'studious rambles', but the sixth realise their cause is lost when they see him returning with his books, 'walking unsteadily, with a queer, stupid look on his face'.[12]

Then one of the scholarship papers is stolen from the Doctor's study on the eve of the examination. Simon, the clown of the novel, reports having seen Greenfield coming out of the Doctor's study at the time in question. As readers, we know Greenfield has been looking for the Doctor to tell him of Stephen's exploits, but Simon has already leapt to the wrong conclusion and is quick to cast aspersions. This time, Oliver strikes him, only adding to the suspicion that surrounds him. Wraysford and Pembury do not join in with the general condemnation, but with Greenfield refusing to defend himself against Simon's intimations, their support is half-hearted and the friendship between Greenfield and Wraysford begins to crumble. When the results are announced, Greenfield has triumphed. 'I must say,' eulogises the Doctor, 'the examiners and I are astonished and highly gratified with this really brilliant performance. 'Astonished' is loaded with dramatic irony, and the fifth-formers, far from celebrating their champion, greet him with a 'general sneer of contempt'.[13] Greenfield, who never minds too much what the world thinks, does nothing to defend himself, 'Because I don't choose, and it would be no use if I did'.[14] The fifth form sends him to Coventry, but, outwardly at least, it seems to have no effect; in fact, such is his stoic bearing of the situation and his refusal to show any guilt or penitence, that it is his accusers who begin to feel ashamed. As the boys leave for Christmas, Pembury begins to see how everybody may have been mistaken: 'He doesn't act like a guilty person. Just fancy, Wray . . . if you and I and the rest have been making fools of ourselves all the term!'[15]

So it is that after Christmas, things begin to change. Now it is time for the examination for the Waterston Exhibition. Wraysford and Loman are candidates again, and unexpectedly Greenfield also puts his name forward. He knows that if he wins it will perhaps be accepted that he did not cheat in the Nightingale; and the fifth-form boys see the same, and are uneasy about how they have behaved towards him. Even before the results are announced (Greenfield triumphs, but insists that Wraysford takes the

---

12. *The Fifth Form at St Dominic's*, chapter 19.
13. *The Fifth Form at St Dominic's*, chapter 24.
14. *The Fifth Form at St Dominic's*, chapter 27.
15. *The Fifth Form at St Dominic's*, chapter 29.

prize), Wraysford makes up with Greenfield, and little by little the others admit they have been wrong. Soon, since this is a school story, Greenfield and Wraysford are heroes in the football match against the County, but for Loman the tide turns in a different direction. The hapless Simon lets on that Loman has been a regular visitor to The Cockchafer and he is forced to resign as a monitor. He manages at last to pay back all he owes to young Cripps, though to do so he has to borrow from Greenfield and Wraysford, hating them even more for their generosity: 'For a mean person nearly always detests an honest one, and the more open and generous the one is, the meaner the other feels in his own heart by contrast.'[16] Then, the stolen examination paper is found in Loman's 'Juvenal' and, though nothing can be proved, the boys are left to draw their own conclusions.

Thus the novel moves to its climax. Young Cripps produces Loman's promissory note, which he has previously feigned to destroy, and demands that the debt be repaid again. Seeing no way out other than disgrace, Loman goes missing. It is Greenfield who discovers him at night in a storm and coaxes him back to St Dominic's. Before they return, Loman insists on telling all that the reader already knows, and in doing so offers the moral of how one small sin leads inexorably to others and to disaster:

> Cripps had used his advantage to drive the boy from one wickedness and folly to another – from deceit to gambling, from gambling to debt, from debt to more deceit, and so on. How drinking, low company, and vicious habits had followed . . . and how, when the critical moment came, he yielded to the tempter and stole the paper.[17]

Loman hovers between life and death, but Reed's world is different from Farrar's world, and after four weeks he recovers and goes away 'truly penitent, looking away from self and his own poor efforts to Him, the World's Great Burden Bearer, whose blood "cleanseth us from all sin" '.[18] Only Oliver Greenfield shakes his hand as he leaves.

The 'last words' of the final chapter move the action five years on. The St Dominic's cricket team has beaten the County by five wickets – and the captain is Stephen Greenfield. Watching are Tony Pembury (now the editor of a well-known paper), Simon ('a vacant looking-young man with a great crop of whiskers and puffy cheeks'), Wraysford (a popular tutor at his Cambridge college), and Oliver Greenfield (a rowing blue in his last year at Cambridge and now a 'rising man'). Cripps has left The Cockchafer, and

---

16. *The Fifth Form at St Dominic's*, chapter 33.
17. *The Fifth Form at St Dominic's*, chapter 37.
18. *The Fifth Form at St Dominic's*, chapter 37.

Loman, after five years farming in Australia, is coming home. Without any sense of piety and personifying forgiveness, Oliver says, 'When he does, I tell you what: we must all make up a jolly party and come down together and help him through with it.'[19]

The Fifth Form at St Dominic's weaves together the stories of Stephen Greenfield, Oliver Greenfield, Horace Wraysford and Loman, maintaining the reader's interest as it opens up views into the various levels of school life; although originally published in parts, it avoids being episodic in nature. It is also fair to say that, with the possible exception of *Stalky & Co.*, the subject of the next chapter, Reed's stories were rarely equalled. There is no doubt that he benefited from the way the public school system had developed since the time of *Tom Brown's Schooldays*. There was more order and more acceptance of a hierarchy among the boys that does not depend on physical superiority. The fags may go on strike in *The Fifth Form at St Dominic's*, but there is no rebellion. The headmaster, Dr Senior, rarely intervenes; when he does, he behaves quietly and firmly, but he prefers to leave things to the instinct and good sense of the pupils. The heavy religious content of *Tom Brown* and (in particular) *Eric* has diminished, though there is a strong moral emphasis and a sometimes too intrusive narrator to make sure that it is noted. As a character, Oliver Greenfield has greater depth than the usual stereotype, and we discover in him qualities that at first were unexpected. Friendships are restored, and even enemies are forgiven. Above all, after the misery of *Eric*, this is an optimistic novel, in which everything turns out right in the end.

---

19. *The Fifth Form at St Dominic's*, chapter 38.

Chapter 4

The Imperial Story

Rudyard Kipling – *Stalky & Co.* (1899)

The second half of Victoria's reign was dominated by the expansion and administration of the British Empire. There were wars to be fought and uprisings to put down. Patriotism was all, and with it the willingness to die for Queen and Country. It was up to the public schools to educate and inspire their pupils appropriately; and, increasingly, 'appropriate' came to mean an unquestioning acceptance of authority and a selfless commitment to play for the team. In 1856, on a visit to Eton College, the Duke of Wellington was said to remark, 'It is here that the battle of Waterloo was won!' Later, in 1881, in a swipe at the cult of athleticism that had grown up in the public schools, Matthew Arnold rejoined, 'Disasters have been prepared in those playing-fields as well as victories; disasters due to inadequate mental training – to want of application, knowledge, intelligence, lucidity.'[1] Kipling's Stalky would have heartily agreed.

Surprisingly, however, the Empire was rarely an explicit ingredient of Victorian schoolboy fiction and as a story of Empire Rudyard Kipling's *Stalky & Co.* (1899) stands apart; even so, it has no time for the sort of sentimental jingoism of the time, characterised in Sir Henry Newbolt's poem 'Vitaï Lampada' (1897), in which a cricket match at Clifton College is seen as preparation for imperial adventure:[2]

---

1. Matthew Arnold, 'An Eton Boy', in *Fortnightly Review*, June 1881.
2. In fact, the action described in 'Vitaï Lampada', the Battle of Abu Klea in Sudan,

> The river of death has brimmed his banks,
> And England's far, and Honour a name,
> But the voice of a schoolboy rallies the ranks:
> 'Play up! play up! and play the game!'[3]

Nor does *Stalky & Co.* have any truck with the conservative and moralising school story. Kipling thought little of *Tom Brown's Schooldays* and *The Fifth Form of St Dominic's*, but it is *Eric* and Farrar's subsequent novel, *St Winifred's*, given to Stalky by his Aunt on his sixteenth birthday, that are especially derided for their excess of emotion and religion. In the short story 'The Brushwood Boy' (1895), Kipling describes the education of its idealised hero Georgie Cottar: 'the school was not encouraged to dwell on its emotions, but rather to keep in hard condition, avoid false quantities and to enter the army direct'.[4] *Stalky & Co.* is an expanded prospectus for such beliefs and it is not a comfortable read.

Stalky & Co. is not a novel in the usual sense, but a collection of nine individual short stories that first appeared in different magazines between 1897 and 1899. The order in which the stories are collected is not the order of their original publication, and the story that might have introduced the collection, 'Stalky', is not included at all. There were later to be four more stories and *The Complete Stalky & Co.,* which added these and 'Stalky', was published in 1929.[5]

Like both *Tom Brown's Schooldays* and *Eric, Stalky & Co.* is in part autobiographical. It is set in the United Services College at Westward Ho!, Devon, which Kipling attended from 1878 until 1882. It was a new foundation, set up in 1874 by a company of retired Army and Navy officers with the main purpose of preparing often unpromising boys for entry into Sandhurst, Woolwich and Dartmouth, at a modest fee[6] ('We *aren't* a public school,' says Flint. 'We're a limited liability company payin' four per cent. . . . We've got to get into the Army – or get out').[7] There were no frills, social pretensions or (surprisingly) military trappings, and both food and accommodation were sparse. Initially there were about sixty pupils at the College (who had often either failed to gain entry into public schools, or had been expelled from them)

---

was another glorious failure for the British.

3. Sir Henry Newbolt, 'Vitaï Lampada' (1897).
4. Rudyard Kipling, 'The Brushwood Boy' (London, 1895).
5. Rudyard Kipling, *The Complete Stalky & Co.* (London, 1929). The text of a further Stalky story, 'Scylla and Charybdis', has since been discovered.
6. After the Army Act of 1871, Service commissions and promotion had to be obtained by aptitude and examination rather than by wealth, and although the public schools began to open 'Army classes', they were not within everyone's means.
7. Rudyard Kipling, 'A Little Prep', in *Stalky & Co.* (London, 1899).

and at its peak the roll grew to over 200; many of the pupils were sent home from India, where their parents were soldiers or civil servants. At first sight it seems to have been a strange decision to send Kipling to the College. There was never any question of his becoming a soldier (he was very short-sighted), but his parents, who lived in Bombay, knew the College's headmaster, Cormell Price, and could not afford the fees of an established public school. To begin with, Kipling was horribly bullied, but after his first year the unexpectedly liberal atmosphere began to suit him: he did not have to take part in organised games and his talent for writing was encouraged.

The College was housed in a terrace of twelve seafront boarding houses. A corridor was built to connect the houses and there was enough space for a school hall and a gymnasium, but no chapel – let alone as a focal point. Cormell Price, who had run the 'Army class' at Haileybury, was as unconventional as his school. Unusually for headmasters of the time, he was not in holy orders, nor even a committed Christian. He was a left-wing pacifist leading a school that produced soldiers and (despite the vivid accounts in *Stalky & Co.*) he rarely administered corporal punishment. But he was good at his job. He was respected by the boys – even by the real-life Stalky and Co. – as he didn't allow anything to get in the way of extra tuition and he had his ways of negotiating on behalf of his potential officers: 'The Head often ran up to town, where the school devoutly believed he bribed officials for early proofs of the Army Examination papers.'[8] Price retired in 1894 and, as the Indian rupee devalued and public school supply caught up with military demand, numbers at the College dwindled. In 1904, only thirty years after it had opened, it amalgamated with the Imperial Service College, Windsor, which in turn was absorbed by Haileybury College, Hertfordshire, in 1942.

Stalky and Co. are three fifth-form pupils who inhabit Number 5 Study in Mr Prout's house and are very different from the upright heroes of the *Boy's Own* serials. They are in their final year at the College. Stalky is based on the young Major-General Lionel Dunsterville and is the manipulator of the group; McTurk is inspired by George Beresford, an aesthete, who reads Ruskin and would become a noted photographer; and Beetle, who reads and writes poetry, is the embodiment of the teenage Kipling. In each story Stalky engineers an escapade that challenges public school convention, represented by the housemasters, Prout and King; but the risks are calculated and punishment is accepted without complaint. In fact, Stalky and Co. have developed a *modus vivendi* with the masters, and it is only when this is challenged that they come into significant conflict ('Leave them alone or calamity will overtake you,' the chaplain

8. 'A Little Prep' in *Stalky & Co.*

warns his colleagues).[9] Everything in *Stalky & Co.* works on a secular, even humdrum level. There is no suggestion that the boys souls are ever in danger; no prayers are said (even by the chaplain); no-one suffers very much or dies (except later, in battle). Nor is there any truck with such things as the 'honour of the house' and 'fairness', and King's view that 'by games, and games alone, was salvation wrought' is summarily dismissed.[10] So in an important way *Stalky & Co.* is surprisingly modern, in its selfishness if nothing else (though a hundred years on the archaic schoolboy slang, laced with Latin and French maxims, and the Devon dialect, can be off-putting). Whereas most late-Victorian school stories (like *The Fifth Form at St Dominic's*) still have a whiff of the earnestness of *Tom Brown* and *Eric* about them, Kipling believed that school life has little significance beyond the boundaries of its small world.

'In Ambush'

One of the striking characteristics of *Stalky & Co.* is the way in which the stories are largely told through dialogue. The authorial narrator is much less obtrusive than we have seen so far and offers no overt moralising (what moralising there is, is put into the untrustworthy mouths of the masters, while the Head offers less conventional and more pertinent advice). But in their conversation the boys become dramatised narrators, taking the weight of the storytelling, and as readers we are encouraged to see the action from their usually anarchic point of view.

The first of the stories, 'In Ambush', tells how Stalky and Co. set off for an afternoon of reading and smoking.[11] On Colonel Dabney's land, which bristles with forbidding notices, they discover an idyllic spot on the cliff edge, which is described in a rare passage of magical prose:

> He parted the tough stems before him, and it was as a window opened on a far view of Lundy, and the deep sea sluggishly nosing the pebbles a couple of hundred feet below. They could hear young jackdaws squawking on the ledges, the hiss and jabber of a nest of hawks somewhere out of sight; and, with great deliberation, Stalky spat on the back of a young rabbit sunning himself far down where only a cliff-rabbit could have found foot-hold. Great grey and black gulls

---

9. 'The Impressionists' in *Stalky & Co.*
10. 'An Unsavoury Interlude' in *Stalky & Co.*
11. Unusually, smoking was permitted at the United Services College. This was a commercial more than a moral choice since the London 'crammers', its main competitors, also allowed pupils to smoke.

screamed against the jackdaws; the heavy-scented acres of
bloom round them were alive with low-nesting birds, singing
or silent as the shadow of the wheeling hawks passed and
returned; and on the naked turf across the combe rabbits
thumped and frolicked.[12]

What is striking here is the gentle assault on our senses: the 'window' that
gives a view across the sea to Lundy Island, the frolicking rabbits and the
birds wheeling overhead, the 'heavy-scent' of the flora and the cacophony
of sound from the sea 'nosing the pebbles', 'the hiss and jabber' of hawks,
the scream of gulls and jackdaws, the song of the low-nesting birds, and
the thump of rabbits. It is a sparkling medley of alliteration, assonance and
onomatopoeia, just held back from excess by Stalky's casual spitting on the
sunbathing rabbit below. But when Dabney's gamekeeper attempts to shoot
a fox, McTurk, descended from Irish gentry, is incensed and, trespasser or
not, complains loudly to Colonel Dabney – no longer a College boy but a
'landed man speaking to his equal', 'deep calling to deep'.[13] Unexpectedly,
Stalky and Co. are befriended by the Colonel, treated to beer and food, and
given the run of his estate.

Much of the comedy of *Stalky & Co.* comes from the ingenious plotting
of Stalky and the verbal fireworks that ensue. So when on one of their
subsequent expeditions the boys realise that the masters are planning to
follow them ('we'll be *suivi*'), Stalky lures them on to Dabney's estate,
where they are apprehended by the lodge-keeper, and Foxy, the College's
Sergeant, roped in for the pursuit by King and Prout, becomes the fall
guy: 'Who'm yeou to give arders here, gingy whiskers? . . . Yiss, I reckon us
knows the boys yeou'm after. They've two long ears an' vuzzy bellies, an you
nippies they in yeour pocets when they'm dead.'[14] Then the hapless Foxy
is harangued deliciously by Dabney as a trespasser disturbing the game
birds. It is as if they are back in the army and the Colonel is addressing an
insubordinate sergeant:

> Why – why – why, ye misbegotten poacher, ye'll be teaching me
> my A B C next! Roarin' like a bull in the bushes down there!
> . . . Ye've a furtive, sneakin', poachin' look in your eye, that 'ud
> ruin the reputation of an archangel! Don't attempt to deny it!
> Ye have! A sergeant? More shame to you, then, an' the worst
> bargain Her Majesty ever made![15]

---

12. 'In Ambush' in *Stalky & Co.*
13. 'In Ambush' in *Stalky & Co.*
14. 'In Ambush' in *Stalky & Co.*
15. 'In Ambush' in *Stalky & Co.*

All the time Stalky and Co. are listening from the gatekeeper's cottage, where they are being treated to strawberries and cream. Convulsed in laughter, Beetle has a crochet-work anti-macassar stuffed in his mouth, Stalky buries his head on the horse hair pillow, and McTurk 'is eating the rag-carpet before the speckless hearth'.[16]

On their return to College, Stalky and Co. are accused by the masters of all kinds of 'misdeeds', 'vices', 'villainies', and 'immoralities', but, threatened with a beating and sure of their ground, they appeal to the Head, as is their right. Briefed by Foxy as to what has actually happened, the Head sees it all clearly and, in spite of the boys' carefully preserved innocence, he perpetrates, as he acknowledges, 'a howling injustice' – 'six apiece' (but not very thoroughly executed) – and offers them the loan of his paperback books. King and Prout, it seems, suffer a far more hurtful verbal lashing. 'I swear I'll pray for the Head tonight,' says Beetle.[17]

On one level in 'In Ambush' the reader is drawn to side with Stalky and Co. as rebels against the establishment. They are the ones who tell the tale. But for all the satisfaction we may derive from their triumph, the story is uncomfortable. It is not the refusal of McTurk to support the house matches and to humour poor Prout that is objectionable, but the 'sneer' with which he expresses himself. There is a lot of sneering and gloating in 'In Ambush' and the other stories, betraying an unattractive self-satisfaction in Stalky and Co. It goes further than schoolboy fun and displays an utter lack of concern for others ('*Jamais j'ai gloaté comme je gloaterai aujourd'hui*,' says Stalky in 'An Unsavoury Interlude').[18] And although Stalky and Co. may be the heroes in the book, in the College they are regarded as bullies, who have deliberately set themselves apart: ' "They've no following in the school, and they are distinctly – er brutal to their juniors," said Prout'.[19] It is an irony of which Kipling – a master of irony – must surely have been aware.

'Slaves of the Lamp' and 'The Moral Reformers'

When, in 'Slaves of the Lamp', King interrupts a rehearsal of Aladdin and belittles Beetle, Stalky plans revenge. A volley from his catapult from the darkened study assaults Rabbits-Eggs, the local carrier, peppering the rotten cannon of his cart and causing his horse to wheel in the shafts. When King, who is berating Beetle in the approving presence of Manders minor, stands in the gas-lit window to investigate, he becomes the target

16. 'In Ambush' in *Stalky & Co.*
17. 'In Ambush' in *Stalky & Co.*
18. 'An Unsavoury Interlude' in *Stalky & Co.*
19. 'In Ambush' in *Stalky & Co.*

of the enraged Rabbits-Eggs: 'Yiss, yeou, yeou long-nosed, fower-eyed, gingy-whiskered beggar! Yeu'm tu old for such goin's on. Aie! Poultice yeour nose, I tall 'ee! Poultice yeour long nose!'[20] A hurled flint shatters the window and hits Manders minor; another gives Beetle the excuse to knock over a candle-lamp and drip grease on the Persian rug. When King exits to summon Foxy, Beetle guides Manders's bleeding head over the Latin papers on King's table, covers the doorknob with the blood, scars a set of 'Gibbon' as if hit by a flint, and spills ink and gum over the floor. There is again something unnaturally sadistic in Beetle's adding to the destruction of King's belongings – more than might be caused by King's recent insults. This, I think, is the bullied Beetle and the bullied Kipling taking revenge for all the bullying they have suffered themselves. Meanwhile, relaxing in a steaming bath, Stalky ponders the evening's success: ' "Moi! Je! Ich! Ego!" gasped Stalky. "Wasn't it beautiful?" '[21] There could be nothing more self-satisfied than that.

Even so, there remains a score for Stalky and Co. to settle with the younger boys in the house: 'three brisk minutes accounted for many silkworms, pet larvae, French exercises, school caps, half-prepared bones and skulls, and a dozen pots of home-made sloe jam' – a rout of an entire school life and of jam from a distant home. In the story's conclusion, McTurk says of King, 'He begins by bullying little chaps; then he bullies the big chaps; then he bullies some one who isn't connected with the College, and then catches it.'[22] The irony is still at work.

And it is in 'The Moral Reformers' that Stalky and Co. move from bullying the little chaps to bullying the big chaps. Reverend John, the College chaplain, pays a visit to Study 5 to alert them to some bullying that is going on in the house. Beetle recalls his own miserable experience of being bullied ('corkscrew – brush-drill – keys – head-knucklin – arm twistin' – rockin – Ag Ags')[23] and now it seems history is repeating itself with Campbell and Sefton making young Clewer's life a misery. With the chaplain's suggestion that Stalky and Co. might put a stop to it 'in any way you please', they apply their minds to the business. The idea of making Clewer their study-fag is quickly dismissed ('He's a dirty little brute,' says McTurk; and then, in another swipe at Farrar's sentimentality, 'We ain't goin' to have any beastly Erickin'. D'you want to walk about with your arm round his neck?').[24] Then Stalky hatches a plan. Using the sham bullying

20. 'Slaves of the Lamp' in *Stalky & Co.*
21. 'Slaves of the Lamp' in *Stalky & Co.*
22. 'Slaves of the Lamp' in *Stalky & Co.*
23. 'The Moral Reformers' in *Stalky & Co.*
24. 'The Moral Reformers' in *Stalky & Co.*

of Beetle as bait, Campbell and Sefton are tricked into joining in and are 'joyously' trussed up to take on Beetle and McTurk in a cock fight. But once the pair are immobilised the atmosphere changes, becomes threatening.

The ensuing scene is like something out of a CIA rendition. For Beetle and Kipling, this is more revenge for what once happened to them: ' "Molly Fairburn" of the old days could not have done better.' Not only are Campbell and Sefton subjected to all the named but never described tortures, but they are also brutalised psychologically. When it seems they are broken, the punishment continues at a more ferocious but always calculated pitch: 'Now we're goin' to show you what real bullyin' is', as Stalky and Co., with two boxing gloves, rock each of their victims to sleep.[25] Sefton's moustache – or at least some of it – is burned and shaved away, and work continues with cricket stump and strap until the victims are made to sing a chorus of 'Kitty of Coleraine' 'à la Clewer'. 'I've had it done to me', says Beetle coldly; and throughout the whole sickening business, and the helpless tears and the appeals for mercy, comes the refrain, 'The bleatin' of the kid excites the tiger.'[26] Just as Campbell and Sefton have been motivated by Clewer's misery, so Stalky and Co. seem to be driven on by the suffering they inflict. We will meet their like again in Jack Merridew and his savages in William Golding's *Lord of the Flies* (1954), the subject of chapter 8.

For readers, 'The Moral Reformers' is particularly challenging. What starts as the chaplain's hope to save Clewer from further unhappiness, turns into an intensity of violence that cannot be justified by the outcome. The conclusion has to be not that Stalky and Co. put an end to bullying in the College, but that their own propensity for bullying is heightened, that bullying breeds bullying, and that the cycle continues. The chaplain and Head are complicit in this, and their comfortable agreement to regard the whole affair as boys educating each other and as 'a little business which we have agreed to forget' simply will not do.[27]

The Flag of Their Country

It is strange that the United Services College displayed no outward signs of militarism and had no cadet corps. Drill was only used as a punishment. As the chaplain advises the Head: 'It – it isn't the temper of the school. We prepare for the Army'; and, as Perowne says, 'I'm not goin' to ass about the country with a toy Snider.'[28] For these boys, war is not a game. In 'A Little Prep', we learn that 'nine of us to date' have been killed in action, and here,

25. 'The Moral Reformers' in *Stalky & Co.*
26. 'The Moral Reformers' in *Stalky & Co.*
27. 'The Moral Reformers' in *Stalky & Co.*
28. 'The Flag of Their Country' in *Stalky & Co.*

in 'The Flag of their Country', we are told that Hogan will die in Burma and Perowne will be shot in Equatorial Africa by his own men. When the College's governors insist on the setting up of a cadet corps, it drills without uniforms and behind closed doors – accepted only as an expedient to avoid drill at Sandhurst in the future.

The Head appears to know in advance that the visit of Mr Raymond Martin M.P. to lecture the College on patriotism will be a disaster: he fails to enlighten the visitor about the nature of his audience ('he seemed to know so much already,' he says ironically) and he introduces him 'in a few colourless words'.[29] And so it turns out. As Martin gets into his jingoistic stride, he declares that the boys must look forward 'to leading their men against the bullets of England's foes; to confronting the stricken field in all the pride of their youthful manhood', not beginning to understand that these are things 'that boys do not discuss even with their most intimate equals'.[30] At the climax of his speech, he unfurls and waves the union flag, expecting rousing cheers, but is met with silence; for the boys, the flag is 'a matter shut up, sacred and apart'.[31] 'A Jelly-bellied Flag-flapper,' says Stalky.[32] When Foxy suggests the Cadet Corps should march in the open, using the flag as its own, Stalky dismisses the troops, runs out 'white to the lips' and 'blubs'.[33] Here is a powerful restating of the central tenet of *Stalky & Co.* – the rejection of all the 'flumdiddle' that characterised public schools in the late nineteenth century – but it is hardly enlightened either. It is a one-off, sitting outside the development of the school story, which would indulge again in sentimentalism and before long in the mis-selling of glorious death in the First World War.

*

I have said that *Stalky & Co.* is an uncomfortable read, and this is because it is hard to be sure of its moral centre. It does a fine job of debunking the sentimentality of Victorian public schools and school stories, their cult of athleticism, and their jingoism, but it seems to celebrate instead self-satisfaction, bullying, cruelty, and lawlessness. Prout and King may be worthy targets for satire, but, when the laughter stops (and sometimes should we be laughing anyway?) Stalky and Co. are unpleasant young men whose smartness and resourcefulness are always directed at others' expense. I would like to think that Kipling is being deliberately ironic and that we

---

29. 'The Flag of Their Country' in *Stalky & Co.*
30. 'The Flag of Their Country' in *Stalky & Co.*
31. 'The Flag of Their Country' in *Stalky & Co.*
32. 'The Flag of Their Country' in *Stalky & Co.*
33. 'The Flag of Their Country' in *Stalky & Co.*

are tricked into siding with Stalky and Co. when we should see that they are as unworthy as their victims, the damaged products of a College and of a system that has lost its way and become absurd. Yet I do not believe this is the case. The final story, 'Slaves of the Lamp – Part II', describes Stalky's exploits as an army officer in the Khye-Kheen Hills. He is still breaking rules and resorting to ruses similar to his schoolboy japes, showing that, for all his faults, it is ingenuity, self-confidence and ruthlessness, and not public school 'flumdiddle', that defend the Empire. Perhaps Stalky complements Waugh's Paul Pennyfeather (in *Decline and Fall*),[34] a statement that so-called 'public school values' are valueless in the real world, where only the unpleasant likes of Stalky and Co. will win. More importantly, it seems likely that, whatever his intention, Kipling had not yet got over the bullying he had endured at the College, nor the miserable foster-life he had endured before that, and that *Stalky & Co.* is at root about getting even, about revenge, about outsmarting smartness and delighting in inflicting pain. As Beetle, he appears to bask in Stalky's reflected glory, or is just grateful to be safe as an acolyte; and Stalky, the supreme egotist, must have loved it.

---

34. See 'Introductory: Decline and Fall' below.

Part II

A Sense of Endings

Introductory: Decline and Fall

Part II is about the changing fortunes of boys' boarding schools in the first part of the twentieth century and the slow death of the boys' school story.

At the beginning of the century, public schools continued to prosper – tough, competitive, not very academic, brimming with unwarranted self-confidence and educating the leaders of the nation. Nowhere was the latter more evident than in government, where cabinets were dominated by public school old boys, and in the First World War, when boys were coming straight from the classroom to command troops many years their senior on the front line. A little later, the public schools were denounced by left-leaning intellectuals like Lytton Strachey, George Orwell and Graham Greene, and eminent alumni queued up to complain of the brutality of their alma mater. Even before the First World War there was pressure for change, though in most schools it was strongly resisted, and after 1918 the schools continued largely as before. J.F. Roxburgh, the first headmaster of Stowe School (founded in 1923) recognised how the system had become outdated and understood the role of the newer foundations in 'progressively modernising, liberalizing and humanizing' boarding school methods, but he was decried by fellow headmasters for his pains and had little effect on the wider system.[1]

---

1. J.F. Roxburgh, 'The Public Schools and the Future', in *The Headmaster Speaks* (London, Kegan Paul, Trench, Trubner, 1936), p. 228.

However, after the Second World War the society that the public schools served was disappearing. The days of privilege were largely gone; class divisions were being eroded; the British Empire was shrinking, and there was no longer the need for a supply-chain of administrators and military officers; and as fewer colonials were needed and the armed forces shrank, there was no call for the government to pay boarding school fees for its employees. There were also the challenges of the state secondary schools, necessitated by the raising of the school leaving age to fifteen (1947) and sixteen (1972), and of the new raft of grammar schools established by Butler's 1944 Education Act. With free, high-quality academic education open to the brightest children, the middle classes were questioning the need to pay school fees for a product whose time seemed to have passed.

But there were other, self-inflicted reasons for the post-1945 decline of public schools that were still living in a bygone age, and nowhere are these more evident than in Humphry Berkeley's *The Life and Death of Rochester Sneath* (1974). In 1948, Berkeley, then an undergraduate at Cambridge, reinvented himself as the headmaster of the non-existent Selhurst School and wrote outrageous requests to his fellow public school heads. They were so out of touch and so full of their own self-importance that all but two were taken in and replied with such pomposity (and, of course, courtesy) that unwittingly they created a more biting satire of the eccentricities, snobbery and gullibility of their outdated establishments than anyone else could have done. The headmaster of Sherborne School, A.G. Wallace, on learning that a Sherborne boy had stolen a Selhurst cap, wrote a profuse apology – 'I shall catch the culprit right enough. . . . There is absolutely nothing to be said in my view in defence of such barbarous behaviour' – and continued to pursue the matter for some time after Sneath had been exposed and killed off.[2] The new headmaster of Rugby, Arthur fforde, was genuinely grateful for reams of Sneath's 'good and servicable [*sic*]' advice on how to run a public school, covering such everyday matters as suicide (of a housemaster after elopement with a matron), the greater disciplinary effect of a glass of sherry over a beating (Sneath is rather sensible here) and 'hysterical outcries against homosexuality'.[3] To the headmaster of Oundle School, Graham Stainforth, Sneath recounted a problem with rats:

---

2. Humphry Berkeley, *The Life and Death of Rochester Sneath* (London: Harriman House, 1993), p. 22.

3. *The Life and Death of Rochester Sneath*, p. 19.

no less than sixty-four rats of various shapes and sizes have been discovered in the precincts of the School with the result that three Matrons have had nervous breakdowns, and the wife of the Chairman of the Board of Governors, who was lunching with me and my wife, had a fit of hysteria upon seeing no less than six of these creatures, and collapsed in a heap, having to be carried away in a blanket. . . . At present the operations against rats are being conducted by the School Chaplain, in the form of a shooting expedition.

Stainforth was a model of composure ('It certainly seems to be a very unfair hazard on top of all the other troubles of a Headmaster!') and attached a note from his bursar that recommends regular attention from 'The BRITISH RATIN Co. Limited, Station Place, Letchworth'.[4]

Thus, notwithstanding the misplaced self-confidence of Sneath and his ilk, the changed educational scene, Attlee's radical government and post-War austerity meant public schools were at last forced to reinvent themselves if they were to survive. They had become an endangered anachronism.

Stories of the Early Twentieth Century

The first years of the twentieth century saw no sign of the storm of school stories abating. Perhaps most engaging of the Edwardian era is the Teddy Lester series, written by John Finnemore (1863-1915), who had been a school teacher since the age of seventeen; he was, too, a regular contributor to *Boy's Own* and *Boys' Realm*. There were six Teddy Lester novels, published between 1907 and 1921 (two of them were published posthumously). Sport is central to all of them, but as well as excelling on the games field, Lester, a popular hero, takes a stand against bullying and is the epitome of fairness and decency.

Also of note in this period is the contribution of P.G. Wodehouse, who began his career as a writer of popular school stories. His prize-winning (but trivial) essay 'Some Aspects of Games Captaincy' was published in February 1900 in *The Public School Magazine* and was followed by other articles on public school games. His first substantial school story, *The Pothunters*, was serialised in the same magazine in 1902. After the demise of *The Public School Magazine* later that year, Wodehouse's stories were published in *The Captain*, which targeted a similar audience of schoolboys from public and preparatory schools. *A Prefect's Uncle* (1903), *The Gold Bat* (1904), *The Head of Kay's* (1905), *The White Feather* (1907) and *Mike* (1909) all made their first appearance as serials in *The Captain*.

4. *The Life and Death of Rochester Sneath*, pp. 41-42.

Mike, the most accomplished of Wodehouse's school novels, is a humorous account of life at two very different public schools at the beginning of the twentieth century. It falls into two distinct halves, reflecting the fact that the first half (set at Wrykyn) began life as the serial *Jackson Junior* and the second half (set at Sedleigh) as the serial *The Lost Lambs*.[5] As in the Teddy Lester series, the emphasis is on sport, at a time when a sporting hero could still get away with most things. It is, I think, a shame that *Mike* is often dismissed as Wodehouse juvenilia. Admittedly it has its weaknesses: in particular, the join between the Wrykyn and Sedleigh sections jars, and Mike, a deliberately understated hero ('He resembled ninety per cent of other members of English public schools')[6] is overshadowed by Wyatt (at Wrykin) and Psmith (at Sedleigh). But, for all that, the novel uses and satirises the conventional school story to sparkling effect, poking fun at the more exaggerated accounts of Victorian public school life and at the clichés of the genre. In a nice metafictional touch, which alludes to the formulaic nature of the school story, Psmith asks Mike, 'Are you the Bully, the Pride of the School, or the Boy who is Led Astray and takes to Drink in Chapter Sixteen?'[7] On his moral journey, punctuated by a catalogue of farcical events that only Wodehouse could have conjured, Mike comes to understand 'the public school spirit' at Wrykin, but has to learn it all over again when he arrives at Sedleigh. He never does a stroke of work in the classroom, never accepts authority, and eventually staggers off with Psmith to engage in further illicit adventures. After *Mike*, there was not much further for the conventional public school story to be developed, though Frank Richards's inescapable Billy Bunter, the subject of chapter 5, waddled steadfastly through *The Magnet* from 1908 to 1940, at which point a wartime lack of paper resulted in a long suspension.

There were also a number of novels written either for adults (who had enjoyed *Tom Brown's Schooldays* and *Eric* in their youth and wanted more of the same), or for the nebulous adult and teenager crossover audience, that are important as context. I mean such novels as Horace Annesley Vachell's, *The Hill: A Romance of Friendship* (1905), in which John Verney and Reginald Scaife struggle for the attentions of the 'blood' Harry Desmond (this is the closest the boys' school story comes to a love story, though with homosexuality a taboo subject, the relationships are romanticised and so sanitised); E.M. Forster's *The Longest Journey* (1907), which compares

---

5. *Jackson Junior* was serialised in six parts between April and September, 1907; *The Lost Lambs* was serialised in six parts between April and September, 1908.
6. P.G. Wodehouse, *Mike* (London: A. & C. Black, 1909), chapter 41.
7. *Mike*, chapter 32.

the unfeeling and authoritarian life of the public school (Sawston), with
the golden, intellectual life of Cambridge and the liberating spirit of rural
England; and Hugh Walpole's *Mr Perrin and Mr Traill* (1911), which is
played out in the stifling atmosphere of the staffroom of Moffats, a second-
rate Cornish public school. Perrin, old and set in his ways, comes into
conflict with Traill, a young and idealistic new master, and the jealousies
explode when Traill becomes engaged to Isabel Desart, for whom Perrin has
harboured secret longings.

G.F. Bradby's witty novella *The Lanchester Tradition* (1913) is in the same
vein and strikes against the conservatism of public schools. It describes how
the new headmaster of Chiltern School, Flaggon, sets about the dangerous
business of modernising (or at least rescuing) Chiltern, where there is 'a certain
immutability and fixity of things, an as-it-was-in-the-beginning-is-now-and-
ever-shall-be attitude towards life' and where 'any change in the hour of a
lesson or the colour of a ribbon is regarded as an outrage on the Lanchester
tradition' (Lanchester being Flaggon's most illustrious predecessor). On
arrival, Flaggon discovers a culture of indiscipline, bullying and cribbing;
snobbery ('rich men are content to pay large fees in order that their sons may
have the privilege of being educated, exclusively, with the sons of other rich
men'); pupils whose 'gait and manner which, if not exactly insolent, at least
suggested a complete absence of anything like awe in the presence of their
headmaster'; and senior masters (led by the overbearing Chowdler) who will
brook no change and expect to control him as they had his predecessor.[8]

But the novel also works on another level. Bradby was an assistant master
at Rugby School and in writing about Chiltern he was also writing about
Rugby, which still worked in the shadow of Thomas Arnold, even though,
as we have seen, the Doctor's reforms had been traduced across the whole
public school system in the sixty years after his death. For all his radical
and reforming zeal, Arnold was now regarded as a conservative and as the
creator of a public school system that ironically reflected few of his actual
ideals. Like Lanchester:

> Nothing is so paralysing . . . as the memory of a great man.
> If I want a new Latin prose book, I can't have it because Dr
> Lanchester taught out of the old one; and if I want a window
> that will open, it is impossible because Lanchester didn't believe
> in ventilation. . . . Of course . . . it's only his ghost that annoys
> me. The man was an educational reformer, but the ghost is only
> a glorified cricket 'pro'.[9]

---

8.   G.F. Bradby, *The Lanchester Tradition* (London: John Murray, 1913), chapter 1.
9.   *The Lanchester Tradition*, chapter 10.

In the end, Flaggon is able to face down his critics, root out the unnamed 'evil' (presumably homosexuality), expel a raft of troublesome pupils, and dismiss Chowdler, whose appeal to the School's Council only fails through the Chairman's casting vote. Although some believe that the Lanchester Tradition has 'received its death blow', others see that it has been 'disinterred and given a new lease of life'.[10]

It is important to try to distinguish between the public school myth – the often optimistic view of public school life portrayed in the conventional school story – and the reality. A number of autobiographical stories purport to paint pictures of how things really were in some very different individual schools, but these also have to be read with caution. Shane Leslie's *The Oppidan* (1922) looks back at life at Eton College in 1899-1902. By Leslie's account, the College was a thoroughly unpleasant place (though Leslie does not see it that way), full of prejudice and lamenting its changing pupil body: 'Good wine and good blood and, for that matter, a good House at Eton went together'; there was no room for even 'the nicest Jews or the best-born cosmopolites'. Arnold Lunn's more clear-sighted *The Harrovians* (1913) is based on diaries kept by the author during his time at Harrow School in 1902-1906. Later, in *The Loom of Youth* (1917), the subject of chapter 6, the seventeen-year-old Alec Waugh describes his career at Sherborne School in the years leading up to the First World War. At the time, *The Loom of Youth* was regarded as scandalous, but in spite of its sometimes clumsy prose it gives a convincing and not altogether unflattering account of an adolescent's life at public school as the First World War approached.

The final chapters of *The Loom of Youth* see boys and masters leaving for the trenches, and the War is also the backdrop to, for example, Beverley Nichols's *Prelude* (1920) and Ernest Raymond's *Tell England* (1922). There is again something of autobiography in Paul, the hero of *Prelude*. The setting of Martinsell is based on Marlborough College, where Nichols had been a pupil, but either Marlborough was far ahead of its time or, more likely, the school life that Nichols describes is more fantasy than reality. Paul is an extrovert, a musician, an actor, a dancer. One might have thought all this would bring down the lasting opprobrium of his peers, but instead he gradually wins acceptance. In the closing pages, Paul's extravagant manner and buoyant optimism are carried into the trenches, and quite without irony he praises Martinsell for leading him to almost certain death. The action of *Tell England* is divided between school (the imaginary Kensingstone) and the front line: the one is a preparation for the other. In spite of the horrors of both, Rupert, the narrator, loves

10. *The Lanchester Tradition*, chapter 14.

it all, and the colonel's impassioned call to arms is delivered without irony: 'Eighteen years ago you were born for this day. Through the last eighteen years you've been educated for it. Your birth and breeding were given you that you might officer England's youth in this hour. And now you enter upon your inheritance.'[11] As well as emphasising the 'youth' of the soldiers, there is something chilling in the idea that Kensingstone has 'educated' Rupert for this. We are reminded, I think, of the writing of another Rupert (Brooke), who in his sonnet 'Peace' sensed the same destiny:

> Now, God be thanked Who has matched us with His hour,
> And caught our youth, and wakened us from sleeping.[12]

One of the most moving public school books of the period is *Letters from a Headmaster-Soldier* (1918) by Harry Sackville Lawson. Lawson, who was headmaster of Buxton College, Derbyshire, felt it his duty to leave Buxton in 1915 and enlist, sending regular letters back to his pupils from the trenches. In his first letter, he writes:

> I wish I could be with you in person to say goodbye to you all, and to hand over my Headmastership to my successor. Instead, I'm writing from a dug-out, to the sound of guns, the sort of message I want you to have before Term ends. . . . I've got one thing in particular to say to you all, just the main thing we've talked about together in its different bearings in the past, just the one important thing which keeps life sweet and clean and gives us peace of mind. For whether I have been talking to a boy alone, or to a class in its class-room, or to the school met together in the New Hall, I have found opinion quite clear and quite decided as to what the game is and what the game is not.[13]

There is another echo here of Brooke's 'Peace', which describes England's youth as 'swimmers into cleanness leaping'. Lawson, who was the inspiration behind Osborne, the schoolmaster-soldier in R.C. Sherriff's play *Journey's End* (1928), died of wounds in France in February 1918.

---

11. Ernest Raymond, *Tell England* (London: Cassell, 1922), Part II, chapter 1.
12. Rupert Brooke, 'Peace', in *The Works of Rupert Brooke* (Ware: Wordsworth, 1994), p. 144. In *The Happiest Days* (Manchester: Manchester University Press, 1988), p. 217, Jeffrey Richards points out that Ernest Raymond testifies in his autobiography to the influence Brooke's sonnets had on him.
13. Harry Sackville Lawson, *Letters from a Headmaster Soldier* (London: H.R. Allenson, 1918).

The often sentimental accounts of public school heroes in the First World War were in tune with most public opinion and literature of the time. When we look back from a century on, our perspective has changed. We see the glory overshadowed by the futility and the waste. We see the wholesale slaughter of public school alumni, who had been educated in loyalty, patriotism and self-sacrifice, but had scant understanding of the War they were destined to fight; more than that, we see how the public school story inspired the same values in those who had only read about the schools. None of this is surprising: there was a need to justify the waste, and for the duration of the War and some years after the Armistice the truth was too hard to bear. All this is put into illuminating perspective in Peter Parker's *The Old Lie: The Great War and the Public School Ethos*[14] and Anthony Seldon and David Walsh's *Public Schools in the Great War.*[15]

Between the Wars

After the First World War, Bunter soldiered on, but there were few other notable public school stories. First, more children were now attending school, so stories about it, however different it was from their own experience, no longer caught the imagination so strongly. Secondly, in the more hedonistic years of the 1920s, the public school world and all it represented lost much of its fascination and glamour, and maybe there was little appetite for more of the same. Evelyn Waugh's *Decline and Fall* (1926), whose opening chapters perhaps tell the most deliciously funny school story of all, is more of a satire of 1920s society than it is of schools of the time. However, it also attacks its shadowy central character, Paul Pennyfeather, the reluctant schoolmaster at Dr Fagan's outrageous Llanabba Castle. Pennyfeather's public school education has bestowed on him only charming manners, an innocence of the real world in which he is quite out of his depth, and a willingness always to take the blame for others without demur, whether in the case of his supposed indecency at Oxford (he was debagged by drunken members of The Bollinger Club) or his unwitting involvement in Margot Beste-Chetwynde's white slave trade. In *The Crazy Fabric*, A.E. Dyson comments:

> An education conducted along impeccably Arnoldian lines has turned him into a wasteland character, without convictions, without insight into evil, without any felt or understood values.

14. Peter Parker, *The Old Lie: The Great War and the Public School Ethos* (London: Constable, 1987).
15. Anthony Seldon and David Walsh, *Public Schools and the Great War* (Barnsley: Pen and Sword Military, 2013).

> Given the loneliness of modern man as well, he seems fated to
> mistake appearance for reality; to become an incarnation of the
> liberally nurtured innocent abroad.[16]

Stalky would have agreed absolutely. Thirdly, children's literature as a wider
genre became more popular, in part because of the mixture of realism and
fantasy in the work of E. Nesbit and the very different colonial adventures
of Percy Westerman. Between the Wars, Arthur Ransome wrote about what
children can get up to outside school and away from their parents, starting
a vogue for 'camping and tramping' novels. There were also the inevitable
war stories, with Captain W.E. Johns's Biggles (from 1932) flying his way
through the first half of the century.

After the Second World War, Frank Richards's Bunter reappeared in
a welter of novels (from 1947 to 1967)[17] and television series (fifty-
two episodes were broadcast between 1952 and 1961), as well as on
radio and stage (though Greyfriars had changed not at all). Otherwise,
with public schools in temporary decline, interest in the boys' school
story was largely centred on Anthony Buckeridge's tales of Jennings and
Linbury Court (1953-94), which (like *Mike* and *Billy Bunter*) also began
as a popular series, but on radio, and had huge success. Buckeridge was
a master of comedy, much in the style of Wodehouse, and his novels
about preparatory school life had wide appeal both at home and abroad.
As well as humour, they have a warmth and generosity about them,
and Linbury Court is sufficiently removed from reality to capture the
imagination of children everywhere. Another comic triumph (for adults)
based on the preparatory school world were H.F. Ellis's *The Papers of
A.J. Wentworth, B.A.* (1949), *The Papers of A.J. Wentworth, B.A. (Ret'd)*
(1962), and *The Swan Song of A.J. Wentworth* (1982), which began as
articles in *Punch* from 1938. A very different and less well-known series
set in a preparatory school is William Mayne's quartet of choir school
novels: *A Swarm in May* (1955), *Choristers' Cake* (1956), *Cathedral
Wednesday* (1960) and *Words and Music* (1963). Mayne was one of the
most original and powerful writers for children in the latter part of the
twentieth century. His school stories are among his earliest work, but
already they display the extraordinarily resonant use of language, the
close observation, and the dislocation of time that became his hallmarks
in later, less accessible writing. Novels of Buckeridge and Mayne are the
subject of chapter 7.

---

16. A.E. Dyson, *The Crazy Fabric* (London: Macmillan, 1965), p. 189.
17. Although *The Magnet* ceased publication in 1940, a dispute between its publisher,
    Amalgamated Press, and the author resulted in Bunter's lengthy suspension.

Part II concludes with another 1950s preparatory school story, but an unlikely one – William Golding's *Lord of the Flies* (1954). I feel justified in including it here both because it is so often part of school English syllabi and because Golding decided to write it as an antidote to such 'island' books as *Treasure Island, Coral Island,* and *The Swiss Family Robinson,* which he had been reading to his children at bedtime. As in the novels that inspired it, the island setting of *Lord of the Flies* is the ultimate 'world apart'. How would well-educated and well-mannered boys, initially smart in their uniforms, really behave when cast away from parents, teachers, and a civilisation that is itself under threat?

Chapter 5

The Popular School Story

Frank Richards – 'The Making of Harry Wharton' (1908) and *Billy Bunter at Greyfriars School* (1947)

Not many children today have any interest in Billy Bunter and Greyfriars School, and stories about them are now out of print. Yet for much of the twentieth century he was the world's best-known schoolboy. Bunter's creator, Charles Hamilton (writing as Frank Richards), was also the author of the *St Jim's* school stories (writing as Martin Clifford) published in *The Gem* from 1906, the *Rookwood* stories (writing as Owen Conquest) published in *Boys' Friend Weekly* from 1915, and the early *Cliff House* stories (writing as Hilda Richards), featuring Bessie Bunter and published in *The School Friend* from 1919 (see Introductory, Part III). It is estimated that during his lifetime he wrote at least 60,000,000 scholastic words.

Bunter made his debut on 15 February 1908 in 'The Making of Harry Wharton' in the first edition of *The Magnet* and was a weekly presence until the comic folded in 1940. He featured in 1,670 episodes. The readership of *The Magnet* was very different from that of *The Captain* and was largely drawn from middle-class children at less expensive 'private schools' and from working-class children; it was not from the public schools themselves. Although Bunter was to become popular with readers, he was initially only an amusing character among the crowd. It was fifteen years before he became a leading player (in terms of narrative), and even then Hamilton/Richards continued to rotate the central character of the stories to offer different perspectives and to avoid any staleness (unlike Reed's *St Dominic's* serials, each of the early Bunter stories was complete in itself, though later the same plotline could run for eight or even sixteen weeks).

George Orwell and 'Boys' Weeklies'

Greyfriars, a third-rate public school near Friardale in Kent, is built on the ruins of a monastery dissolved by Henry VIII. With its old stone building, the emphasis on discipline and hierarchy, the strict moral code of schoolboys, the juvenile slang, and the liberal use of the cane, it shares much with the public schools and public school stories of the early twentieth century. In an essay about 'Boys' Weeklies', George Orwell sums up the world of Greyfriars thus:

> The year is 1910 — or 1940, but it is all the same. You are at Greyfriars, a rosy-cheeked boy of fourteen in posh tailor-made clothes, sitting down to tea in your study on the Remove passage after an exciting game of football which was won by an odd goal in the last half-minute. There is a cosy fire in the study, and outside the wind is whistling. The ivy clusters thickly round the old grey stones. The King is on his throne and the pound is worth a pound. Over in Europe the comic foreigners are jabbering and gesticulating, but the grim grey battleships of the British Fleet are steaming up the Channel and at the outposts of Empire the monocled Englishmen are holding the niggers at bay. Lord Mauleverer has just got another fiver and we are all settling down to a tremendous tea of sausages, sardines, crumpets, potted meat, jam and doughnuts. After tea we shall sit round the study fire having a good laugh at Billy Bunter and discussing the team for next week's match against Rookwood. Everything is safe, solid and unquestionable. Everything will be the same for ever and ever.[1]

For Orwell, Greyfriars is an image of the world of Empire, its 'posh' upper classes still 'cosy' as the storms rage outside. Foreigners are 'comic' and 'jabbering' (although Hurree Singh is entirely accepted by his schoolmates – he is, after all, the Nawab of Bhanipor – his exaggerated English is turned into a politically incorrect comic highlight); 'niggers' are kept at bay; all

---

1. George Orwell, 'Boys' Weeklies', in *Horizon* (London: March 1940). Reprinted in George Orwell, *Inside the Whale and Other Essays* (London: Victor Gollancz, 1940).

that matters is the success of the school's football team.[2] Even though in the real world there had been the First World War and the depression of the 1930s, and the Second World War was now beginning, at Greyfriars everything is 'safe' and 'solid'. Nothing will ever change.

G. J. B. Watson, writing from the perspective of an Irish boy who was always conscious of the real danger of an Orangeman with a half brick, agrees with Orwell:

> I was an avid reader of public school stories, my favourite being a book called *Teddy Lester and his Chums*. . . . The appeal lay in the notion of codes and rules, especially as those applied to enmity. You might have to fight, that is, but if you did, it would be with boxing gloves in a ring, with a proper referee, and afterwards hands would be shaken. Even the cads and bounders subscribed to the notion of 'fair play'. As a boy, I would not have had worries about the comic foreigners of Europe or the black or yellow peril. But what this England of the mind offered, in its atrocious way, was an image of security so powerful that the rules of sad experience and the much greater experience and the much greater literature I read subsequently could never quite expunge it. . . . A complacency even. . . . Perhaps an arrogance.[3]

Ironically, for all the sense of 'security', 'complacency', and 'arrogance', in the same month that Orwell's essay appeared, *The Magnet* ran out of paper and closed, taking Bunter with it; but after the War was over the 'fat owl' was resurrected as if time and history did not exist. At Greyfriars, a new school year began each September, but for Bunter's entire fictional life he was aged fifteen and never escaped from the Remove.

Orwell goes on to highlight the snobbishness of Richards's work (which he sees as part of its appeal to young readers who want to imagine themselves as public school boys), its cult of athleticism (hardly fair, since at Greyfriars competitive sport was not compulsory) and its 'plagiarism' of earlier school stories. He suggests the Greyfriars stories were written to such a rigid formula because, although published under Richards's name, it would have been physically impossible for one man to sustain the prodigious output. He also bewails the dearth of writing for children displaying more left-wing attitudes: if children are influenced for life by their early reading, an unmitigated diet of conservative values and beliefs is hardly a balanced literary diet.

---

2. At Greyfriars, the boys play football, not rugby, which again suggests a nod to readers who did not attend public schools themselves.
3. G.J.B. Watson, 'England: a Country of the Mind', in R.P. Draper (ed.), *The Literature of Region and Nation* (London: Palgrave Macmillan, 1989), pp. 154-155.

Although Orwell's essay is mostly affectionate in tone, Hamilton was outraged. In his reply (writing as Frank Richards) he confirms, not altogether truthfully, that he alone was the author of the various stories under his pen names (on occasion, when he missed deadlines on account of a gambling expedition, another 'hand' had to be employed). He also rejects utterly the charge of plagiarism, which I think is a pity (though plagiarism is perhaps the wrong word): whether it was done consciously or unconsciously, the distant echoes of earlier classics in the Greyfriars stories seem to me to be one of their strengths. Hamilton may say that his Mr Prout has nothing to do with Mr Prout in *Stalky & Co*, but the inclusion of Tom Brown, Bob Cherry and Harry Wharton[4] on the roll of Greyfriars, all of whom feature in some way in *Tom Brown's Schooldays*, can hardly be a coincidence, and Jeffrey Richards usefully draws attention to Hamilton's additional debt to the novels of Thackeray, Farrar, Reed, Wodehouse and Vachell.[5]

In other respects, too, I think Hamilton/Richards comes out of the exchange rather badly. He admits that thirty years on, he does look back fondly to the world of 1910 and has no intention of moving his stories forward in time: 'the world went very well then. It has not been improved by the Great War, the General Strike, the outbreak of sex-chatter, by make-up or lipstick, [or] by the present discontents'. He does prostrate himself before the aristocracy: 'noblemen generally are better fellows than commoners . . . the higher up you go in the social scale the better you find the manners and the more fixed the principles'. He does think that 'foreigners *are* funny': 'Take Hitler, for example – with his swastika, his "good German Sword", his fortifications named after characters from Wagner, his military coat that he will never take off until he marches home victorious: and the rest of his fripperies out of the property box.' And, blind to his own conservatism, he intones: 'Mr Orwell hopes that a boys' paper with a left-wing bias may not be impossible. I hope that it is, and will remain, impossible. Boys' minds ought not to be disturbed and worried by politics.'

Orwell's point, confirmed rather than denied by Hamilton/Richards, is that by 1940 the Greyfriars stories had become stuck in a time warp (though, to be fair and as Sneath revealed, most public schools had become stuck there as well). But in fact Orwell was being kind: Hamilton/Richards's

---

4. In *Tom Brown's Schooldays*, chapter 5, Tom's coach arrives in Rugby 'in a style which would not have disgraced "Cherry Bob" . . . or any other of the old coaching heroes'. In chapter 9, Wharton is referred to by Dr Arnold as a 'slight and weak' head of house.

5. Jeffrey Richards, *Happiest Days* (Manchester: Manchester University Press, 1988), pp. 275-276.

style had transformed, without any sense of irony, into something more exaggerated and cartoon-like; and Greyfriars and its inhabitants, by accident rather than design, had turned into a parody of public school life in fact and fiction. Isabel Quigly calls it 'a cloud cuckooland';[6] Jeffrey Richards calls it 'a beguilingly attractive image of an idealised world'[7] – which is more sympathetic but amounts to much the same thing. So Hamilton/ Richards played to his particular audience, and little by little Greyfriars was translated into a wholly imaginary place designed to appeal to boys who were unlikely to go there – an adventure playground that provided an escape from the drudgery of everyday life.

'The Making of Harry Wharton' (1908)

Thus 'The Making of Harry Wharton', the first of the Greyfriars stories, is very different in style and tone from the later ones, and in particular from the post-War novels. It is the sole content in the first edition of *The Magnet*, running to ten chapters and 20,000 words, and tells how Harry Wharton is sent to Greyfriars by his uncle and guardian to give him the discipline he needs. To begin with, Wharton rebels against Greyfriars, but the tale is a moral one about how, after a number of hard lessons, he comes to embrace his new school.

As we might expect, the adventure opens on the school train, where Wharton fights with Nugent, only to rescue him when the 'hack' taking Nugent from the station at Friardale to Greyfriars is in collision with a car on a narrow bridge and he is thrown into the raging river below. But in spite of Nugent's efforts, Wharton repeatedly refuses his friendship. He falls foul of the bully Bulstrode, smashing his camera and refusing to pay for it; eventually he throws a cup of hot tea over him in the Hall and is caned savagely by his form-teacher, Quelch, for his pains. When he tries to run away, he is followed by Nugent and the pair are attacked by a 'footpad' after their money. In protecting Wharton, Nugent is struck by the villain's cudgel, but this time Wharton realises the situation is his fault and helps Nugent, now his friend at last, back to Greyfriars:

> 'I have been a fool!'
>   'Exactly! Come, give me your arm, and let's get back!'
>   And Nugent leaning upon the new boy's arm, moved towards the school. Harry Wharton made no resistance. The die was cast for him now; he was to return to Greyfriars, to take up the

6. Isabel Quigly, *The Heirs of Tom Brown* (London: Chatto and Windus, 1982), p. 249.
7. Jeffrey Richards, p. 277.

thread of life there again.

'You're coming?' said Nugent joyfully.

'Yes.'

'Good for you! Make up your mind to it, old fellow, and I can promise you that you'll find Greyfriars a ripping place. The Remove don't like you now, but we'll stick together, and bring them round. Is it a go?'

'Yes, yes!'

And the two juniors – friends now, and for life henceforth – shook hands upon the compact. And so Harry Wharton faced his difficulties again, to fight his battle out, with a true chum by his side to help him to win.[8]

It is a sentimental ending, crammed not only with careless verbal clichés but with the promise of friendship and all the moral clichés of the school story as well.

Billy Bunter of Greyfriars School (1947)

In 1940, the wartime rationing of paper led to the closure of *The Magnet*, leaving Hamilton/Richards without an outlet for his writing. Worse, the Associated Press owned the copyright of Greyfriars and its characters, and, as a consequence, Bunter, who was at the centre of the final *Magnet* story, disappeared until an agreement was reached between author and publisher in 1947. It was then that Hamilton/Richards adopted the novel form, out of necessity as much as choice. There were to be thirty-eight novels published between 1947 and 1961, as well as adaptations on radio, television and stage.

Billy Bunter of Greyfriars School (1947) is the first of the Greyfriars novels. It begins like this:

'BUNTER!'

Mr Quelch's voice was not loud, but deep.

It was heard distinctly by all ears in the Remove form-room at Greyfriars School: excepting, apparently, one pair of very fat ears.

Billy Bunter did not answer.

It was the second time Quelch had called his name. Quelch seldom had to call on any boy in the Remove twice. Now he had called twice, and still in vain. Bunter was silent.

---

8. Frank Richards, 'The Making of Harry Wharton', in *The Magnet*, 15 February 1908.

There was a stirring in the Remove, as fellows turned their
heads to look at Bunter, wondering why he did not reply.
Really, it was not safe for any Remove man to pass Quelch by
like the idle wind which he regarded not. Yet there sat Billy
Bunter, staring straight at his form-master through his big
spectacles, but otherwise not deigning to take the slightest
notice of him![9]

Given the popularity of the very much larger than life character of Bunter
in *The Magnet* stories, it was a shrewd marketing strategy of Hamilton/
Richards to put him emphatically at the start and centre of his first Greyfriars
novel – 'BUNTER!' – but it was equally unfortunate. Here Bunter becomes a
grotesque; he has 'fat ears' and we are to be reminded time and time again
of his fatness (in this brief chapter alone, Bunter is 'the fat junior' and 'the
fattest member of his form' and 'the fat owl', and he is woken when Skinner
pulls his 'fat ear'); he has 'big glasses', which will reflect the sunlight and
'gleam almost like headlights', disguising his closed eyes. Later in the novel
we are told that although Bunter does sleeping very well, he is no good at
games, he is no good in class and is no good at telling the truth ('You could
chuck up the execrable fibfulness, and try your hand at esteemed veracity!'
suggests Hurree Singh).[10] Since school stories are all about the importance
of games and telling the truth, making Bunter the hero, or at least the anti-
hero, was a dangerous tactic. As in *Stalky & Co.*, as readers we are faced
with a moral dilemma: where should our sympathies lie?

The slow build-up of tension, when nothing much happens but we
wait in anticipation, is typical of the Greyfriars novels. Quelch's opening
exclamation is, in fact, his second attempt to rouse the sleeping Bunter, but
it passes him by 'like the idle wind which he regarded not' (the allusion is
to Brutus in Shakespeare's *Julius Caesar*).[11] Bunter is likened to 'Epimenides
himself' and his snores to 'Wagnerian music'. Similarly, Quench's frown is
compared to the wonderfully alliterative 'frightful, fearful, frantic frown of
the Lord High Executioner' in Gilbert and Sullivan's *The Mikado*, while his
look 'might have been envied by the fabled basilisk'. These references to
other writers and classical myth are unlikely to be picked up by the child
reader, but for the adult reader they add a playful richness.

When Bunter has been shaken from his slumbers, declaring that after
the Battle of Worcester Charles II had obviously hidden in the pub on
the Courtfield Road (what other Royal Oak is there, after all?), the novel

9. Frank Richards, *Billy Bunter of Greyfriars School* (London: Charles Skilton, 1947),
    chapter 1.
10. *Billy Bunter of Greyfriars School*, chapter 10.
11. William Shakespeare, *Julius Caesar*, IV, 3, 68-9.

proceeds through a catalogue of scrapes and thefts: Bunter stealing Smithy's jam and being caught eating it in Quelch's study; Bunter stealing Wharton's cake and eating it in the box room; Bunter being threatened with expulsion ('there would be a lot of dry eyes when he went!');[12] Bunter failing at his Latin translation; Bunter being caned by Quelch – many times; Bunter stealing Coker's hamper, and, as a consequence, being tricked by Bob Cherry into thinking that the local policeman has come to arrest him; Bunter spilling ink in Quelch's study and letting Vernon-Smith (up to his own gummy mischief) take the blame; Bunter waiting for a postal order that never comes (and when it does, at last, having to use it to pay for Coker's hamper); Bunter stealing Mauly's jam and scoffing it 'not wisely, but too well':[13]

> In the study armchair was stretched a rotund form. It was that of Billy Bunter. His face was ghastly. It looked as it might have looked on a Channel steamer on a rough day. Bunter's fat paws, both sticky, were pressed to his extensive waistcoat. And he groaned. He gurgled. Something, evidently, was amiss with Bunter.
>
> The gimlet-eye spotted what was amiss. On the study table stood an enormous jam jar – nearly empty! Beside it lay a sticky tablespoon!
>
> Bunter was as sticky as the jar and the spoon! Often and often was Bunter sticky – but never in his sticky career had he looked as sticky as he did now.
>
> 'Bless my soul!' repeated Mr. Quelch. 'Bunter!'
>
> 'Oh,' gasped Bunter. 'Oooo-er!'
>
> He did not rise from the armchair. He couldn't!
>
> 'So this,' said Mr Quelch, 'is how you have been occupied, Bunter, when you were specially excused from detention to play cricket.'
>
> 'Ooooogh!'
>
> 'You have been eating jam - !'
>
> 'Moooooooh!'
>
> 'Which I have little doubt you have purloined from some other study.'
>
> 'Grooogh!'[14]

This episode is typical of the novels. The writing is extraordinarily visual and aural: we see and hear exactly what Quelch sees and hears when he visits No. 7 study, though we are likely to be more amused than the

12. *Billy Bunter of Greyfriars School*, chapter 8.
13. William Shakespeare, *Othello*, V, 2, 342.
14. *Billy Bunter of Greyfriars School*, chapter 34.

schoolmaster. The caricature is unmistakable – 'rotund form', 'fat paws', 'extensive waistcoat'. The 'form' is 'that of Billy Bunter'. The jam jar is 'enormous' and a tablespoon is Bunter's weapon of choice. It is the work of a verbal cartoonist – almost in the style of Dickens, though not at his best. Notice the repetitions – how we are told that something was 'amiss' and how Quelch 'spotted what was amiss'; how 'sticky' is repeated 'often and often' (six times, to be precise). Notice Bunter's onomatopoeic groans – and 'Quelch' has an old-fashioned squelchiness about it, suggesting battered mortarboard and mildewed gown. And notice how the narrative voice intrudes frequently and unnecessarily: 'Something was evidently amiss with him' and 'He did not rise from the armchair. He couldn't!'

All such escapades are loosely tied together in the novel's plot by Bunter trying lamely to avoid a bad report and 'the sack'. He is only saved when, hiding up a tree to drop a vengeful bag of soot on Quelch, he sees his form-master being attacked by the ne'er-do-well Nosey Jenkins and comes to the rescue by jumping on the assailant 'with the effect of a particularly powerful steam-hammer'.[15] So his 'genuine old British pluck' saves the day,[16] the villain from the outside world who has threatened the equilibrium of Greyfriars is overcome, and Bunter's reprieve is accompanied by a large box of toffees.

But, for all the outrageous humour, the ending of *Billy Bunter at Greyfriars* is unsatisfactory, with Bunter stuffing himself with the ill-earned sweets – 'Groogh! Ooogh! Woogh' – and lauded as 'the brightest ornament' of the Remove: 'Next term the happy Owl would still be Billy Bunter of Greyfriars School!'[17] It means, of course, that Bunter lives to eat another day, and if Hamilton/Richards were satirising the public school story and there were even a deliberate touch of irony in this final sentence, there would be no discrepancy. But Greyfriars is not St Trinian's and Bunter is not a teenage revolutionary bent on overturning the system. Moreover, he is so thieving, underhand and deceitful, so keen to avoid work and sport, and so quick to take advantage of the good nature of his friends, that he cannot just be enjoyed as an amiable rogue; and Hamilton/Richards was so fiercely on the side of all those public school values of discipline (beatings become a tasteless joke), honesty, loyalty, trust, industry, etc. – that the ultimate celebration of both the unacceptable characteristics of public schools and of Bunter as a comic hero leaves a sense of moral confusion. In the novels at least, Jeffrey Richards's argument that Bunter is 'the antithesis of the system . . . whose discomfiture affirms its virtues' is unsatisfactory.[18]

15. *Billy Bunter of Greyfriars School*, chapter 37.
16. *Billy Bunter of Greyfriars School*, chapter 37.
17. *Billy Bunter of Greyfriars School*, chapter 38.
18. Jeffrey Richards, p. 212.

By the time the last Bunter novel was published in 1961, England had altered beyond all recognition, and public schools were beginning to reinvent themselves for the new age; but Greyfriars and its increasingly self-absorbed and two-dimensional inmates remained resolutely the same. Thus, as the twentieth century drew to a close and the Greyfriars stories drifted out of print, what had been among the most popular school stories ever began to seem rather silly to all but a devoted band of adult enthusiasts, as did Hamilton's belief that as a storyteller he ranked above such 'duds' as Thackeray, Scott, Shaw, Ibsen and Chekhov.[19] It is not, I think, surprising that his millions and millions of words have mostly been consigned to history.

---

19. Frank Richards, 'Frank Richards Replies to George Orwell', in *Horizon* (London, May 1940).

Chapter 6

The Schoolboy's Story

Alec Waugh – *The Loom of Youth* (1917)

Alec Waugh's *The Loom of Youth* (1917) is a non-fiction novel that describes the seventeen-year-old author's time at Sherborne School in 1911-1915. The hero of the novel, Gordon Caruthers, is Waugh's thinly disguised self, and this is his story from his arrival as a bewildered and lonely new boy at Fernhurst (Sherborne, moved from Dorset to Derbyshire), to his leaving after the outbreak of war. Along the way, Caruthers revels in and suffers the highs and lows of a rebellious adolescent as he is swept along in an ebbing stream of public school values, sometimes ecstatic, sometimes apathetic, and sometimes determined to kick against the demands for conformity and unbending loyalty.

The novel provoked a storm of protest. It was not that Waugh said anything new and there was by now some pressure for change in an educational system that had become increasingly outdated. However, the bullying and the beatings, the worship of sporting heroes (whose prowess gave them licence to behave as they wished), the outdated curriculum that was further undermined by the universal custom of cribbing, and the deep friendships between pupils celebrated in novels such as Vachell's *The Hill* (1905) were all acceptable when dressed up as fiction, and even more acceptable if the practices were softened by laughter. But *The Loom of Youth* was different. Not only did it follow Lunn's *The Harrovians* in attempting to describe public school life as it really was, but it also dared to allude (though never explicitly) to the almost inevitable and usually fleeting homosexual relationships between adolescent boys enduring a monastic life. Worse, perhaps, it dared to question the whole notion of the 'public school spirit', the suppression of the individual in favour of a greater good, at a time when young public school officers were dying in the trenches and there was a growing debate about the futility of the drawn-out War. For all this, it is best read not as a protest novel, but as the account of a confused adolescent kicking against the mixed messages of the school world that he loves as much as hates. Not surprisingly, *The Loom of Youth* is replete with the indignant exaggerations of youth, along with repetitions, clichés, overdone set pieces about the failings of public schools, expressions of guilt and self-doubt, and passages of mawkish sentimentality ('At fifteen one is apt to be sentimental'),[1] but as a whole it is engaging and often clear-sighted.

The novel is divided into four parts, each one describing a year in Caruthers's career in School House. The opening chapter is entirely conventional. Caruthers experiences 'supreme happiness' when he arrives at Fernhurst (by train, naturally) and his future seems 'full of possibilities', but it is not long before he feels lonely and miserable. As he listens to the dormitory conversation, he understands the overriding importance of sport and getting into the 'Fifteen'. Lovelace, the captain of House games, is more highly respected than Clarke, the academic (and ineffective) head of House; Buller, the games master, is a 'splendid person . . . he had the strong face of one who had fought every inch of the way'.[2] Thus Caruthers quickly learns to recognise the public school type: 'their conversation was entirely on games, scandal and the work they had not done'.[3]

Caruthers also recognises that the bloods (the sporting heroes) are wont to proposition other boys. Meredith, a prefect and blood, hangs out with the useless Davenham; 'Johnson's a simply glorious man. Only a bit fast; and that doesn't matter much'. ('In a farewell lecture, Gordon's preparatory school master had given him to believe that it mattered a good deal, but he was doubtless old fashioned.')[4] Towards the end of term Caruthers is propositioned by Meredith but turns him down. Then, in the following term, Jeffries is bunked because the Chief (headmaster) finds out 'all about me and Fitzroy'. Before he leaves, Jeffries addresses Caruthers and his friends in a contrived set piece:

> Who made me what I am but Fernhurst? Two years ago I came
> here as innocent as Caruthers there; never knew anything.
> Fernhurst made me worship games, and think that they alone

1. Alec Waugh, *The Loom of Youth* (London: Methuen, 1917), Part III, chapter 4.
2. *The Loom of Youth*, Part I, chapter 2.
3. *The Loom of Youth*, Part I, chapter 3.
4. *The Loom of Youth*, Part I, chapter 3.

mattered, and everything else could go to the deuce. I heard
men say about bloods whose lives were an open scandal, 'Oh,
it's all right, they can play football.' I thought it was all right
too. Fernhurst made me think it was. And now Fernhurst, that
has made me what I am, turns round and says, 'You are not fit
to be a member of this great school!' and I have to go. Oh, it's
fair, isn't it?[5]

The point that Jeffries makes, and which most offended contemporary
critics, is that homosexuality at Fernhurst was not something that went
on among a minority of ne'er-do-wells, but was the overt practice of the
shining sportsmen who represented the best of the public school system.
Waugh left Sherborne in 1915 after his own involvement in a homosexual
affair (the headmaster suggested that his father remove him), and although
there is (in Part IV of the novel) an account of Caruthers's friendship with
Morcombe, the unseemly end to Waugh's school career is not recounted
directly. But here Jeffries is speaking for the author, reflecting his anger
at Fernhurst's hypocrisy and the unfairness of it all (in fact, the entire
novel can be read as Waugh's explanation and justification of his apparent
'crime'). At the end of the school year, Meredith, 'the fastest fellow in
the school', performs heroically in his final cricket house match and is
congratulated by the Chief that night after prayers; his well-known
indiscretions don't seem to matter. Caruthers wishes there were more men
like Meredith in School House, which says much about the change that
has come over him.

Caruthers's second year at Fernhurst is described in Part II. For
Caruthers, it is the year that he enjoys most – after he has settled into the
strange and introspective public school world and before he has to take on
its responsibilities. So, in a half-echo of Shelley's rebellious hero in 'Ode
to the West Wind', he plunges into Fernhurst life: 'All ignorant he went
his way; careless, arrogant and proud.'[6] He is confirmed into the Church
because it is the conventional thing, but it has no effect on his behaviour.
He shares a study with the outwardly louche but thoughtful Tester, for
whom 'Wrong and right are merely relative terms': this has a greater effect
and he begins 'to look on things which he once objected to as quite natural
and ordinary'.[7] He has to clear out of the study when Tester wants to be
alone with Stapleton, and at the end of the Easter term he asks Tester to
return the favour.

5. *The Loom of Youth*, Part I, chapter 5.
6. Percy Bysshe Shelley, 'Ode to the West Wind' (1819).
7. *The Loom of Youth*, Part II, chapter 1.

Otherwise it is a time of ragging, cribbing and sport. The unfortunate object of much of the ragging is the ineffectual Rudd (unpardonably, he did not play 'footer'). When he is attacked in his study, one of his chairs and a table are wilfully destroyed, and he is buried in a foot of waste-paper from the adjacent store. In the tuck shop, the serving girls are roundly abused; on Field Day, two Fernhurst boys are reported for using foul language and the school loses a half-day as a result (the idea of a protest strike gains little support); each week, the Extra French class degenerates into chaos. Caruthers gains a reputation for disregarding authority. He puts the chapel organ out of action and gets into trouble for cribbing (in an example of the recurring intertextuality, and echoing *Stalky & Co.*, he comments complacently, 'This isn't a St. Winifred's sort of school. It will only mean a bad report').[8]

The narrator reflects on how the public school system destroys individuality and turns out a man who 'is slack, easy-going, tolerant, is not easily upset by scruples, laughs at good things, smiles at bad, yet he is a fine fellow'. To be a leader means 'blind worship at the shrine of Athleticism. Honesty, virtue, moral determination – these things mattered not at all'.[9] Clearly much of this is self-justification, but Betteridge warns Caruthers that he is making a fool of himself and at the end of the summer term Tester accuses him of wasting his time and indulging in the pettiness of Fernhurst life. He reads him Swinburne's poetry and Caruthers is enchanted: the world is changed for him and he realises 'how far he himself was below the splendour of it all'.[10] In all this, the novel shifts uncomfortably between the over-intrusive narrative voice and stilted dialogue, but, whatever Caruthers's faults, there is no doubt that Fernhurst has become outdated, philistine and complacent. The masters see their pupils 'going to the dogs' simply because they are following accepted customs, but they cannot see that the fault lies in the customs and not the pupils. They have forgotten what it is like to be young and want the boys to view life through middle-aged spectacles. They teach Vergil, Tennyson and Browning – 'the comforts of old age' – rather than the poetry of rebellion and physical beauty of Byron, Swinburne and Rossetti.

In another example of intertextuality, Part III opens with a discussion of Lunn's *The Harrovians*. At first Caruthers recognises the truth of Lunn's descriptions of public school life, but when a storm of criticism erupts in the press, he begins to doubt himself. It is always alumni who fight against change at their alma mater, and Old Harrovians were no exception, sending

8. *The Loom of Youth*, Part II, chapter 3. See Frederic Farrar, *St Winifred's* (1862).
9. *The Loom of Youth*, Part II, chapter 3.
10. *The Loom of Youth*, Part II, chapter 3.

angry letters that rejected Lunn's claims about an already decadent system: the Harrow they remember is 'pure and manly' with an atmosphere of 'clean, healthy broad-mindedness' (that word 'clean' again). However, what if the fault lies not with Harrow but with Lunn, or not with the public schools but with Harrow? What if Harrow and Fernhust are exceptions in their decadence, and the system itself is beyond reproach? What if Lunn and Caruthers/Waugh have got it all wrong? By chance, during the last week of the summer holidays, Mr Ainslie, an Old Harrovian, comes to dinner. Ainslie has been a contemporary of Lunn's at Harrow and Caruthers asks him if Lunn's is a true account. 'Absolutely,' replies Ainslie, 'and it's as true to the life of any other Public School. They are all much the same, you know, at the root.' So Fernhurst, which Caruthers loves, is after all the victim of a rusty old system.[11] Rogers, the school's chaplain, who (in a nice irony) also commands the Cadet Corps and who can see no fault in the system, denounces *The Harrovians* in chapel.

However, Caruthers is an unreliable witness. In his second year he has been, by his own confession, 'objectionable' and, as we have seen, his friends have warned him of his unreasonable behaviour. Now, in his third year, he revels in the status and privileges of being in the sixth form but continues on his wayward path. When he is engaged in another wrecking expedition in Rudd's study, Rudd brands him a coward and challenges him to join a nocturnal and out-of-bounds visit to the Pack Monday Fair. It is a challenge that Caruthers is too proud and still too fond of notoriety to resist.

At the Fair (which reminds of Tom Brown's similar expedition), Caruthers meets Emmie, a local girl, and the evening passes in a frenzy 'of warm hands, and of fierce, wild horses'.[12] On one level, for Caruthers at least, the Fair is an image of all the excitement, freedom and ordinary life that are the antithesis of life at the School. But his attitude to Emmie is patronising, the Abbey and the School tower above all the 'tawdry glitter',[13] and the next day the Fair seems to be a nightmare, not a dream. It reaches out to Caruthers with 'cold, clammy hands' (compare Emmie's 'warm hands' of the night before); he is haunted by images of 'shrieking showmen's booths, blinding with tawdry yellow eyes'; and 'Emmie's hoarse laugh grated on his ears'.[14] Later Caruthers will see the Fair in a different way, as the day 'he had finally burnt the old garments and put on the new . . . the funeral pyre of his old life. . . . A glorious end; no anti-climax'.[15]

---

11. *The Loom of Youth*, Part III, chapter 1.
12. *The Loom of Youth*, Part III, chapter 2.
13. *The Loom of Youth*, Part III, chapter 2.
14. *The Loom of Youth*, Part III, chapter 2.
15. *The Loom of Youth*, Part III, chapter 8.

For the moment, however, Caruthers continues in what the narrator describes as a 'Jekyll and Hyde business'.[16] Symptomatic of his double life is the challenging of the old public school order by the new, played out by Fernhurst's masters. The aptly named Buller ('the Bull'), who is in the mould of Chowdler in *The Lanchester Tradition*, believes that Fernhurst and its sport mean everything.[17] Caruthers recognises that there is 'something essentially noble in so unswerving a devotion' (as Flaggon does of Chowdler) and although he fights against the subservience that Buller demands, he cannot help admiring and respecting him and all that he represents.[18]

In sharp contrast is the new master, Ferrers, whose radical ideas are soon challenging the Fernhurst establishment. At a meeting of the Stoics Society, he takes part in a debate on Classical and Modern Education; not only does he turn up late, but he wears 'a soft collar'. His performance is a revelation:

> Classics men do very well in the Foreign Offices, but they can't think. . . . We want originality; and the classics don't give it. . . . What did I learn from classics? – only to devise a new way of bringing a crib into form. . . . Is that an education? No, we want French . . . Maths, that's the stuff. . . . Makes them think.[19]

Burgess, who is supporting the Classics, can only comment that the public school man should be too gentlemanly to want to succeed in business. Later, Ferrers arranges for the Stoics Society to read Stanley Houghton's play *The Younger Generation*, about the conflict between overly strict parents and their three children who all demand their freedom.[20] The housemasters are outraged but the reading goes ahead with only School House attending. Afterwards the Chief, who is a quiet influence for good and reason in the novel, and is wise enough to steer the School between the Scylla of tradition and the Charybdis of progress, asks for a copy of the play and endorses Ferrers's choice. Under Ferrers's guidance, Caruthers begins to read widely and, from believing in the pre-eminence of sport, comes to find that ideas are more attractive. But the narrator reflects that, for all its faults, the public school system has done Caruthers no harm and will bring him many gifts, and that while his grounding in the classics has been invaluable, he has been able to move on quickly enough to prevent

---

16. *The Loom of Youth*, Part III, chapter 5.
17. The character of Buller is based on G.M. Carey, an Old Shirburnian who had played in five rugby test matches for England (1895-96) and now taught at the School.
18. *The Loom of Youth*, Part III, chapter 1
19. *The Loom of Youth*, Part III, chapter 1.
20. Stanley Houghton, *The Younger Generation* (London: Sidgwick and Jackson, 1910).

him from becoming trapped by them. Thus Part III ends on a measured and optimistic note. Caruthers's three years at Fernhurst have somehow untangled the threads of his adolescence and they can now be woven into the man on 'the loom of youth'.[21]

Such hopes are unfulfilled and in Part IV Caruthers's school career and the novel both end in anti-climax. As Caruthers and Ferrers watch cricket at the Oval during the holidays, war is declared and there is a sense of excitement. 'A war is what we want,' says Ferrers. 'It will wake us from sleeping; stir us into life; influence our literature. There's a real chance now of sweeping away the old out-worn traditions'[22] (again, compare with Brooke's 'Peace': 'Now, God be thanked Who has matched us with His law, / And caught our youth, and wakened us from sleeping').[23] When Caruthers returns to Fernhurst he finds that it is already a very different place. The senior boys and the younger masters have departed for the army and Caruthers's ambition to be captain of School House is fulfilled two years earlier than he had dared hope. But now it means little. The Corps takes on a new importance, though has little of the urgency that histories of the time suggest.

In the midst of the Fernhurst gloom, characterised by the onset of winter, Caruthers becomes friends with Morcombe and is tempted 'to plunge himself into the feverish waters of pleasure. . . . No one would mind. . . . Unless, of course, he was caught' (which, of course, Waugh was, but Caruthers was not).[24] Then news comes that Jeffries, the blood who had been caught and expelled in shame from Fernhurst, has been killed. Tester pays a visit and tells the War as it is: 'There's nothing glorious. . . . It's bloody, utterly bloody.'[25] He knows he will not return to Fernhurst again. Caruthers immerses himself in games, although he finds it hard to summon up much enthusiasm. Buller suggests angrily that failure on the pitch will mean death in the trenches, but for the boys such talk is a sham and the Stoics Society overwhelmingly condemns the worship of games.

So Caruthers's time at Fernhurst comes to an end, not with the ignominy that marked Waugh's leaving, but, conventionally, with a triumphant innings in the house match final – though by now it is rather meaningless. There is the emotion of the last chapel service that 'has been done to death by the novelist'; the promises to keep in touch with friends that

---

21. *The Loom of Youth*, Part III, chapter 8.
22. *The Loom of Youth*, part IV, chapter 1.
23. Rupert Brooke, 'Peace' (1914).
24. *The Loom of Youth*, Part IV, chapter 3.
25. *The Loom of Youth*, Part IV, chapter 4.

will not be kept; the unspoken farewell to Buller – 'so essentially big, so strong, so noble' – which suggests more respect than the hurried word with Ferrers; and the symmetry of the train steaming out of the station to which it had brought Caruthers as an innocent three years before.[26] For all his confusions, Caruthers leaves with a quiet confidence, and a silent recognition of all Fernhurst has given him and of his love for the place, whatever its faults.

A hundred years on it is hard to see why *The Loom of Youth*, which is essentially a youthful outburst and a self-justification, should provoke such outrage, even given its inconvenient timing. But the public schools were so linked up with political power, with the Church (both Anglican and Catholic), and above all with the War effort, that to criticise them was to strike at the very roots of society. The immediate controversy was not quite the end of the story: a robust defence of the public schools against Waugh's charges was made by two other schoolboys, in Martin Browne's *A Dream of Youth* (1918)[27] and Jack Hood's *Heart of a Schoolboy* (1919),[28] and Waugh was to write further about his schooldays in 'The Public Schools: the Difficulties of Reform' (1919),[29] *Public School Life* (1922)[30] and *The Early Years of Alec Waugh* (1962).[31] And although, in the years after the War, the changes to the curriculum that had been recommended by the Clarendon Commission back in 1861 were gradually introduced and there was some softening of attitudes, even a second global conflict and the end of Empire would for a time fail to stir the public schools from the complacency that would threaten their survival.

---

26. *The Loom of Youth*, Part IV, chapter 6.
27. Martin Browne, *A Dream of Youth* (London: Longmans, Green & Co., 1918).
28. Jack Hood, *Heart of a Schoolboy* (London: Longmans, Green & Co., 1919).
29. Alec Waugh, 'The Public Schools: the Difficulties of Reform', in *English Review* 28 (January-June 1919), pp. 220-228.
30. Alec Waugh, *Public School Life* (London: Collins, 1982).
31. Alec Waugh, *The Early Years of Alec Waugh* (London: Cassell & Co., 1962).

Chapter 7

The Preparatory School Story

Anthony Buckeridge – *Jennings Goes to School* (1953)
and *Jennings at Large* (1977)
William Mayne – *A Swarm in May* (1955)

After the First World War, in a changed world, the boys' school story went into decline, but in the 1950s and 1960s it enjoyed a brief revival in Anthony Buckeridge's inimitable tales of Jennings and Darbishire, and William Mayne's novels, set in a minor key, about life in a choir school. Until then, preparatory schools had largely escaped literary attention, but Buckeridge and Mayne created far more benign establishments than most schools of fact and fiction. The boys are content and there is none of the unattractive arrogance and aggression, and none of the tortured adolescent relationships, that characterise fictional public schools.

Anthony Buckeridge – *Jennings Goes to School* (1953)

Buckeridge wrote from experience. After working in preparatory schools in Rhyl and Suffolk, he bought into Vernon House, an ailing school in Brondesbury, London, and became its headmaster. A year later, with the outbreak of the Second World War, Vernon House evacuated to Northamptonshire, but when hostilities were over it was no longer viable and amalgamated with St Lawrence College, Ramsgate, where Buckeridge was employed to teach English. It was there that his writing career began to flourish:

> Merely by keeping my eyes and ears open as I walked round
> the school and noted what was happening, I gathered a store

of material which I could shape to suit the personality of my characters. Much of the comedy came from noting the different way in which a situation would be viewed from the adult and the youthful point of view. For example, boys will explode with hilarity at some fatuous joke which leaves Mr Wilkins baffled.[1]

In 1948, Buckeridge sent the script of a radio play featuring Jennings as its main character to the BBC. The producers of *Children's Hour* recognised its potential and commissioned a series of six plays, beginning with *Jennings Learns the Ropes*. There were eventually sixty-two *Jennings* radio plays, written between 1948 and 1960, and these are the basis of many of the twenty-five *Jennings* novels. The main tranche of novels was published between 1953 and 1977.

It is an irony that Buckeridge, who was a man of left-wing views, should focus his writing on the exclusive preparatory school world, for which he had little political sympathy:

> Had my father survived the war . . . I would certainly not have been sent to boarding school, for the Buckeridge family would never have subscribed to the hierarchical tradition of sending children away to school to have their rough corners rubbed off and thereby moulded into potential members of the political establishment. Rather the reverse![2]

But for Buckeridge, Linbury Court was simply a 'world apart', an imaginative setting for high jinks, sanitised of the worst aspects of boarding school existence, which would transport his readers away from those dull post-War years and which for him became a refuge from an unhappy personal life.[3]

Jennings Goes to School (1953) is the beginning of the series of *Jennings* novels and is based on the scripts of three radio plays: *Jennings Learns the Ropes*, *Jennings Raises the Alarm* and *Jennings and the Poisonous Spider*. Unlike in most school stories, there is little sense of Linbury Court's physical appearance, which may have much to do with the radio origins; instead, Buckeridge encourages readers to 'alter the shape of the building so that it becomes, in imagination, your own school. Jennings' class-room will be your class-room; his desk, your desk.'[4] This suggests that the intended primary

---

1. Anthony Buckeridge, *While I Remember: An Autobiography* (London: David Schutte, 2nd revised edition, 1999), p. 74.
2. *While I Remember*, p. 26.
3. Buckeridge married Sylvia Brown, whom he had met in Rhyl, in 1936, but became increasingly unhappy. The couple divorced in 1962 and Buckeridge then married Eileen Selby, who survived him.
4. Anthony Buckeridge, *Jennings Goes to School* (London: Collins, 1953), Introduction.

audience was one of preparatory school boys, but in the event, the novels
proved just as popular with children (and adults) who had never attended a
boarding school. They were even translated into a dozen languages (including
Indonesian and Chinese) and read in countries where boarding schools do not
exist. Readers found in them a different and more exciting school than their
own, where the characters are larger than life, where there are more pranks
than lessons, and where both children and staff are essentially kind to each
other (in spite of Mr Wilkins's outbursts of temper). There can be no happier
school than Linbury Court for children to attend in their imagination and
today the novels still attract a small, albeit dwindling, following.

In the opening chapter, the school train brings Jennings to Linbury
Court, near the fictional town of Dunhambury in Sussex. He is greeted
by Mr Carter, the best of all schoolmasters, who is full of good humour,
patience and common sense, and who provides the moral centre of the
series. He also meets Darbishire, the clergyman's son, who becomes his
close friend and accomplice in his various escapades. Tea on that first
day is a bemusing introduction to prep school life: the pecking order and
assumed seniority of boys who have arrived at Linbury Court just a few
months ('donkeys' years') before; the schoolboy slang, incomprehensible to
outsiders; the nicknames. Even their own names are not quite what they
were in the home life that they have left behind:

> 'Here, you, what's your name?'
> 'Charles Edwin Jeremy Darbishire,' said the small edition of
> his father, in capital letters.
> 'You can keep the Charles Edwin Jeremy, you won't be
> needing it,' said Venables.[5]

After tea on that first day, the boys each write a postcard to reassure
their parents that they have arrived safely (even if their parents have
brought them by car). Jennings has much to report and his seventh
attempt reads:

> Dear Mother
> I gave mine in to Mr cater Darbsher has spend 4½ of his my
> healthser ticket was in my pocket he said I had got bubnick plag
> it was a jok he is called Benny Dick toe I think it is. We had
> ozard of wiz for tea Atkion says wiz is good and oz is garstly so
> do I. Love John.
> P.S. Temple is a brain, he is short for dogs boody.[6]

---

5. *Jennings Goes to School*, chapter 1.
6. *Jennings Goes to School*, chapter 1.

Although largely unpunctuated, it is a neat summing up of prep school and an interpreter (which the bemused Mr and Mrs Jennings do not have) would report that Jennings has given his pocket money to Mr Carter to pay into the school 'bank', but that his new friend Darbishire has already spent 4½d of his own allowance. Jennings's health certificate ('healthser ticket'), part of the ritual of returning to boarding school, is found in his blazer pocket. Mr Carter, whose nickname is Benedick (because of the grace he says after meals – 'Benedicto benedicata' – has made a joke about Jennings not having bubonic plague, though in a better, inadvertent joke Jennings has already renamed it 'bucolic' plague. In the slang of Linbury Court, anything good is 'wizard' and anything bad is 'ozard' (derived somehow from 'The Wizard of Oz'), and jam, which is especially nasty, is simply called 'ozard'. One of the older pupils, Temple, is known as 'Bod': his initials, C.A.T., have perversely led to the name 'Dog', lengthened to 'Dogsbody' and shortened to 'Bod'. Thus Jennings's extraordinary attempt at letter-writing highlights how he is already immersing himself in the strange logic and language of his surroundings and is typical of the glittering humour that suffuses the *Jennings* novels. Child readers are likely to miss some of the verbal jokes, but they revel in the startling exclamations for which Jennings is best known – 'Fossilized fishhooks!', 'Crystallised cheesecakes!', 'Grusome hornswoggler!', and 'Super-wizzo-duper!' – though these occur more in later novels after Buckeridge had learned how quickly conventional schoolboy slang can date.[7]

In line with the plays on which it is based, *Jennings Goes to School* is loosely divided into three episodes – Jennings's and Darbishire's running away (which in the end results in Jennings becoming a schoolboy hero, denting the pecking order, and avoiding a 'bashing-up' which wasn't going to happen anyway); the fire practice, when Jennings is asked to use his initiative; and the incident of the poisonous spider, whose capture leads by a tortuous route to the cancelling of the cancellation of a football match and Jennings scoring the winning goal by mistake. The episodes are skilfully interwoven and between them fill Jennings's first term, but otherwise there is no sense of a plot in which characters develop and lessons are learned.

In his *Autobiography*, Buckeridge suggests that one of the mainsprings of his comedy lies in allowing situations to develop a little further than they would in real life – so, for example, in chapter 3 Mr Carter follows Jennings and Darbishire in their unlikely escape from Linbury Court instead of dully stopping them at the outset. Another of the mainsprings of his comedy lies in boys saying and doing things 'which to them are perfectly logical,

---

7. Some later editions nevertheless updated Buckeridge's original slang, to the outrage of a number of original readers.

but appear incomprehensible to an adult who lacks the facility of looking into the developing mind and interpreting what is going on there'.[8] This is illustrated in chapter 5 when the headmaster decides to hold a fire practice and lets the boys use their initiative. What he expects is for the normal orderly descent from the dormitories via the 'Pennetra' escape mechanism. But Jennings, who as a new boy has never been instructed on the workings of the machine, comes up with a different solution. So while the occupants of Dormitory 4 crawl around on the floor swathed in damp towels to avoid the imaginary smoke, he telephones the fire brigade – with the most hilarious consequences.

I have already suggested how school stories are often about the uncomfortable business of growing up, but in the *Jennings* novels, as in the *Billy Bunter* stories and novels, this is simply not the case. In *Jennings Goes to School*, Jennings enters Linbury Court at the beginning of the Christmas term at the age of 'ten years, two months and three days last Tuesday' and remains the same irrepressible character at the end of it, planning 'the wizardest of prangs' for the journey home. In the same way, the first three novels follow Jennings's escapades through the school year, and the pattern is generally repeated, sometimes spilling over into the following Christmas term. But Jennings always remains a ten- or eleven-year-old, always remains in Form 3, and always remains in Dormitory 4. Jennings, Darbishire and their friends never lose their innocence and exuberance (and if lessons are learned they seem to be quickly unlearned); and Mr Wilkins is never able to control his explosive outbursts or to think before acting. So Linbury Court is a sort of idyllic 'neverland' in which nobody grows up and similar games are played in a delightful loop. It is somewhere that we revisit because we know just what to expect, and the sameness is part of the enjoyment.

In the final chapter, Mr Carter is writing reports and confronting the age-old problem of schoolteachers – how to tell at least some of the truth without causing offence. Not surprisingly, Carter leaves Jennings's report until last: what should be said of running away, calling the fire brigade, hunting poisonous spiders, and driving Mr Wilkins into 'rare baits' that 'touch ozard cubed, in five second bursts'? It was always going to be the trickiest report, but it is a masterpiece of disingenuousness, cliché and understatement: 'He enters very fully into all out-of-school activities, and takes a lively interest in the corporate life of the school. . . . He has a vivid imagination and definite qualities of leadership, but these traits must be carefully guided into the right channels.'[9]

---

8. *While I Remember*, p. 78.
9. *Jennings Goes to School*, chapter 13.

With the report finished, Mr Carter has the job of rejecting the appalling detective story that Jennings and Darbishire are submitting for the school magazine. 'Choose a subject that you really know something about,' he advises. 'Try describing your first term at school.' The two boys think he's 'super-screwy squared': nobody would want to read stories about them. 'If you think it's such a good idea, why don't you do it yourself?' asks Jennings, as politely as he can. But Mr Carter is inspired: ' "I might," Mr Carter replied unexpectedly. "It's certainly an idea." '[10] Thus at the very end of the novel we are faced with the suggestion that the kindly and ever-reliable Mr Carter, perhaps as Buckeridge's alter ego, has been the narrator all along, and will be the narrator for the rest of the series. This metafictional twist explains further the unworldliness of Linbury Court. We have been in the hands of a storyteller who is himself a fictional character with superhuman patience and without an axe to grind. He can look at the goings-on around him with an amused sense of detachment. Luckily he not only understands small boys but has a sense of the ridiculous as well.

Jennings at Large (1977)

I have argued that Jennings lives in a 'neverland' and never grows up, but this is not quite true. Certainly he always remains in Form 3 and Dormitory 4, does not get much past his eleventh birthday, and retains his unquenchable spirit to the last; but there is a sense in the later novels that things have subtly changed. *Jennings at Large* (1977) is the last of the main tranche of Jennings novels and is the only one to take Jennings outside the classroom for a sustained period. It begins with an end-of-term camping trip, and when Jennings ties a guy rope to the bumper of the minibus and Mr Wilkins drives away with the tent in tow, it seems we are on familiar ground. But after a week of schoolboy mayhem, Jennings goes off to spend the holidays with his Aunt Angela, a social worker who lives in a seventh-floor council flat in Gaitskell Court, south-east London.[11] It is in these insalubrious surroundings that Jennings encounters Emma Sparrow, a girl of his own age who lives with her parents in the flat immediately above. Emma has collected a menagerie of stray animals against the rules of the Housing Department and Jennings has to help her to smuggle them to a new home. When he suggests lowering them out of the window to Aunt Angela's flat, we are treated to one of the most memorable scenes in the *Jennings* series. Mrs Pratt and Mrs Plumrose, serial complainers, are

---

10. *Jennings Goes to School*, chapter 13.
11. Hugh Gaitskell was leader of the Labour Party and Leader of the Opposition, 1955-1963.

visiting Aunt Angela to moan about children playing football in the yard, only to discover goldfish in the washing-up bowl, a spiky hedgehog under the tea towel, and a colander that moves across the top of the washing machine propelled by the tortoise beneath. The climax comes when a cage of hamsters arrives outside the window:

> For some seconds the visitors were too paralysed with shock to do anything but point and gibber. Then Mrs Pratt found her voice.
>
> 'Look what's in the cage,' she shrieked. '*Rats!*'
>
> Her cry was echoed by Mrs Plumrose. 'Rats! Rats at the window, trying to get in. Keep them off! Take them away! Quick.'[12]

The upshot is that Jennings arranges for the menagerie to be moved to Mrs Hockin's animal sanctuary, which the boys have come across on their camping holiday – but not before the chaos of a fund-raising fair and a sponsored run at Linbury Court, and a confrontation with Mrs Hockin's gun-toting neighbour, Major Rudkin.

'How do I know what's going to happen next term?' asks Jennings in the final paragraph. 'We'll just have to wait and see what happens, shan't we?'[13] *Jennings at Large* might have pointed to a new life for Jennings – and for Emma Sparrow – outside school, but it was not to be, and after a fourteen-year hiatus and the publication of *Jennings Again!* (1991) and *That's Jennings* (1994), both of which lack the breathless quality of their predecessors, the boarding school story very nearly comes to an end.

William Mayne – *A Swarm in May* (1955)

A Swarm in May (1955), William Mayne's first significant novel, is set in a cathedral choir school and was followed by *Choristers' Cake* (1956), *Cathedral Wednesday* (1960) and *Words and Music* (1963). Written in a spare but rich prose, it transforms the by then tired model of the boarding school story into something fresh and mysterious, although it only hints at the extraordinary depth of Mayne's later work.

Like the *Jennings* novels, *A Swarm in May* is about life in a traditional boys' preparatory school, but there the similarity ends. Whereas, the Jennings novels present a series of outrageous episodes, with little in the way of plot to hold them together, here there is a serious intent and a clear narrative thread. The characters are more rounded and more realistic

---

12. *Jennings at Large*, chapter 5.
13. *Jennings at Large*, chapter 15.

than Buckeridge's caricatures, and the language has a poetic richness that is almost entirely missing from Linbury Court. Although *A Swarm in May* has its humorous moments and verbal jokes, there is little of the uproarious comedy that characterises Jennings's journey through Form 3, and so perhaps it is not as immediately appealing to the young reader.

A Swarm in May is dominated by the performance of church music, and its antecedents lie more with the moral and specifically Christian tales of Victorian times. It also displays two aspects that were to become central to Mayne's later work: the importance of physical location (unlike in the *Jennings* novels) and the mystery of time, which shifts and sometimes becomes muddled. The first aspect in particular chimes with the tradition of the boarding school story, helping to create that sense of otherness. In the opening chapter, the Cathedral itself, with the school nestling beside it, is established as a central but isolated living presence within which the story unfolds. It is compared to a ship on its moorings, unmoving, while all around it moves, and linked only by two or three gangplanks to life beyond:

> It stood in grass like a ship anchored in a green swell: the uneven lawns swept away from the walls in bow-waves and eddies, flurries and wakes; yet nothing moved, and across the tides of grass was stretched in two or three places a gangplank of a path to the door.[14]

In such rich images, the sea continues to lap unobtrusively throughout the novel, when, for example, the sounds of the organ become alive, 'whirlpooling in the round apse . . . spring-tiding over the choir screen . . . and losing themselves in breakwaters of chairs in the nave';[15] when the inside of the Cathedral is compared to a 'sunless cool cave with its eternal wash and flow of quiet feet like the pebbled edge of the sea';[16] and later when the Cathedral 'gathered into itself, like a sea shell, the sounds of stillness, as if the echoes of the day had been unable to escape'.[17] In the final chapter, the image returns more forcefully as everything comes right and the organ voluntary rises to a crescendo:

> those in the beehive went down through a sea-storm of sound, as Dr Sunderland built and rebuilt enormous endeavours and sent out convoys of melodies, only to wreck them on rocks of

14. William Mayne, *A Swarm in May* (Oxford: Oxford University Press, 1955), chapter 1.
15. *A Swarm in May*, chapter 3.
16. *A Swarm in May*, chapter 4.
17. *A Swarm in May*, chapter 10.

harmony, and beat them down with wind and waves. He carried
his voyage out of these dangers, into the smooth trade winds,
and by the time everyone had come down from the tower into
the transept, the music was landlocked on a far coast; and the
sailors dancing on the shore.[18]

The narration sparkles with other imagery too: an omelette looks like a
'prehistoric moon';[19] a chair is 'whimpering' under Dr Sunderland's weight;[20]
the echo of a dropped book in the cathedral would 'flit like an audible bat
round each pillar'.[21] But in spite of the drama of the organ music, and the
never-ending surprises of the prose, *A Swarm in May* is mainly a calm and
reflective voyage of discovery, as past intertwines with present, a puzzle that
has lasted for hundreds of years is finally solved, and as the last notes fade
away, 'In the midday Cathedral there was peace under the echoes.'[22]

The action takes place during the school's Easter holidays. But, holidays
or not, sung services in the Cathedral must go on, and the boarding
choristers are returning early to take over from the dayboys who have
already taken their turn. There is thus an absence of lessons (apart from
copious stints of Extra French and Extra Latin), the atmosphere is relaxed
and homely, and the boys' adventure is implicitly encouraged. On the first
evening, there is an informal supper in the kitchen; there is a spur-of-the
moment trip to the seaside, when the headmaster is buried up to his neck
in sand and decorated with shells; and later there is a trip to the country to
blow off steam before term starts. Perhaps it is this situation that allows *A
Swarm in May* to be a gentle book, unusual for a boys' school story, with
a routine that is often domestic rather than institutional. However, the
trappings of boarding school life are never far away. There are the familiar
routines of dining and dormitory, the caravan of unpacked trunks, each
with its own history, being carried away for storage (and home life with
them), duty patrols, cricket nets, music practice, the ritual 'rest' after lunch,
the strict 'pecking order' among the boys, and the sprinkling of benign
schoolboy slang ('Chiz', 'Well done ye' and 'Unwell done ye').

The small cast of *A Swarm in May* is made up of recognisable school-
story characters. Four members of staff are in evidence (they are all
bachelors in this male-oriented society): Mr Ardent, the headmaster, whose
name evokes Victorian evangelism; Dr Sunderland, the large, breathless
and kindly organist and choirmaster ('Tweedledum'), a lonely figure, apart

18. *A Swarm in May*, chapter 21.
19. *A Swarm in May*, chapter 1.
20. *A Swarm in May*, chapter 1.
21. *A Swarm in May*, chapter 3.
22. *A Swarm in May*, chapter 21.

from the boys, who provides much of the novel's good sense and most of its comedy; Turle, the equally large and curmudgeonly porter ('Tweedledee'); and Mr Sutton ('Brass Button'), the eccentric and irascible Latin master, who has taught generation after generation (including, it transpires, the Bishop). Among the choristers, the focus is on just six: Trevithic (the head chorister); Owen, the inoffensive Welsh 'singing boy', who eventually becomes the Beekeeper; Iddingley (the youngest, and annoying); Dubnet (affable and not very clever); Madington (the swot); and Kelsey (full of himself and a bully). The Bishop turns up at the end of the novel to preside over the Cathedral's annual beekeeping ceremony and to offer a wise, if opaque, moral to an explicitly moral tale.

John Owen is the central character, but in the preparatory school world he is shorn of his first name almost immediately. A familiar railway journey brings him from home to the other world of school. Returning late, he is ushered into the darkened Cathedral grounds by the somewhat sinister Turle – the 'gatekeeper' – leaving behind him 'town and shops, home and holidays, other people and far places'.[23] We learn nothing of his home life, which is an irrelevance here, though his Welshness makes him something of an outsider. As the youngest 'singing boy' in the school (since his junior, Crew, is away with mumps), it falls on him to take on the traditional role of Cathedral Beekeeper. Legend has it that before the Reformation, Prior Tollelege, one of the monks in the monastery, had kept bees in a secret place in the Cathedral to provide wax for candles; there was even the story that a boy had been sealed up with the bees and left to die. Although there have since been no bees in the Cathedral for 400 years, and it is now lit by electricity, there remains an annual ceremony in which the chorister Beekeeper presents the Bishop with a beeswax candle. But in addition to learning and reciting a Latin text, the ceremony involves singing an introit – and Owen has 'more dread than anyone else of being asked to sing a solo'. So the task passes to Iddingley, who is the smallest singing boy. 'You're a really dull passage,' says Iddingley in choir-school language, 'almost a monotone, and I expect Mr Ardent will blow you up later'.[24]

As Iddingley predicts, Mr Ardent is unimpressed by Owen's ducking out: 'it was your duty to be Beekeeper, and I think you will regret having missed the opportunity. . . . Your first duty here is to the Cathedral and its services'. Mr Ardent (who is himself in holy orders) is given the role of moral guide in the novel. 'Thoughtlessness in anything is irresponsibility,'

23. *A Swarm in May*, chapter 1.
24. *A Swarm in May*, chapter 3.

he tells Owen;[25] and later, 'Life is real, life is earnest'.[26] Mr Sutton is even more outraged by Owen's attitude and is seemingly vindictive as well. In a scene reminiscent of Mr Wilkins at Linbury Court, 'Mr Sutton shook the music in Owen's face with a sharp movement that certainly meant Brass Button would thump him in a moment. Mr Sutton was very angry. Owen would have taken the music, but Mr Sutton threw it over his head into the passage' – but here the tone is sharper, even cruel, and Owen weeps.[27]

From here, the novel becomes an account of Owen's journey to redemption, as he and Trevithic discover secret passages in the Cathedral and find the place where Prior Tollelege kept his bees. Owen also discovers Prior Tollelege's key attached to a strange orb that, when warm, produces a scent that has the magical effect of attracting and calming bees. This explains how, according to the legend, Prior Tollelege was able to prevent his bees from flying away and how he was never stung by them. With the help of Dr Sunderland, who keeps three hives of bees in his own garden, Owen finds that he too can carry bees on the orb without being stung: it seems like a sort of magic. So he changes his mind and decides to take part in the Cathedral ceremony after all and to present the Bishop with a real swarm for his blessing. Iddingley surrenders the role of Beekeeper and Mr Sutton not only coaches Owen to recite an appropriate Latin script, but also stands ready at the presentation with a bicycle pump filled with water in case the bees need a calming spray.

Thus in the final chapter a changed and benign Mr Sutton declares that Owen is 'a credit to us all' and 'splendidly courageous'. The Bishop sees in him the works of God and explains that whatever happened to Prior Tollelege after the dissolution of the monasteries, the position of Beekeeper has survived, 'not lost or dead, but asleep'. That, he says, has now been brought to life again in Owen, who wonders if he will be 'a ghost of all future ages'.[28] It is characteristic of Mayne to conflate time in this way, with more than a hint of another temporal dimension. So the novel tells of how Owen, and each one of us, inhabits and is inhabited by the past, and will in turn be part of the future as well, for which there could be no more fitting setting than a cathedral, with its prayerful stones that have stood for centuries, and an ancient school with its own peculiar traditions. When Trevithick hears a distant thump (in fact, the swell shutters of the organ being closed), his suggestion that Prior Tollelege still moves in the cathedral is not quite a joke.

---

25. *A Swarm in May*, chapter 5.
26. *A Swarm in May*, chapter 8.
27. *A Swarm in May*, chapter 9.
28. *A Swarm in May*, chapter 21.

A Swarm in May is an understated book, whose simplicity is deceptive. Although it is in the didactic spirit of *Tom Brown's Schooldays* and its Victorian imitators, charting Owen's change and growth, it is lighter in touch and moves at a slower pace: God, it seems, is in his Heaven as well as in the Cathedral, and each night the watchman shouts out 'All's Well'.[29] But what sets it apart from and above other school stories are its striking use of language, its sympathy for all its characters, and its uncertain and self-effacing hero. The potential for both preachiness and sentimentality is undercut by a quirky humour, and it is typical that the thrilling and strangely apposite words of the psalms, which weave their way throughout, are accompanied absent-mindedly on the organ by Dr Sunderland with playful tunes that sound remarkably like nursery rhymes.

---

29. *A Swarm in May*, chapter 18.

Chapter 8

The Anti-School Story

William Golding – *Lord of the Flies* (1954)
Giles Cooper – *Unman, Wittering and Zigo* (1958)

It may seem surprising to find a chapter on William Golding's *Lord of the Flies* (1954) in a book about school stories – not least because there is no school in this extraordinary and powerful novel. But *Lord of the Flies* explores what might happen if the authoritarian structures around which schools are built were stripped away. Although the popular and lasting image of the novel is of a band of marauding, raggedy and ultimately murderous children, this is not how it begins.

Like the *Jennings* novels, *Lord of the Flies*, is written from experience. Before its remarkable success, Golding had had three novels rejected for publication. The last of these, *Short Measure*, is described in some detail by John Carey in *William Golding: The Man Who wrote 'Lord of the Flies'*.[1] Set in a British boarding school, it owes much to Golding's early years as a teacher at Bishop Wordsworth's School in Salisbury. The hero, Philip Stevenson, a newly appointed English and Drama teacher, is, according to Carey, a hostile self-portrait – negligent, untidy, drunken, and misogynistic – and 'the Remove's disruptive tactics are depicted in such detail that it seems possible they were drawn from life'.[2] Undeterred by the rejections, Golding thought it would be a good idea if he 'wrote about children on

---

1. John Carey, *William Golding: The Man Who Wrote 'Lord of the Flies'* (London: Simon and Schuster, 2009).
2. Carey, p. 148.

an island, children who behave in the way children really would behave'.[3]

In the first chapter, the aeroplane evacuating a party of disparate schoolboys from an atomic war has crashed on a deserted island, so, as in other school stories, the characters inhabit their own world that, more than ever, is cut off from the real world outside. There are other familiar ingredients too: the close friendship that develops between Ralph and Piggy, the 'feminine' traits of Simon, the bully in Jack, schoolboy slang. *Lord of the Flies* is very much in the tradition of the moral tale in which the boys face up to challenges, learn and change, but here, although there is rescue, there is no happy ending. Rather than making the boys into better, civilised people, ready to take their place in adult society, the experience of the jungle and the lack of a figure or system of authority to control them turns them into savages, both mirroring and satirising the world from which they have come.

The opening paragraph introduces us to twelve-year-old Ralph, the novel's hero, whose drab school uniform is out of place in the jungle, with its creepers, broken trunks and exotic bird life: 'Though he had taken off his school sweater and trailed it now from one hand, his grey shirt stuck to him and his hair was plastered to his forehead.'[4] When he jerks up his stockings, it is 'an automatic gesture that made the jungle seem for a moment like the Home Counties'.[5] Within moments, however, Ralph is ripping off 'the weight of his clothes' until he stands naked on the beach.[6] Here, for a moment, there is the thrill of exchanging the shackles of school, symbolised by the uniform, for a new and exotic freedom, but as he frolics and lolls in the shining lagoon, Piggy, the fat, bespectacled boy, crawls out of the undergrowth behind him. His ungrammatical speech marks him out as a 'scholarship' boy'; he is despised by the other middle-class children, but it is he who understands the hopelessness of the situation: 'Nobody don't know we're here. . . . We may stay here until we die.'[7] Slowly, as Piggy pleads that they must do something, Ralph's dream fades and the adventure takes on a grimmer complexion. Freedom becomes a worse sort of captivity and Ralph finds that 'to put on a grey shirt once more was strangely pleasing'. It is no longer an encumbrance, but a reassurance.

When Ralph sounds the conch, the boys who stumble out of the jungle are mainly in school uniforms: 'grey, blue, fawn, jacketed or jerseyed' – with 'badges, mottoes even, stripes of colour in stockings and pullovers'.[8]

---

3. Carey, p. 149.
4. William Golding, *Lord of the Flies* (London: Faber and Faber, 1954), chapter 1.
5. *Lord of the Flies*, chapter 1.
6. *Lord of the Flies*, chapter 1.
7. *Lord of the Flies*, chapter 1.
8. *Lord of the Flies*, chapter 1.

Here, though, the uniforms speak of difference rather than sameness: the boys come from diverse schools and at this stage there is nothing to bind them together. The exception is the cathedral choir, controlled by Jack Merridew, with each member dressed in a black cassock bearing a long silver cross, and a square black cap with silver badge. When the choir is seen fumbling along the sand, it is 'something dark'; then it is a 'creature', presaging the animal violence to come. It is united by shared experience: once Simon fainted 'at matins over the precentor'; Jack is chapter chorister, head boy and can sing C sharp. Piggy collects names, establishing a semblance of order and bringing each boy into individual focus; but the formality of school, its wiping away of individuality, is never far away – ' "Kid's names," said Merridew. "Why should I be Jack? I'm Merridew." '[9] To Jack's mortification Ralph is elected leader, not least because he holds the conch shell, which has become the symbol of authority – whoever holds it is in charge and has the right to speak. Ralph, Jack and Simon go off to explore. It is like a game, their pleasure reflected in their language: 'Wacco'; 'Wizard'; 'Smashing'; and, when they interrupt their ascent of the island's mountain to send a boulder crashing into the forest below, 'Wacco!', 'Like a bomb!', 'Whee-aa-oo!'.[10]

When the explorers return, Ralph calls another meeting. There are no grown-ups, so they will have to look after themselves. They cannot have everyone talking at once, so 'We'll have to have "Hands-up" like at school'; and, while they are waiting for rescue, they'll have a good time 'like in a book' – '*Treasure Island*', '*Swallows and Amazons*', '*Coral Island*'.[11] The similes show them grasping for a link back to the familiar. But, as the novel develops, life on the island is not like it is in these comfortable books. The children get dirty and sunburnt; they defecate; Piggy is asthmatic, obese and short-sighted; Simon is an epileptic; Jack is a bully and at every opportunity slams his sheath knife threateningly into a tree; and the small boy with the mulberry-coloured birthmark has seen a beastie, a snake-thing (with the suggestion of the devil-serpent in Eden) that came in the dark and from which they cannot escape, however hard they try to deny its existence. Like other 'island' literature, *Lord of the Flies* is almost inevitably imperialist in tone, as the boys attempt to bring the order of an English school to their new surroundings. Stefan Hawlin suggests that 'The boys are determined, like all good colonisers before them, to maintain standards

---

9. *Lord of the Flies*, chapter 1.
10. *Lord of the Flies*, chapter 1.
11. *Lord of the Flies*, chapter 2. In the first draft of *Lord of the Flies*, Enid Blyton's *The Island of Adventure* is also included, but Blyton's nanny state would hardly have been convincing here.

of Englishness and to distinguish themselves from the natives.'[12] But here it all goes horribly wrong: although there are no natives, the boys lose their Englishness and turn into 'painted niggers'.

Under Ralph's leadership, and guided by Piggy's good sense, the boys make a fire to attract the attention of a passing ship and build shelters on the beach. But when a ship sails across the horizon and there is the potential for rescue, Jack and his choir are hunting in the forest; although they have killed a pig, they have let the fire out. So there comes the confrontation between Jack and Ralph, between tempting excitement and dull practicality, between evil and good in the human psyche, which lies at the heart of the novel.

In chapter 8, Jack brings the confrontation to a climax, demanding that he become leader, and the world of savagery and school collide: 'He's not a hunter [he says of Ralph]. He'd never have got us meat. He isn't a prefect'. It seems the boys will remain loyal to Ralph: 'I'm not going to play any longer', says Jack, a humiliated child again, as he runs off along the beach and into the forest.[13] But others slip away to join him and, in what becomes a sexual frenzy, they kill another pig. Jack decapitates it and the head is placed on a stick as a gift to the beast, whatever the beast may be.[14] But the gift morphs into the beast itself, the 'Lord of the Flies', and reveals its true identity to Simon: ' "Fancy thinking the Beast was something you could hunt and kill!" said the head. . . . "You knew, didn't you? I'm part of you? . . . I'm the reason why it's no go?" '[15] But the beast speaks in the unmistakeable voice and language of a schoolmaster: 'I'm warning you. I'm going to get waxy. D'you see? You're not wanted. Understand? . . . So don't try it on, my poor misguided boy, or else – '.[16] Simon suffers an epileptic fit and when he awakes he discovers that the 'beast' the littleuns have seen is nothing of the sort, but the body of an airman dragged along by his parachute, and he makes his way back to the beach to reassure the others.

Meanwhile, Jack, buoyed up by the killing, offers 'meat' and 'fun' to the children and becomes the *de facto* leader, with Ralph deserted by all except Piggy and the twins. In the first climax of the novel, while beneath thunder and lightning Jack's tribe continues to celebrate the success of the hunt in a terrible Bacchic dance ('Kill the beast! Cut his throat! Spill his blood!'),

12. Stefan Hawlin, 'The Savages in the Forest: Decolonising William Golding', in Harold Bloom, ed., *Lord of the Flies: William Golding*, Modern Critical Interpretations series (London: Chelsea House, 2008), pp. 71-84.
13. *Lord of the Flies*, chapter 8.
14. *Lord of the Flies*, chapter 8.
15. *Lord of the Flies*, chapter 8.
16. *Lord of the Flies*, chapter 8.

Simon emerges from the jungle, but in the frenzy he is mistaken for the beast, and is torn to death by 'teeth and claws'.[17] His body is taken by the sea, a haloed, Christ-like figure, accompanied by 'bright' angels, and with 'silver' and 'marble' resonant of the Church.[18] It seems even Ralph and his companions are involved in the murder, and although the next morning they try to blot out their involvement, 'Memory of the dance that none of them had attended shook all four boys convulsively.'[19]

The second climax comes when Ralph, Piggy and the twins confront Jack and his tribe, demanding the return of Piggy's glasses that have been stolen as the only means to make fire. Ralph has wanted to revert to the schoolboys that they all used to be and go 'looking like we used to, washed and hair brushed – after all we aren't savages really and being rescued isn't a game'.[20] But by now Jack and his tribe are no longer playing and have become real savages: the uniform that once bound them together as an orderly choir has been replaced by a uniform of war-paint and they enjoy 'the liberation into savagery that the concealing paint brought'.[21] Facing the savages, Ralph makes a desperate attempt to cling to civilisation, blows the conch and calls an assembly, but he is defeated variously by 'laughter, silence and painted anonymity'.[22] Piggy takes the conch and appeals for the world they have left behind: 'I got this to say. You're acting like a bunch of kids. . . . What is better to have rules and agree, or to hunt and kill?'[23] In Golding's pessimistic imagination, the bully will in the end triumph over a civilised democracy (as he feared would happen in the actual Cold-War world) and a crowd of kids without rules will surrender to the beast and revert to savagery. As if to prove the point, Roger releases the rock that scatters the assembly and knocks Piggy to his death forty feet below.

That night Ralph confronts the pig's skull, the 'Lord of the Flies', for the last time. It gleams 'as white as ever the conch had done'.[24] With the conch destroyed, the beast has gained absolute power; even when Ralph smashes the skull in two, it lies grinning mockingly at the sky. As he cowers alone in the darkness, the novel nearly comes full circle, but doesn't:

> Might it not be possible to walk boldly into the fort, say – 'I've got pax,' laugh lightly and sleep among the others? Pretend they were still boys, schoolboys who had said 'Sir, yes, Sir – and worn

17. *Lord of the Flies*, chapter 9.
18. *Lord of the Flies*, chapter 9.
19. *Lord of the Flies*, chapter 10.
20. *Lord of the Flies*, chapter 11.
21. *Lord of the Flies*, chapter 11.
22. *Lord of the Flies*, chapter 11.
23. *Lord of the Flies*, chapter 11.
24. *Lord of the Flies*, chapter 12.

caps? Daylight might have answered yes; but darkness and the horrors of death said no.[25]

On the island, they have all been transformed utterly from the people they once were; even being boys, let alone schoolboys, is now a pretence.

So Jack sets light to the jungle to drive Ralph from his lair. Ralph runs desperately along the beach, but when he stumbles and falls it is at the feet of an astonished naval officer, not a killer. Ironically, it is smoke from the fire made with Piggy's stolen glasses, employed with such murderous intent, and not the impotent beacon, that has attracted the attention of a passing battle cruiser. Suddenly the hunters are again the schoolboys as Ralph has wished. 'Fun and games,' remarks the officer, with unintended irony, and then:

> 'I should have thought that a pack of British boys – you're all British aren't you? – would have been able to put up a better show than that – I mean –'
> 'It was like that at first,' said Ralph, 'before things – '
> He stopped.
> 'We were together then –'
> The officer nodded helpfully.
> 'I know. Jolly good show. Like the Coral Island.'[26]

The officer's voice is the clear voice of Empire, and of the schoolmaster (though a more genial one than the 'Lord of the Flies'), and the mention of Coral Island takes us back to that first excited anticipation of an island adventure 'like in a book'. But in spite of the brave efforts of Ralph, Piggy and Simon, it hasn't been a 'jolly good show', and while the officer gives them time 'to pull themselves together', Ralph, surrounded by 'little boys' who shake and sob, weeps 'for the end of innocence, the darkness of man's heart'.

With few exceptions, school stories tell of children learning to live together under the rule of law, finally leaving school as responsible citizens. Some stories go further and suggest that children are capable of making and upholding their own rules (see, for example, Enid Blyton's *The Naughtiest Girl in the School*, 1940, discussed in chapter 11), or even running their own school (as in William Mayne's *No More School*, 1965). But *Lord of the Flies* turns the structure and morality of the school story on its head. Here, as uniforms are discarded, order is undermined and rules are broken, Golding sets out to explode the romantic concept of man's innate goodness. The pessimism of his vision is made complete by the manner of the boys' arrival

---

25. *Lord of the Flies*, chapter 12.
26. *Lord of the Flies*, chapter 12.

on and leaving of the island. Both the crashed aeroplane and the 'trim cruiser' speak of the savagery of the adult world, obliterated in part, no doubt, by the atomic bomb, as surely as the island is reduced to 'a burning wreckage'. Thus the story of the disintegration of the society on the island because of the 'beast' within is also an allegory for the disintegration of the outside world that has chosen war over peace.

Giles Cooper – *Unman, Wittering and Zigo* (1958)

Giles Cooper's radio play *Unman, Wittering and Zigo* (1958)[27] – later adapted for stage and screen – brings the savagery of *Lord of the Flies* into the classroom itself and is a more obvious satire on the public school system that stands for 'Church and Empire' and turns out 'a normal, decent type of Christian oaf'.[28] The boys are called 'men' and are 'never a problem, given discipline'; CCF, sport and chapel (you get a 'bumming' if you don't attend) are central to their lives; and dormitories are named after imperial heroes like Kitchener and Rhodes.

Cooper, an Anglo-Irish playwright, had previously adapted *Lord of the Flies* for the radio and its influence on his play is clear. At Chantrey, an isolated boarding school, the senior master, Pelham, has fallen from the nearby cliff-top in fog and has been killed. His young and inexperienced replacement, John Ebony, struggles for acceptance among the staff and to control Nadia, his errant wife. Worse, his class resents him and becomes impossible. When Ebony threatens to keep the boys in for detention on a Saturday afternoon, they claim that Pelham's death wasn't in fact accidental: after he tried to give them a detention, they struck him with a rock and pushed him from the cliff. Though Ebony is unsure of the truth, he soon gives in to their bullying and, in return for a quiet life, allows them to do little work, places bets for them at the local bookmakers, and promises to award them dishonestly high marks in their exams. But when he attempts to investigate Pelham's death and to discover the class ringleader, the boys turn their attention to Nadia – though, because she offers them cigarettes and shows she is not on the side of the establishment, they fail to press home their attack. In the final scene, as the parents 'gather round the dead innocence of their children' (a haunting reminder of 'the end of innocence' in *Lord of the Flies*), it is left to Cary, the cynical art master, to draw the uncomfortable moral:

---

27. Giles Cooper, *Unman, Wittering and Zigo* (1958). References are to Nelson's Dramascript series (London: Thomas Nelson, 1971).
28. *Unman, Wittering and Zigo*, scene 23.

CARY Authority, my old Ebony, is a necessary evil, and every bit
   as evil as it is necessary.
JOHN But if it was Pelham . . . and me . . . the masters, then why
   doesn't it happen all the time?
CARY It does, my dear fellow, but thank heaven not in schools.[29]

So Ebony realises that the ringleader he has searched for, who has
'dominated' the children, given them a 'corporate will' and apparently
turned them into murderers, is not one of them, but the 'authority' figure
– Pelham, and then himself.

   In the cinema, Lindsay Anderson's film *if* (1968), with screenplay by
David Sherwin, was also indebted to *Lord of the Flies*. It is the story of
an insurrection at a British public school and again satirises the public
school system. Three boys, who are fed up with bullying by the prefects
(the 'whips'), decide to rebel, bringing down not only the bullies but the
whole system that has bred them. On Founder's Day they start a fire in
the school hall, driving everyone from the building; there is then a surreal
gunfight between the rebels (who have found automatic weapons in a store
room) and teachers and parents (who arm themselves from the Cadet Force
store), but instead of winners and losers, the violence fades to a red word
on a black screen: 'if'. Made and released during the student unrest of the
1960s, it caught the mood of the time. Public schools and stories about
them simply could not escape the zeitgeist.

*

Lord of the Flies did not in itself change the direction of the school story.
There were many other factors in play that between them ended for a
time the fascination with the boarding school. However, it did show
that schools (and society) rely on the tacit agreement of the majority to
submit to the rule of law and that such agreement was beginning to break
down. Soon the 1960s – a rebellious age in the western world, which
brought new and welcome freedoms – would present huge challenges in
education. Schools became increasingly child-centred. In primary schools,
the influential Plowden Report championed 'learning by doing' in place
of the old 'chalk and talk'.[30] In secondary schools, the ideological battle
between old-fashioned intolerance and progressive tolerance was played
out very publically in 1960-1965 at Risinghill, an Islington comprehensive
school led by a radical headmaster, Michael Duane: 'Does Sparing The

---

29. *Unman, Wittering and Zigo*, scene 29.
30. *Children and their Primary Schools* – a *Report* of the Central Advisory Council for
   Education (England) (London: Her Majesty's Stationery Office, 1967).

Rod Breed Crime?' asked one sceptical newspaper headline.[31] Children, no matter how they behaved, suddenly had rights. Parents, who had previously stayed outside the school gates, wanted to know and influence what went on inside, often challenging the authority and judgement of the establishment. There was an upsurge in parent-teacher organisations and parent governors. Teachers no longer knew best and ceased to be respected figures in the community. Even the toughest and surest of public schools had to move with the times and the totems of corporal punishment and 'fagging' gradually disappeared. This was all justifiable if children, whatever their faults, are innately good; however, if Golding is right, and beneath the uniform they are savages, any weakening of rules and blurring of boundaries run the risk of handing control back to the bully and the mob. But, what if, as Golding half suggests and Cooper and Sherwin posit more explicitly, it is the disciplined environment, which is meant to protect children from themselves, that actually reinforces their worst traits, makes them coalesce as a mob, and turns them into thugs? These are intractable problems, but fifty years on the most successful schools have, it seems, established a middle way of give and take, without giving or taking too much.

---

31. The story of Risinghill is told in Leila Berg's *Risinghill: Death of a Comprehensive School* (Harmondsworth: Penguin Books, 1968).

Part III

Girls' Schools and their Stories
Introductory: Morals, Manners and Mediocrity

Until the middle of the nineteenth century, education for girls had been neglected, especially since the closing of the convent schools during the Reformation. Some upper- and middle-class girls were taught at home by a governess and there were a few small boarding schools like Miss Teachum's Academy (see Introduction). However, by the 1840s the middle classes were beginning to demand education for their daughters as well as for their sons – though at first girls' education still meant the imparting of domestic and social skills as a preparation for married life, whether at home or as a wife of Empire. This led to a proliferation of private girls' schools, where the emphasis was on inculcating in young ladies the best of morals and manners, the ability to make polite conversation and manage a household, and the temperament to be good and subservient companions. Even the advent of free state education later in the century failed to dent the popularity of such schools: however bad the standards in their classrooms, they had social cachet, which for most parents was of greater importance. This state of affairs continued into the first half of the twentieth century and even beyond.

Fortunately, however, the growing movement for women's emancipation also led to the foundation of a raft of impressive day schools. The Queen's College for Women in Harley Street, London, founded by the social reformer

F.D. Maurice in 1848,[1] was in the vanguard and was followed in 1871 by the
North London Collegiate School for Ladies, founded by Miss Frances Buss,
an alumna of Queen's College. The Taunton Commission (1868) found
that girls' schools were usually inferior to boys' schools and recommended
that all towns with more than 4,000 inhabitants should have a high school
for girls. As a result, the 1869 Endowed Schools Act enabled girls' schools to
benefit from charitable endowments, opening the way for the establishing
of the Girls' Public Day School Company in 1872 and the Church Schools
Company in 1883. By 1905, the Girls' Public Day School Company had
founded thirty-seven schools and the Church Schools Company a little less
than half that number.[2] There were also boarding public schools for girls
(many privately owned at the outset and later becoming charitable trusts).
Cheltenham Ladies' College (1853) was the first of note, though it did
not make its mark until Miss Dorothea Beale, another alumna of Queen's
College, arrived as headmistress in 1858 and faced down domestically-
minded parents. Other notable foundations included, for example, St.
Leonard's, Fife (founded in 1877), Roedean (Sussex, 1885), Wycombe
Abbey (Buckinghamshire, 1896), St Felix (Suffolk, 1897), Downe House
(Berkshire, 1907), Moreton Hall (Shropshire, 1913), Benenden (Kent,
1923), and Felixstowe College (Suffolk, 1929; closed 1994). Since there
was no other model, they borrowed much from the boys' public schools
– the organisation by 'house', the prefect system (though prefects at girls'
schools never seem to have wielded the almost unbridled power of their
male counterparts), and the considerable emphasis on team games. More
about the history of girls' schools can be found in Gillian Avery's *The Best
Type of Girl – A History of Girls' Independent Schools,* which is immensely
readable and more gripping than most girls' school stories.[3] Also consigning
fiction to the shade are Julie Welch's *Too Marvellous for Words! – The Real
Malory Towers Life* and Ysenda Maxtone Graham's *Terms & Conditions –
Life in Girls' Boarding Schools, 1939-1979.*[4]

---

1. See chapter 1. F.D. Maurice was, with Thomas Hughes and Charles Kingsley, a
    leading Christian Socialist.
2. Today the Girls Public Day Schools Company has become the Girls' Day School
    Trust; it is one of the richest charities in the United Kingdom and runs twenty-six
    schools. The Church Schools Company has become The United Church Schools
    Trust and operates thirteen schools, only five of which are now exclusively girls'
    schools.
3. Gillian Avery, *The Best Type of Girl – A History of Girls' Independent Schools* (London:
    Andre Deutsch, 1991).
4. Julie Welch, *Too Marvellous for Words! – The Real Malory Towers Life* (London:
    Simon and Schuster, 2017); Ysenda Maxtone Graham, *Terms & Conditions – Life
    in Girls' Boarding Schools, 1939-1979* (London: Abacus, 2017).

Meade, Brazil, and the 'Big Three'

The first significant girls' school story of Victorian times was L.C. Meade's lavender-scented *A World of Girls* (1886). But it was Angela Brazil, with her more daring and attractive heroines, who started the landslide of girls' school stories that was to engulf the inter-War years. Both novelists are considered in chapter 9. Brazil was followed by the 'Big Three' of girls' school fiction, Elsie J. Oxenham, Dorita Fairlie Bruce and Elinor M. Brent-Dyer, all of whose output was phenomenal.

Elsie Oxenham (1880-1960) really began the extended girls' school series. The first of what was to become the *Abbey* series is *Girls of the Hamlet Club* (1914), which is centred on Miss Macey's School. New girl Cicely Hobart discovers that pupils from the local hamlets are looked down on by the rest of the school and cannot afford the deliberately inflated subscriptions to the school clubs. So she sets up the secret 'Hamlet Club' (motto: 'To be or not to be'), whose members indulge in Oxenham's own hobby of country dancing. The Club comes to the rescue when the cast of the school play falls ill, revealing its existence but allowing the show to go on. Not only does the novel highlight the social divisions between the wealthy town dwellers and the not-so-wealthy country folk (many of the Hamlet Club members are despised scholarship girls – in most girls' schools, class was still more important than brains), but it also contrasts urban and rural values: Oxenham's championing and description of the Buckinghamshire countryside has an almost Wordsworthian flavour.

There was never, in fact, an Abbey School. Six years after *Girls of the Hamlet Club*, *The Abbey Girls* (1920), introduces cousins Joy and Joan Shirley to Miss Macey's School – through the good offices of Cicely Hobart. Joy has inherited Abinger Hall and Joy has inherited the ruined abbey in its grounds, so they become the 'abbey girls' and the series takes off.[5] The early novels relate the schoolgirl adventures of Joy, Joan and their friends; later we follow them into adult life, with their daughters now attending Miss Macey's. But, in an attempt to avoid too much repetition, the plots sprawl away from Miss Macey's and, as the series drags on, the quality begins to fade.

My own favourite of the 'Big Three' is Dorita Fairlie Bruce (1885-1970), whose five separate series (*Dimsie*, *Nancy*, *Springdale*, *Toby* and *Sally*) are each nicely contained. *Dimsie Moves Up* (1921), which is about the Anti-Soppist Society at the Jane Willard Foundation, is discussed in chapter 10. There is even less soppiness in Josephine Elder's outstanding *Evelyn Finds*

---

5.   The abbey was based on Cleeve Abbey, Somerset, which Oxenham moved to the Buckinghamshire/Oxfordshire border, close to Miss Macey's School.

Herself (1929), discussed in the same chapter. This is set in a day school and deals in a serious way with schoolgirl friendship and the pleasures of the academic life.

In 1925, Elinor M. Brent-Dyer (1894-1969) unleashed the interminable *Chalet School* series that outruns even the Abbey series. There were originally fifty-eight titles, and even then the characters spill into other of Brent-Dyer's novels. Since her death, the series has continued to grow, with fresh authors contributing a further twenty novels that slot into the original timescale, not to mention a prequel and four sequels. Between 1938 and 1948 Brent-Dyer ran her own school – The Mary Roper School – in Hereford, but it was not successful and unsurprisingly, given the demand for her books, she ended up as a full-time author.

The extraordinary Chalet School world began with *The School at the Chalet* (1925), in which 24-year-old Madge Bettany decides to start a school in the Austrian Tyrol, where the clean air will benefit her sickly younger sister, Joey. In less than two months, the Chalet School opens with its first nine pupils, of whom six live locally. 'My father says that the English schools are deficient in education, but they give girls a more healthy life,' says Gisela, pointing out that schools in Austria and Germany have much longer hours. For good measure, she adds, 'And they have no games'.[6] The first term at the Chalet School passes quickly and is packed with action: as well as the usual escapades – the spilled red ink, the French chalk on the piano keys, the dormitory pranks and the vaselining of the blackboards – there are the dramas of Juliet's abandonment by her parents, the thunderstorm in the mountains, Grizel's running away, and the train crash in the final chapter, where the school party is helped by Dr James Russell. However, as well as the romance of the Austrian countryside and its colourful inhabitants, the real interest of *The School at the Chalet* is that the focus is not on its international cast of spirited schoolgirls (not least Joey, a tomboy, who, in spite of her weak constitution, is at the heart of most of the action), but on young Madge Bettany struggling with her responsibilities as a headmistress.

The second term at the Chalet School is described in *Jo of the Chalet School* (1926). The magic of 'word of mouth' means that the roll has grown to an improbable thirty-three pupils, and another chalet provides a 'junior house'. Part of the novel's charm is its description of an Austrian winter and Christmas (though there are also Joey's rescue of a St Bernard puppy and a flood that threatens to engulf the school). As the title suggests, Joey begins to take centre stage. When she and her friends play truant to attend

6. Elinor M. Brent-Dyer, *The School at the Chalet* (London: W. and R. Chambers, 1925), chapter 5.

the local ice carnival, it is by chance that she falls conveniently into the path of James Russell, who avoids slicing through her fingers by falling on top of her. In the final chapter, after an unseen whirlwind romance, Madge becomes engaged to Russell (Dr Jem) and, although she resolves to stay as headmistress for the foreseeable future, the reader can sense the way things are going. What could be nicer:

> 'Nice!' Joey repeated her words rapturously. 'It'll be gorgeous!
> – Oh, Madge, it's just the very nicest and splendidest of all our adventures!'
> Madge looked down at the slender ring on her left hand, where a sapphire glowed in the sunshine, blue as the waters of the Tiernsee under summer skies, and smiled softly to herself. 'I think so, too!' she said.[7]

For a time, Joey becomes the central character of the series, gradually cured by the Austrian air and surviving near death in *Rivals of the Chalet School* (1929). She marries Dr Jack Maynard (Dr Jem's partner in the nearby sanatorium), produces eleven children, and, like her creator, becomes a writer of children's stories. In 1939, the Chalet School escapes to Guernsey to avoid the Nazis (*The Chalet School in Exile*, 1940), then escapes again to Herefordshire (*The Chalet School Goes to It*, 1941). A further seven novels see the Chalet School on an island off the south-west Coast of Wales, before it settles in the Oberland in Switzerland in the 1950s (the political situation in Austria precluded a return to its original home). Each time, Joey moves with it and eventually some of her children take over as leading protagonists. Inevitably, the later novels in this mammoth series have little more to say and resort to the hackneyed transforming of disruptive girls into paragons of virtue, but the fact that the Chalet School was from the outset especially 'apart' meant that Brent-Dyer could go on writing about it while ignoring the changes in society around her.

The mantle of girls'-school series fiction was taken up by Enid Blyton, who wrote in even barer prose. Blyton wrote her school stories during World War II and its aftermath, but they are deliberately escapist and it is as if the War does not exist. Her three series – *The Naughtiest Girl*, *St Clare's* and *Malory Towers* – are considered in chapter 11. Altogether more challenging and satisfying are Antonia Forest's Kingscote novels: *Autumn Term* (1948), *End of Term* (1959), *The Cricket Term* (1974) and *The Attic Term* (1976), which have a complexity, depth and irony that are missing from most other girls'-school stories. *Autumn Term* is the subject of chapter

---

7. Elinor M. Brent-Dyer, *Jo of the Chalet School* (London: W. and R. Chambers, 1926), chapter 25.

12. Thereafter, Penelope Farmer's *Charlotte Sometimes* (1969) tells how Charlotte (in a 1950s boarding school) changes places with Clare (a pupil at the same school at the end of the First World War), but its language is uncomfortably archaic and there is no insight into the life of the school in either period.[8] More recently, Harriet Martyn's *Balcombe Hall* trilogy (1982-1984) and the fourteen short novels of Anne Digby's *Trebizon* series (1978-1994) return to the old boarding school clichés (Digby daringly introduces boys as well), but they have little to add to a literary fashion whose time had passed.

Popular Stories

The success of the boys' weekly papers *The Magnet* and *The Gem* (see chapter 5), which also had a considerable readership of girls, encouraged the Amalgamated Press to launch a sister paper, *The School Friend*, in 1919. Charles Hamilton/Frank Richards was asked to contribute the main story and, now as Hilda Richards, he developed the character of Bessie Bunter, Billy's sister, and a whole cast of girls, good and bad, in the eternal Fourth Form of Cliff House. But even Hamilton/Richards could not meet the copy deadlines and what worked for boys did not work for girls: Billy might have been regarded as a clown, but female readers greeted Bessy with contempt. So Hamilton/Richards was replaced by R. S. Kirkham and Horace Phillips (each took over the Hilda Richards pseudonym at different times), who had the task of turning Bessie into a more attractive character and producing the sort of sentimental plots, laced with adventure, that the schoolgirl audience demanded. From 1926, the Hilda Richards mantle was taken up by L. E. Ransome and although in 1929 *The School Friend* was superseded by *Schoolgirl*, Ransome and Bessie Bunter soldiered on until 1932. There was then a two-year hiatus until Bessie returned in 1934, now in the hands of John Wheway. His characters are more realistic and talented than their predecessors – even Bessie becomes a popular and slimmed-down member of the Fourth – and Cliff House is an altogether more attractive place. However, like *The Magnet*, *Schoolgirl* was forced to close in 1940 because of paper shortage. It was *The School Friend* that was revived after the War, but Bessie's innings was over and she was replaced by the lightweight Dilly Dreem.

Meanwhile Horace Phillips, writing as Marjorie Stanton, had been invited to write his own series for *The Schoolgirls' Own*, launched as a companion paper to *The School Friend* in 1921. Phillips, who might have been more at home writing a hundred years earlier, was an exponent of the

---

8. Penelope Farmer, *Charlotte Sometimes* (London: Chatto and Windus, 1969).

'Cinderella' story. His tales of Morcove School, in North Devon, centre on Betty Barton, a poor girl from Lancashire whose fees are paid by a rich (fairy godfather) uncle. When she arrives at Morcove she finds herself sharing a study with the two (ugly) Grandways sisters (Mrs Barton works as a charwoman at the Grandways' mansion and Mr Grandways has tried to evict the Bartons from their home for not keeping up with their rent):

> They stood up, stiff as poles, whilst the languid looks on their proud faces gave place to an expression of fierce disgust.
> 'What's this!' gasped the elder of the two at last.
> 'You know what it is,' answered the younger sister. 'It is the Council school girl! Our charwoman's kid – come to this school!'
> Then all I can say is,' said Cora Grandways fiercely, 'she has come to the wrong shop! But what does it mean, Judith? How dare they have Council school girls at a school like this! How dare they!'[9]

At the end of this first episode, Betty resolves to face down her enemies with 'flashing eyes' and 'heroic spirit', and as if there are not already sufficient clichés, 'Will she sink or swim?' asks the teaser for the following week's paper. The Morcove saga ran until 1938 (with its last two years in *Schoolgirl*), but by then the world had changed and there was nowhere left for it to go. It is also worth pondering why the majority of popular girls' school stories (as opposed to girls' school novels) were written by men and whether a failure to empathise fully with the schoolgirl reader contributed to their relative lack of success.

Not So Innocent

In marked contrast to all these escapist stories for girls are two novels for adults. First, Antonia White's *Frost in May* (1933) is a barely fictionalised account of her experiences at the Convent of Five Wounds between the ages of nine and fourteen. The central character is Nanda Gray, who half embraces the strict Catholic way of life, but still enjoys the normal childhood friendships that the nuns frown on as likely to inspire rebellion. The minutely detailed descriptions of convent life are enthralling and frightening, as the nuns strive to break the girls' human spirit so they can devote themselves to a religious life. The girls at the Convent of Five Wounds are largely from upper-class Catholic families, so their education is not that different from the norm: its object is still to prepare them to be brides – but brides of Christ.

---

9. Marjorie Stanton, 'Scorned by the School', in *The Schoolgirls' Own*, 5 February 1921.

Secondly, Muriel Spark's *The Prime of Miss Jean Brodie* (1961) describes life in a girls' day school – Marcia Blaine – in 1930s Edinburgh. Miss Brodie is a charismatic and eccentric teacher in a conservative school, in love with the married art master and loved by the bachelor one-armed music teacher, whose mistress she becomes for a time because it is more respectable. All this is witnessed by her 'set' of six girls, with whom she discusses art, travel, politics (she has a portrait of Mussolini on her classroom wall) and romance. In contrast to the suffocating conventions, discipline and morality of the time, not to mention the nuns at the Convent of Five Wounds, Miss Brodie is determined to liberate her girls, empowering them to think, feel and live their lives instinctively and creatively. 'I shall remain at this education factory,' she says, when the despairing headmistress tries to persuade her to seek a post in a progressive school. 'There needs must be a leaven in the lump'.[10]

As the Brodie girls move through the school, their characters develop, shaped by their mentor: 'Give me a girl at an impressionable age, and she is mine for life,' she says in chilling echo of the Jesuit belief.[11] In their final year, Rose becomes a model for Mr Lloyd, but every portrait he executes resembles Miss Brodie; yet it is Sandie, Miss Brodie's favourite, who has an affair with him and who betrays Miss Brodie to the headmistress (she is sacked for encouraging fascism). Finally, Sandie leaves Mr Lloyd, taking only his religion with her, and becomes a nun, while Miss Brodie does not perceive Sandy's treachery until her dying moments. Spark tells the story with insight and wit, making *The Prime of Miss Jean Brodie* one of the great novels of the twentieth century, but one wonders how far her portrait of the uninhibited and sexually aware girls at Marcia Blaine in the 1930s is an accurate one, and how far she moves the more enlightened and precocious girls of 1961 back to a very different world.

Given the often extraordinary nature of private girls' schools in the first half of the twentieth century and their even more extraordinary translation into fiction, it is not surprising that the stories about them have become widely satirised – usually employing the sexual innuendo (and more) that the original schools and stories so studiously avoid. Ronald Searle's first *St Trinian's* cartoons appeared in 1941, but it was after the end of World War II, when he was freed from the horror of a Japanese prisoner-of-war camp, that the series took off and was soon translated to screen and stage. St Trinian's is the opposite of the storybook girls' school. According to Searle, a St Trinian's girl 'would be sadistic, cunning, dissolute, crooked, sordid, lacking morals of any sort and capable of any excess. She would also be

10. Muriel Spark, *The Prime of Miss Jean Brodie* (London: Macmillan, 1961), chapter 1.
11. *The Prime of Miss Jean Brodie*, chapter 1.

well-spoken, even well-mannered and polite.' In the same way, 'The staff, behind an extremely old-fashioned facade, conceal equivalent excesses and plenty of lesbianism.'[12] The violence in the post-War cartoons is in part Searle's way of coping with his experiences (many of them were drawn when he was in captivity), but more than that he plays on the patriarchal fears engendered by the growth of girls' education and by the stories that accompanied it. Girls were not to be trusted, nor were their teachers. They would destroy society. Girls' schools were out of control – and hotbeds of lesbianism too.

More disturbing and bordering on the pornographic is *Trouble at Willow Gables* (2002) by Philip Larkin (writing as Brunette Coleman). This was completed just after Larkin had taken his finals at Oxford in 1943, but it was only discovered in 1992 and published with other juvenilia ten years later.[13] The plot uses familiar ingredients: a stolen five pound note; an innocent girl, Marie, wrongly accused and running away; the real culprit, Margaret (who has used the money to bet on a horse and won £100) escaping on horseback – and a resulting night-time search; Margaret saving her drowning friend in the nick of time; and everything ending happily (although the headmistress appropriates the winnings for the school's swimming pool fund). But *Trouble at Willow Gables* also has a darker side and foreshadows the cruel streak in much of Larkin's poetry. Marie is held down by two prefects and savagely beaten by the headmistress; there are suggestive descriptions of girls dressing and undressing; Hilary, a prefect, discovers that Margaret is the real thief but keeps quiet in return for sexual favours. Critics have disagreed vehemently over the novel's worth, and if it had not been written by Larkin, it would probably have been long forgotten.

Another twist on the girls' school story is found in Rosalind Erskine's *Passion Flower Hotel* (1962). In this light-hearted novel, the enterprising 'Passion Flowers' of Bryant House set up a brothel to service the boys from Longcombe School:

> 'All right. . . . But supposing you could bear to, and in fact liked
> it, but happened to get paid?'
>   'Imposs,' said Mary-Rose.
>   'Jamais de la vie,' said Virginia.
>   'Why? Why is it?'
>   'Because,' said Virginia patiently, 'if you felt enough for a man
> to let him –'

12. Russell Davies, *Ronald Searle: A Biography* (London: Sinclair-Stevenson, 1990), pp. 101-102.
13. James Booth (ed.), *Philip Larkin: Trouble at Willow Gables and Other Fictions* (London: Faber and Faber, 2002).

'I could feel enough,' said Melissa throatily, 'for *any* man to
let him do *anything*, after nearly a whole entire stinking creeping
term in this dump.'[14]

This, remember, was written at a time when Elsie Oxenham and Elinor
M. Brent-Dyer were still pouring out their 'topping' tales of schoolgirl
crushes and midnight feasts. In similar vein to *The Passion Flower Hotel* are
Tyne O'Connell's *Pulling Princes* (2003), *Stealing Princes* (2004), *Duelling
Princes* (2005) and *Dumping Princes* (2006), which tell of the experiences
of Calypso, a Californian outsider, at exclusive St Augustine's School, not
far from a fictionalised Eton College, Windsor Castle, and (suggestively)
Puller's Woods. Whatever else has changed over the centuries, social
aspiration is still very much at the heart of the independent school system.

*

Unfortunately, the progress made in girls' education in the first half of
the twentieth century was ill served by the stories written about it. The
core audience of the early novels was not the comparatively small number
of pupils at the private schools that they mainly describe, but girls with
no social standing (some already at work) who fantasised about becoming
aristocratic ladies and longed to have a vicarious presence in the intense
friendships and adventures that were lacking in their own lack-lustre world.
Even some twenty-first century novels remain stuck in a world of privilege
and sentimentality, where the expectation is of a pleasant togetherness
and ladylike behaviour, and ambition is limited to a life of domestic bliss,
though it has to be said that until comparatively recently some girls' schools
continued to mirror the fiction written about them. Elder's *Evelyn Finds
Herself* and, in a different way, Forest's Kingscote novels, are honourable
exceptions, better reflecting the mainstream of girls' independent education,
but pioneers like F.D. Maurice, Frances Buss, and Dorothea Beale, who
as much as anyone served the cause of women's emancipation, deserved
considerably better.

---

14. Rosalind Erskine, *The Passion Flower Hotel* (London: Jonathan Cape, 1962), chapter
    2. Rosalind Erskine is the fifteen-year-old persona created by Roger Longrigg.

Chapter 9

The Girls' School Story

L. T. Meade – *A World of Girls: The Story of a School* (1886)
Angela Brazil – *The Fortunes of Philippa* (1906)
and *A Patriotic Schoolgirl* (1918)

L.T. Meade's *A World of Girls: The Story of a School* (1886) established the model for girls' school stories in the way that Thomas Hughes's *Tom Brown's Schooldays* had done for the boys. Twenty years later, Angela Brazil developed the model, dragging it away from the Sunday School preachiness of the Victorian era, and unleashing the wave of escapist girls' school stories that would have huge appeal for the next half-century.

L.T. Meade –
A World of Girls: The Story of a School (1886)

A World of Girls is heavily influenced by Victorian moral tales (the normal reading matter for girls of the age) and, I think, by F.W. Farrar's *Eric*. However, its incidents are mainly trivial (squabbles and jealousies, a forbidden copy of *Jane Eyre*, a smudged exercise book, a stolen essay, a midnight feast, and, worst of all, a cleverly drawn caricature of the saintly headmistress); there is an abundance of angels, but no threats of hell-fire and damnation; and the emphasis in both the school and the universe is on forgiveness rather than punishment. The school's name, Lavender House, sets the tone for the novel, whose pages are suffused by a heavy and old-fashioned scent.

Meade (1844-1914) was the Enid Blyton of her day. Her output was prodigious: she wrote more than 300 books, both for children and adults, as well as numerous short stories. She produced what publishers asked for and what would sell, and, like Blyton, she was adept at promoting herself and her work. She was sympathetic to the feminist movement and argued especially for girls' access to education. *A World of Girls* is the first of a large number of stories that she set in small, privately owned girls' schools of about fifty pupils. Ironically, considering her feminist views, there is little focus on what goes on in lessons (at Lavender House the girls work in different groups in the same large schoolroom) and there is an assumption that girls' education is about moulding their character and instilling good manners as they prepare for a life of housekeeping.

Hester Thornton begins as the novel's main character. Her mother has been killed in a carriage accident and her overbearing father, Sir John Thornton, finding her unmanageable, is sending her away to school. In the opening chapter, she is saying a tearful goodbye to her infant sister Nan (who will stay at home with Nurse); Nan's irritating baby-speak never rings true and is one of the main weaknesses of the novel (' "Me want more bicky, Hetty" . . . "Me'll skeeze 'oo vedy tight for more" ').[1] On a tearful train journey, Hester believes she is being carried 'from a free life into a prison' and is determined not to like Lavender House. Like so many unwilling girls who will follow in her footsteps, she decides not to be 'reduced to an every-day and pattern little girl . . . and when her father saw that school could do nothing for her . . . he would allow her to remain at home'.[2]

It is dark when Hester arrives, and not even the cheerful hall and blazing fire can raise her spirits. She is greeted warmly by Miss Danesbury, but Annie Forest, with all the appearance of a gypsy girl, lurks in the shadows and picks up on Hester's demeanour: 'Rather tall for her age, but I fear, I greatly fear, a little sulky'. Hester, who is unused to criticism, takes a dislike to Annie and is determined never to forgive her. 'What a horrid, vulgar, low-bred girl', she says, betraying the pride that will be her downfall.[3] Thus Hester, almost without meaning it, disrupts the school's happiness; to make it worse for her, Annie is a favourite of the other girls and enjoys a special bond with Mrs Willis, the headmistress, who has promised the dying Mrs Forest that she will take care of Annie until her father returns. The absent father and the melodramatic reunion are a recurring feature in children's literature from Victorian times to the middle of the twentieth century, owing much to the demands of Empire and two World Wars.

1. L.T. Meade, *A World of Girls* (London, 1886), chapter 1.
2. *A World of Girls*, chapter 2.
3. *A World of Girls*, chapter 3.

Miss Danesbury takes Hester through the baize door from the hall into the school part of the house, and 'warmth, luxuriance and even elegance' give way to 'long, narrow corridors, with snow-white but carpetless floors, and rather cold, distempered walls'.[4] It is an image of the move to a 'world apart' and to the 'prison' that Hester has dreaded. Lavender House, says Mrs Willis, on their first meeting, is 'a miniature world around you; you will be surrounded by temptations; and you will have rare chances of proving whether your character can be strong and great and true'.[5]

In fact, Lavender House turns out to be far more liberal than most Victorian girls' boarding schools. There are no petty rules; the girls are trusted; they are allowed to talk in their bedrooms; they are not watched during play-hours; their mail is not censored. In spring, the school grounds are an unlikely pastoral idyll:

> Sounds of laughter and merriment filled the air; the garden was
> all alive with gay young figures running here and there. Girls
> stood in groups under the horse-chestnut tree – girls walked two
> and two up the shady walk at the end of the garden – little ones
> gambolled and rolled on the grass.[6]

For half an hour each evening, the girls are able to speak to Mrs Willis alone, when she adopts the role of mother and not headmistress, and she spends the whole of each Sunday with them: 'In short, she was like the personified form of Goodness in their midst.'[7] On Sunday evenings, she gathers the older girls together and tells them stories or sings to them, and at bedtime she 'gave a mother-kiss to each of her pupils' (there is a lot of kissing at Lavender House).[8]

Hester settles gradually into school life, doing well at her lessons in spite of her bad intentions, but failing to learn the power of give and take and so failing to make friends. Her argument with Annie becomes more bitter. She is 'taken up' by one of the older girls, Dora Russell, who encourages her in the opinion that Annie is 'under-bred'. But Dora, warns the intrusive narrator, 'possessed in a strong degree that baneful quality, which more than anything else precludes love for others – she was essentially selfish'.[9] Dora is the 'soul of neatness and order',[10] whereas Annie has always been

4. *A World of Girls*, chapter 3.
5. *A World of Girls*, chapter 5.
6. *A World of Girls*, chapter 18.
7. *A World of Girls*, chapter 9.
8. *A World of Girls*, chapter 9.
9. *A World of Girls*, chapter 10.
10. *A World of Girls*, chapter 10.

'the soul of disorder'.[11] Susan Drummond, who shares a room with Hester, also enters the action. She is lazy, greedy and unkempt. As more and more unpleasant tricks are played, and the atmosphere at Lavender House is infected with mistrust, it seems Annie must be the culprit and is 'sent to Coventry'. Hester, her main accuser, finds herself suddenly popular and feels 'particularly virtuous'. However, there are enough clues to suggest that Annie is innocent and the real trouble-maker is Susan Drummond. This dramatic irony has the effect of turning the reader against Hester and directing sympathy towards Annie, who becomes the main focus of the novel. The narrator cannot help commenting in biblical metaphor: 'Poor foolish, thoughtless Hester, she little guessed what seed she had sown, and what a harvest she was preparing for her own reaping by-and-by.'[12]

At the end of the Easter holiday, Hester learns that her father is going abroad and that Nan, although only three-years-old, is to join her at Lavender House. For a while, Nan brings out the best in Hester: 'the hardness, the pride, the haughty spirit were all laid aside'.[13] But Annie is tempted to gain revenge for Hester's cruelty by stealing Nan's heart for herself. On a picnic outing, Nan chooses to go with Annie rather than her sister, and while they are playing she falls from Annie's shoulders and is concussed. That evening, at Nan's bedside, Hester kneels down for her private prayers, but, like Farrar's Eric, 'she found it impossible to pray'; she is overcome with hatred for Annie and her petition to God to make Nan better seems 'to fall flat on the empty air'.[14] When Nan's condition worsens, only Annie is able to nurse her through the crisis – and Hester loathes her for it.

Soon afterwards, with Mrs Willis away, Annie leads a group of her friends to the Fairies' Field for a midnight feast. It is one of the more cloying episodes in the novel, with the moonlit scene as sugary as the meringues and cheesecakes; but beneath the idle chatter, there is a sense of unease. On their way back, the girls are confronted by a gypsy-mother, Rachel, demanding sixpence from each of them for telling their fortunes if she is not to reveal their truanting.

On their return to school, Dora's entry for the essay competition is sabotaged and Annie is suspected. Hester discovers that the real culprit is Susan, but is tempted to say nothing. As in *Eric*, her internal conflict is dramatised as a cosmic struggle: 'Good angels and bad drew near to fight for a victory'; 'her colour came and went as the angels, good and bad, fought

---

11. *A World of Girls*, chapter 11.
12. *A World of Girls*, chapter 14.
13. *A World of Girls*, chapter 22.
14. *A World of Girls*, chapter 24.

hard for victory within her'; and 'Then the good angels went sorrowfully back to their Father in heaven, and the wicked angels rejoiced.'[15] The matter of the midnight feast is discovered and Annie admits to arranging it; however, impulsively and against all logic, Mrs Willis takes this to mean that Annie has also sabotaged Dora's essay. Although Hester knows she should speak out and absolve Annie, she is too proud to lose face by doing so and 'before that day was over she was to experience that awful emptiness and desolation which those know whom God is punishing'.[16]

Hester's punishment from a vengeful God is the stealing of Nan by Rachel, the gypsy-mother, and the remainder of the novel is the story of Annie's rescuing of Nan from the gypsy encampment. Aided by her looks, she disguises herself as a gypsy girl and, having worked her soothing magic on Tiger, the gypsies' dog, she wanders among the tents and discovers the underground passage where Nan is hidden. With Tiger's help, they manage to escape, but Annie's efforts have taken their toll – she is found collapsed in a nearby field and succumbs to a scarcely credible fever.

When news arrives of Nan's safety, Hester confesses everything and forces Susan Drummond to do the same. As Annie hovers melodramatically between life and death, Mrs Willis is at last able to forgive her. Then a handsome, foreign-looking man arrives at Lavender House: it is Captain Forest, who has escaped from a shipwreck and has at last returned to be reunited with his daughter. Nan lies beside Annie, and it is Nan's presence that begins her recovery, just as Annie has assuaged Nan's own fever after her fall. So Annie does not die; Susan Drummond is expelled and no more is heard of her; Annie wins the Essay Competition with her entry 'A Lonely Child', which is 'crude and unfinished', but has 'the merit of real originality' – her appallingly predictable prize is a locket containing 'a miniature of the head-mistress's much-loved face'. Thus, with a nod to romanticism, it is Annie, the gypsy girl with the big heart and 'the soul of disorder', who turns out to be the real heroine.[17] Hester becomes her greatest friend, but otherwise is no longer of consequence. It is enough that her character has been reformed and she has become the 'every-day and pattern little girl' that she was determined not to be.[18]

In its day, *A World of Girls* was hugely popular, chiefly because 'wild' Annie is able to transcend the pettiness of her surroundings, is true to herself, and is brave in her rescue of Nan. However, more than a century on,

15. *A World of Girls*, chapter 31.
16. *A World of Girls*, chapter 39.
17. *A World of Girls*, chapter 11.
18. *A World of Girls*, chapter 2.

it is hard to take the novel seriously. Lavender House and its headmistress are too sentimentally sweet, its plot and characters are too predictable, and its evangelism is overwhelming. But the real disappointment is that Meade, who believed strongly in the need for girls' education, should so trivialise it in her writing. Although others would develop the girls' school story from her whimsical foundations, it was a betrayal from which it would never properly escape.

Angela Brazil – *The Fortunes of Philippa* (1906)

Angela Brazil wrote forty-nine girls' school novels and seventy short stories that were happy and optimistic, concerned friendship and adventure, and gave an entry for girls of every background into a world of privilege that was often entirely removed from their own experience. The first of these, *The Fortunes of Philippa* (1906), is a novel of its colonial time. Philippa Seaton is the only daughter of a doting widower, who is the British Consul and owner of coffee plantations in San Carlos, South America. At the age of ten, Philippa suffers the heart-wrenching fate that awaited such children, making the long sea voyage 'far away over the sea to strangers and to an unknown land' to be educated in England.[19] After spending two years in London with her Uncle Herbert and Aunt Agatha, where she is taught by a governess, the time comes for Philippa to be sent to The Hollies, a privately-owned boarding school of some forty pupils in Derbyshire. Its aim, reports Philippa, sounding like a school prospectus, is 'to combine the very best points of a thoroughly modern course of study with the rigid rules and exemplary behaviour of a past generation'.[20] So Mathematics, Science (in 'a well-fitted laboratory'), Languages, Literature,[21] History and Geography, are part of the curriculum, but so are 'the most exquisite darning and the finest of open hem-stitch', 'balancing books upon our heads', flower arranging, and learning to receive visitors graciously.[22]

On Saturday evenings in winter, Mrs Marshall hosts an 'At Home', 'to form our manners and to fit us for good society',[23] and at the end of term, to put the girls' learning into practice, they act as hostesses to local dignitaries. Judge Saunders does not quite enter into the spirit of the occasion, offering Cathy patronising but sensible advice: 'Just forget all your conversation

19. Angela Brazil, *The Fortunes of Philippa* (London, 1906), chapter 1.
20. *The Fortunes of Philippa*, chapter 4.
21. At the age of twelve, Philippa has knowledge of Spencer, Dryden, Pope and the Cavalier Poets, and is attempting to write in their style, suggesting that she already has a sounder grounding than many of today's English Literature undergraduates.
22. *The Fortunes of Philippa*, chapter 4.
23. *The Fortunes of Philippa*, chapter 4.

lessons, and be your natural little self; it's ever so much nicer.'[24] It is often argued that Brazil writes without irony, but I am not sure that this is the case. In *The Fortunes of Philippa*, there is always a flickering authorial humour.

Philippa tells little else of her first year at The Hollies, except that she finds an enemy in spiteful Ernestine Salt and the closest of friends in Catherine Winstanley. She and Catherine become inseparable and the Winstanleys become her surrogate family. Philippa spends many of her holidays at Marshlands, the Winstanley's home, and four of the novel's twelve chapters describe the adventures she and Catherine have with Catherine's brothers.

In her second year at The Hollies, Philippa, now aged thirteen, moves up to the fourth form, where she is taught by the severe Miss Percy. Her best efforts are dismissed and her smallest defects are punished. Says Philippa, no doubt speaking for the author: 'I believe, if people would only realise it, that overwork and ill-health are often responsible for many tiresome habits in growing girls.'[25] The climax of the novel occurs when, having been belittled by Miss Percy for an untidy bedroom, and further punished after she is tripped over in class by Ernestine, she collapses. The doctor diagnoses a case of 'nervous breakdown due to overwork' and the following term the girls notice that the hours of work have been 'considerably relaxed' and that Miss Percy has left. 'I think,' says Philippa [as a mouthpiece for Brazil], 'we really got through as much work as we had done before, if not in the actual number of pages learnt, at any rate in the amount remembered afterwards.'[26]

So the novel ends happily. Miss Percy's replacement, unsubtly called Miss Hope, brings out the best in everyone; on a picnic expedition, Philippa rescues Ernestine from a charging bull, and Ernestine becomes a reformed character; and, in a sentimental ending (which reminds of Captain Forest's entrance in *A World of Girls*), Mr Seaton, presumed drowned in a shipwreck, appears at The Hollies for an emotional reunion with his daughter. He has resigned his consulate, sold his plantations, and now buys and restores a deserted house close to Marshlands. Philippa leaves The Hollies and settles down 'to master the mysteries of housekeeping, and to supply to my father that dear place which my mother left empty long ago'. She adds with probably unintentional irony, 'We do not want to fritter away our lives in that aimless fashion which girls sometimes do when school-days are over'.[27] If the growth of girls' education was in part about equality for women, this is hardly a ringing endorsement.

---

24. *The Fortunes of Philippa*, chapter 8.
25. *The Fortunes of Philippa*, chapter 9.
26. *The Fortunes of Philippa*, chapter 9.
27. *The Fortunes of Philippa*, chapter 12.

For all its success, *The Fortunes of Philippa* has its faults. The structure is episodic. There are only two chapters about life at The Hollies before we are swept away to the chapters at Marshlands that are asides to the main plot. Back at school, the action is confined to a few self-contained episodes: the end-of-term 'At Home', the school play, the poetry competition, the cruelty of Miss Percy and the picnic. The use of a first-person narrator is uncomfortable, with Philippa offering hardly-disguised authorial comment as well as telling her own story. But the gentle humour, the often shrewd characterisation, the feel-good accounts of friendship and the overcoming of bullies (both Ernestine and Miss Percy), and Philippa's final reunion with her father, were enough to point the girls' school story in a new and brighter direction.

Angela Brazil – *A Patriotic Schoolgirl* (1918)

After *The Fortunes of Philippa*, Brazil's school stories take place at a variety of different schools. Thus they differ from the serial novels written by many of the authors who followed her and avoid the danger of following the career of a single heroine who is growing up while satisfying a readership that will, on the whole, stay the same age. *A Patriotic Schoolgirl* (1918), an example of Brazil's later work, was written twelve years after *The Fortunes of Philippa* and is an altogether more assured novel. Brackenfield College, overlooking the sea in the West Country, is a different establishment from Lavender House and The Hollies, and is modelled more on the first of the girls' public schools. At Brackenfield, there are two hundred pupils, divided into three Houses, though in a novel steeped in observation there is surprisingly little physical description of the College itself. For Marjorie and Dona Anderson, both new girls, life seems to be 'a breathless confusing whirl of classes, meals, and callisthenic exercises, with a continuing ringing of bells'.[28] The atmosphere is formal, even repressive, and the good name of the College and its girls is the overriding priority of the headmistress. When the girls venture outside the College's grounds, they either walk in supervised 'crocodiles' or are chaperoned by one of the teachers, and they have to wear regulation 'exeat' uniform ('I feel I'm as much labelled "Brackenfield" as a Dartmoor prisoner is known by his black arrows!' says Marjorie).[29] Visitors are discouraged and even turned away. When a camp is built nearby for German prisoners of war, it seems to be a metaphor for Brackenfield itself. But when the head girl, Winifrede Mason, gives a long, rousing speech about Brackenfield – 'The

---

28. Angela Brazil, *A Patriotic Schoolgirl* (London: Blackie and Son, 1918), chapter 2.
29. *A Patriotic Schoolgirl*, chapter 4.

main thing that we're really striving for is the formation of character. There's nothing finer in the world' – Marjorie realises at last 'all that Brackenfield stood for'.[30]

It was one of Brazil's achievements to create heroines with weaknesses as well as strengths, with opinions of their own, and with a spirit of adventure, rebellion and fun. From the start, Marjorie, aged fifteen, is intelligent, sports-loving (though not always sporting), impulsive, argumentative, and an obvious leader of her peers, whether for good or bad. She despairs of Dona, her younger, less confident sister, who is starting at Brackenfield with her: 'Rouse up, you old bluebottle, can't you? . . . Dona, you're ostriching! For goodness' sake brace up child, and turn off the waterworks! . . . I'll not let you start in a new school nicknamed Niobe'.[31] The mix of cliché and schoolgirl slang is typical of the novel's dialogue.

Marjorie's headstrong nature soon lands her in trouble. She runs off from a 'crocodile' promenading beside the beach to acquire the autograph of a French flying 'ace' who has landed nearby. She organises a midnight birthday party for Irene ('I'm your man if there's any fun afoot,' says Betty; 'Jubilate! What a frolicsome joke!' says Irene).[32] She accidentally provokes a harmless snowball fight with a party of invalid war veterans. She is then on the brink of expulsion for writing a patriotic letter to a soldier in the trenches. For her, the soldier is 'a mere picturesque abstraction, a romantic figure, as remote as fiction'; she 'had a vague idea that the army consisted mostly of public-school boys'.[33] But to her consternation, and to the fury of the Headmistress, the soldier thinks he is being propositioned and suggests 'keeping company' with Marjorie on his return: 'Every pupil here is at least supposed to be a gentlewoman, and that a Brackenfielder could so demean herself as to enter into a correspondence with an unknown soldier fills me with disgust and contempt.'[34]

However, typically of the school story, much of the interest of *A Patriotic Schoolgirl* lies in the up-and-down relationships between the girls themselves. Marjorie gets on well enough with the other girls in her dormitory, though they remain minor players, as does her sister, Dona. But in her second term she develops a particular friendship with new arrival, Chrissie Lang. For some reason, Chrissie doesn't quite fit in: 'It

30. *A Patriotic Schoolgirl*, chapter 12.
31. *A Patriotic Schoolgirl*, chapter 1. In Greek mythology, Niobe died of grief after her twelve children were killed by Apollo and Artemis. Although turned to stone by Zeus, she continued to weep unceasingly.
32. *A Patriotic Schoolgirl*, chapter 7.
33. *A Patriotic Schoolgirl*, chapter 15.
34. *A Patriotic Schoolgirl*, chapter 15.

was really in the first instance because Betty and Sylvia were disagreeable to Chrissie that Marjorie took her up.'[35] Soon their relationship 'flamed at red heat' and the two of them are walking round the school arm in arm, writing 'sentimental little notes to each other'.[36] The general opinion of the form is that Marjorie has 'got it badly'[37] and the pair are known as the 'Turtle Doves'.[38] On a walk to harvest potatoes at Mr Briggs's farm, Marjorie is also befriended by Winifrede Mason and is flattered by her patronage. However, there is no hint of sexual frisson, and when in the end-of-term charades an on-stage kiss seems to be too intense, a discreet cough from the Empress is enough to cut it short. Unless adolescent girls have changed considerably over the last hundred years, the absence in early twentieth-century girls' fiction of any description of turbulent emotions must result more from what could be legitimately explored in public or even in private, and less from how girls (and teachers) actually felt and behaved.

As its title suggests, the action of *A Patriotic Schoolgirl* is played out against the background of war. On the school train, soldiers fill the corridor. At school, food is rationed and sacrifices are made. A number of girls have fathers and brothers serving in the forces (Marjorie's father is at Havre, one brother is at the front in France, another is at sea in *H.M.S. Relentless*, and a third has just left school at Haileybury and is in training), and there is a roll of honour of those relations of past and present girls killed or wounded in action. Marjorie has pictures of Lord Kitchener, Sir Douglas Haig, the Prince of Wales and His Majesty the King beside her bed. The prison camp is built. Marjorie's cousin, whom she and Dona are allowed to visit every fortnight, is a V.A.D. nurse at the hospital, caring for the wounded, but when the girls are allowed to visit they fail to register the suffering that lies behind the soldiers' grim humour and find it all rather exciting.[39] Spoiled Irene can only complain that her riding lessons have been interrupted ('If I don't learn to ride properly while I'm young I'll never have a decent seat afterwards').[40] Marjorie, by contrast, fights against the female stereotype and is impatient to leave school and join in the action – 'I'll nurse, or drive a wagon, or ride a motor-bike with dispatches.'[41]

---

35. *A Patriotic Schoolgirl*, chapter 13.
36. *A Patriotic Schoolgirl*, chapter 14.
37. *A Patriotic Schoolgirl*, chapter 14.
38. *A Patriotic Schoolgirl*, chapter 17.
39. V.A.D. is an abbreviation of Voluntary Aid Detachment.
40. *A Patriotic Schoolgirl*, chapter 7.
41. *A Patriotic Schoolgirl*, chapter 7.

Brazil's novels are often criticised for the looseness of their plots (*The Fortunes of Philippa* is an example), but *A Patriotic Schoolgirl* is carefully constructed. The account in the early chapters of Marjorie's first two terms lulls the reader into a false and easy sense of security. There is no sense that Marjorie's and Dona's friendship with the sickly Eric is more than a sentimental aside, no sense of the identity of the bizarrely named Titania, no sense that Chrissie Lang is taking advantage of Marjorie's good nature, and no sense that the prisoners of war will have a significant part to play in the story. But with Marjorie's illicit visit to the 'Conservatory', a look-out tower on the College roof,[42] the tension at last begins to mount. What is Miss Norton doing there, and what is the meaning of the bicycle lamp that appears mysteriously? 'What secrets were hidden under that calm exterior?'[43] What is she doing sidling into The Royal George (the sort of place no respectable middle-class spinster would frequent) and consorting with 'foreigners' in a local hotel? Why is she so shocked by Marjorie's photograph of Eric and the German prisoners? Worried that Miss Norton may be a German spy, Marjorie takes Chrissie into her confidence and she 'seemed to have taken up the matter with the greatest keenness'.[44] The two set out to gather evidence, but it is easy to miss the ambiguity of 'seemed'. And why is Chrissie beside herself with anger when Marjorie is prevented by the more perceptive Dona from borrowing Leonard's uniform for the end-of-term charade? By chance, Marjorie and Dona discover that Eric lives at The Royal George and Miss Norton is in fact Titania, his well-meaning Aunt. When Chrissie suddenly disappears, the clues fall into place, and it is she, not Miss Norton, who is the German spy.

Apart from two long 'set-piece' speeches by Winifrede Mason, there is little authorial intervention in *A Patriotic Schoolgirl*, but there is, I think, an ironic awareness that implies criticism of the narrow-minded viewpoint of the headmistress and the dull complacency of some of the girls, as well as a championing of Marjorie, whatever her faults. Today, however, it is hard to empathise with Brazil's emotionally naïve pupils, and the attitudes towards the colonial world and the Great War jar (although they were very much of their time for all but the liberal elite). But Brazil was one of the first writers to see things from a child's perspective, and, though not politically a feminist, she was one of the first to allow girls to push boundaries, to take the initiative, to do things that boys do, and to enjoy themselves. It was an appealing mix.

---

42. *A Patriotic Schoolgirl*, chapter 17.
43. *A Patriotic Schoolgirl*, chapter 17.
44. *A Patriotic Schoolgirl*, chapter 22.

Chapter 10

The Anti-Soppist Story

Dorita Fairlie Bruce – *Dimsie Moves Up* (1921)
Josephine Elder – *Evelyn Finds Herself* (1929)

Without meaning it, Angela Brazil launched a wave of schoolgirl fiction that swamped the 1920s and rippled on until at least the Second World War. Literally hundreds of authors produced literally thousands of books, most of which are now forgotten. Just a few examples are Christine Chaundler's *The Fourth Form Detectives* (1920); Dorothea Moore's *The Only Day Girl* (1923); Evelyn Smith's *Marie Macleod, Schoolgirl* (1925); Winifed Darch's *The New School and Hilary* (1926); Joy Francis's *Biddy at Greystones* (1928); Josephine Elder's *Evelyn Finds Herself* (1929); A.E. Seymour's *A Schoolgirl's Secret* (1930); and, most prolifically those by Elsie Oxenham, Dorita Fairlie Bruce and Elinor Brent-Dyer. Here I want to focus on just two. The first is Dorita Fairlie Bruce's *Dimsie Moves Up* (1921), which is typical of the period, revels in the usual trivia of school life (especially sport), but is aware of its own inconsequence and sentimentality. The second is Josephine Elder's *Evelyn Finds Herself* (1929), which, more unusually, is set in a south London day public school, avoids the conventional clutter of escapades, lies and deceit, and is about the nature of friendship and Evelyn's growth as an individual.

Dorita Fairlie Bruce – *Dimsie Moves Up* (1921)

Dorothy Fairlie Bruce was born in Spain in 1885 (hence her pen name, Dorita), but most of her early childhood was spent in Scotland. In 1895, the family moved to London and Dorita was sent to a boarding school, Clarence House, in Roehampton. Clarence House was the model for The Jane Willard Foundation, where Dimsie becomes a pupil, though in the novels it was moved to the Kent coast, which had more possibilities for adventure. Bruce's early short stories include three that are set at The Jane Willard Foundation, and the first Dimsie novel, *The Senior Prefect* (later retitled *Dimsie Goes to School*), appeared in 1921. There were to be nine Dimsie novels and thirteen short stories in all; the final novel, *Dimsie Carries On* (1941), takes place in wartime and finds Dimsie married with two children. Bruce wrote two further substantial school series, both set in the Hebrides – at St Bride's School (1923-44) and at Springdale (1928-39).

Dimsie Moves Up is the second novel in the Dimsie series. Eleven-year-old Daphne Isabel Maitland, hence Dimsie, together with all her friends except Rosamund (whose laziness has caused her to fall behind), have moved up into the Third Division; but their new colleagues, Betty and Joan, warn them against befriending their form teacher, Miss Moffat: 'We're awfully gone on her, Joan and I, and of course we shall have first claim to walk with her or sit next to her, or anything of that sort, having been longer in her form.'[1] Other girls are 'gone on different seniors'; Sylvia Drummond, the head girl, thinks they are 'like lovelorn idiots' and Mabs's mother says that such soppy behaviour is 'a sort of complaint girls get, like measles'.[2] Somehow it all seems more innocent than the close relationships described in contemporary boys' school stories (Alec Waugh's *The Loom of Youth*, for example), but Dimsie and friends are having none of it. Led by Erica, they set themselves up in a secret society 'to protest against – against a lot of silly rot'.[3] They meet in the tool shed and call themselves the 'Anti-Soppist Society'; later, since A.S.S. is an unfortunate acronym, it will be renamed 'The Anti-Soppist League'. The initial rules are:

1. No-one belonging to the Anti-Soppists is on any account to give flowers to the teachers or seniors.
2. No member . . . must sleep with any senior's old hair ribbon under her pillow.
3. Every member must solemnly promise not to kiss any one at all during the term.[4]

1. Dorita Fairlie Bruce, *Dimsie Moves Up* (Oxford: Oxford University Press, 1921), chapter 2.
2. *Dimsie Moves Up*, chapter 2.
3. *Dimsie Moves Up*, chapter 4.
4. *Dimsie Moves Up*, chapter 4.

Thus the Anti-Soppists foreground the usually cloying behaviour of
schoolgirls in the stories written about them. Ironically, however, the main
elements of *Dimsie Moves Up* remain the petty jealousies of school life and
the tensions created by the stealing of close friends.

The villain is Nita Tomlinson, the games captain. She has already
'stolen' Meg from Primrose (who mopes appropriately) and later 'takes
up' Rosamund, Primrose's younger sister, who is nearly expelled from the
Anti-Soppists. Taking a cue from the boys' school stories, games play a
disproportionate part: Nita and Meg as the School's tennis champions;
Nita trying to stop the younger girls playing cricket and nearly sabotaging
their match against the Middle School girls; Nita and Meg entering a
competition at the local tennis club, despite its having been banned by
Miss Yorke, the headmistress, for being an unpleasant place ('They were
bad style all through, tennis and everything,' says Meg after the event);[5] the
loss of the cricket match against Westover High School (which takes up an
entire chapter); the Lower School Match against the Middle School (which
takes up another chapter); the excitement of the water sports. In fact, Nita
is not 'soppy' at all: she enjoys controlling and using people, and the girls
she befriends are discarded when they no longer comply.

Set against Nita is Sylvia, the head girl, whose stylish entry is like something
from an Edwardian romance: 'Sylvia Drummond, cool and dainty in her blue
cotton frock, came slowly down the steps from the open French windows of
the senior schoolroom, and paused on the gravelled terrace to look about
her.'[6] Sylvia is tougher than the portrait suggests and takes the side of the
younger girls in their argument with Nita: 'in the summer term you want
something more sporting [than making up a fairy play], or you'll become soft
and soppy'.[7] She arranges a daily cricket practice and salvages their cricket
match that Nita, out of spite, has tried to squeeze out of the fixtures calendar.

Amidst all this there are the exploits of the irrepressible Dimsie, soft-
hearted, quick-tempered, industrious, resourceful, and courageous. It is she
who dares, unsuccessfully, to put Rosamund's case for promotion to the
Third Division to Miss Yorke (' "I like that child's spirit," she observed, "and
her delightful straightforwardness" ');[8] she who comes to the rescue when
Sylvia sprains her ankle in the thunderstorm; she who makes Nita reinstate
Rosamund in the cricket team; she who, with Pam, goes exploring in the
maze of underground passages; she who is the Lower School champion at the
water sports, saving Erica from drowning before being saved herself by Nita.

---

5. *Dimsie Moves Up*, chapter 19.
6. *Dimsie Moves Up*, chapter 3.
7. *Dimsie Moves Up*, chapter 3.
8. *Dimsie Moves Up*, chapter 2.

After all the turbulent relationships, and as we might expect, everything is sorted out in the final chapter. Benefiting from Dimsie's help with her lessons, Rosamund gains her promotion and will join her friends in the Third Division; Primrose and Meg are close again, and Meg replaces the disgraced Nita as games captain; Nita, who is moving to a school in France at the end of term, visits Dimsie in the sick room and there is a sort of reconciliation ('since I had to save somebody, Dimsie Maitland, I'd rather it was you'); and, as if to prove there is still work for the Anti-Soppists to do, 'she gave her an abrupt kiss before leaving the room'.[9]

Like all the Dimsie books, *Dimsie Moves Up* is pleasant enough, but never surprises and never challenges the reader. It is not quite as twee or melodramatic as most other girls' school stories of the period, and even if it does not quite avoid the soppiness against which the Anti-Soppists warn, it is aware of the irony. Nothing much happens away from the games field except the underground adventure (complete with the secret door in the wardrobe) that diverges from the main plot to enliven the proceedings. At the water sports, the near drownings are no more than a minor inconvenience; no-one dies; and the worst injury and illness are a sprained ankle and a bout of influenza. But Dimsie herself is a feisty heroine in the Tom Brown mould, who will in later novels climb the school ladder with her unquenchable spirit; Nita, in her own words, is 'a pretty average villain';[10] and Miss Yorke, 'a slim, brown-eyed woman with unruly dark hair and a wonderfully kind smile', is a more approachable and sensible headmistress than most of her fictional predecessors.[11] The idea of the girls' school as a 'world apart' is beginning to slip away: 'That old-fashioned boarding-school idea of shutting us up like nuns in a convent is absurd nowadays' (though this is Nita's view and is not much shared by Miss Yorke).[12] God, who has been mainly removed from sight in the real world, is only allowed a single embarrassed appearance when, at the end of the underground passage and overlooking the sea, Dimsie makes a suggestion:

> 'I don't know what you think about it, Pam, but it seems to me it might help things on a little if we prayed for a boat or something of that sort.'
> 'Do you mean out loud?' asked Pam shyly.
> 'Not unless you'd rather. I didn't mean a proper prayer meeting you know, but just quietly in to ourselves.'[13]

9. *Dimsie Moves Up*, chapter 28.
10. *Dimsie Moves Up*, chapter 19.
11. *Dimsie Moves Up*, chapter 1.
12. *Dimsie Moves Up*, chapter 14.
13. *Dimsie Moves Up*, chapter 21.

Even here, there is no sense of impending disaster. In this laid-back, feel-good novel, as Dimsie and Pam wait for a passing ship the seabirds are going idly about their business and far below the waves are enjoying themselves in 'noisy play'.[14]

Josephine Elder – *Evelyn Finds Herself*

Whereas *Dimsie Moves Up* is a story about Anti-Soppists, Josephine Elder's *Evelyn Finds Herself* is itself an Anti-Soppist story. Although it is about the strains of a schoolgirl friendship, and the changes it undergoes, there is little of the soppiness of other girls' school stories. It charts the fractious relationship between Evelyn Ingram and Elizabeth Wainwright, who have been friends since they arrived in the First Form, and Evelyn's search for her own identity. It escapes from the intense and claustrophobic atmosphere of boarding, and its serious intent, the depth of its characterisation, and the accomplishment of its writing make it stand out from other novels of the period. Indeed, in spite of the off-putting sanctimony of its title, *Evelyn Finds Herself* is arguably one of the best school stories for either boys or girls written in the twentieth century.

Josephine Elder was the pen-name of Olive Potter (1895-1988). A doctor by profession, she practised as a general practitioner for sixty years, but (since until comparatively recently patients were wary of being treated by a woman) she found time to write ten school stories and six adult novels as well. Born and brought up in Croydon, Olive Potter attended Croydon High School, one of the Girls Public Day School Trust foundations, probably from the age of seven; on her first day there she met Janet Townshend, who became her close friend. So in this partly autobiographical novel, Croydon High School is the model for Addington High School, and the young Olive and Janet are the inspiration behind Evelyn and Elizabeth.[15]

When the novel begins, it is the start of the autumn term at Addington High. It is a very different place from the Jane Willard Foundation; there are about 400 pupils on the roll, and although hockey plays a prominent part, there is also a considerable emphasis on Evelyn's growing absorption in academic life. Evelyn and Elizabeth, who until now have been inseparable, have moved up into the upper fifth. To look at they are very different. Evelyn is 'slim and springy, and her face, except for its sunburn and its

14. *Dimsie Moves Up*, chapter 21.
15. See Introductory, Part III for comment on GPDST schools. The dedication to *Evelyn Finds Herself* reads: 'To THE GIRLS OF GPDST SCHOOLS this book is dedicated by one of them, in the hope that they may find it life-like, except for the author's licence which allows the matches for the Hockey Cup to take place in the autumn instead of the spring term.'

look of eager intelligence, would have passed unnoticed in a crowd of girls';
Elizabeth, on the other hand, is 'broad and thick-necked, and her square
features had a distinction which might have become beauty as she grew
older'.[16] Their characters are very different too, though as yet they have not
become conscious of it. How they become aware of the difference, and how
their friendship is challenged and nearly destroyed by that awareness, is the
mainspring of the plot.

In the upper fifth, Evelyn realises they are growing up and developing
their own personalities. As she mounts her bicycle, she notices in a new
moment of self-awareness that 'she has quite big legs', while Elizabeth's
are 'simply enormous': 'their owners were not kids any more'.[17] However,
growing up is not easy. Evelyn and Elizabeth have always been in the
hockey teams together, but when the notice for the first match of the
season is pinned up, Evelyn has been left out and her place has been taken
by Amabel, a favourite of Miss Reeve, the games mistress: 'To be in the
first together was their dearest ambition, and it simply had not occurred
to them that one might get in without the other.'[18] Fortunately for them,
another member of the team goes down with influenza; Evelyn plays in the
match and is able to prove her worth. Life goes on and for the rest of their
time in the upper fifth, Evelyn and Elizabeth are as inseparable as ever;
later, however, when Evelyn looks back, she recognises this episode as 'the
very first sign that she and Elizabeth were not one person but two'.[19]

In Part II, Evelyn and Elizabeth move into the Lower Sixth where their
form teacher is Miss Fenton, who is known by the girls as 'Jemima Jane'.
'To thine own self be true,' she tells them, adding crisply, 'If you've got a self
to be true to – most people have not – and have learnt to know what that
self can do, and have the strength to be true to it, you can get anything done
on this earth.'[20] Evelyn and Elizabeth choose to follow separate academic
paths, and although they decide it is fun to have different experiences, it
is perhaps here that Evelyn, without knowing it, begins to set out on the
journey to discover her own self. But the real catalyst is the arrival of pretty,
easy-going Madeleine Summers from soppy St Clare's. After only one term
Madeleine has moved into the upper sixth and is fishing for favour with
the younger girls. It seems that like Miss Reeve, and like Nita in *Dimsie
Moves Up*, she is using people to satisfy her own ego and her need to be

---

16. Josephine Elder, *Evelyn Finds Herself* (Oxford: Oxford University Press, 1929),
    chapter 1.
17. *Evelyn Finds Herself*, chapter 2.
18. *Evelyn Finds Herself*, chapter 2.
19. *Evelyn Finds Herself*, chapter 5.
20. *Evelyn Finds Herself*, chapter 6.

the centre of attention without actually caring for them at all. Elizabeth is particularly outraged: 'I hate people who fish – hate them, *hate* them! . . . To fish, so that you're popular and people think you must be decent just because of that, when you're not a bit really – I think that's absolutely low down and mean.'[21] But it is Elizabeth who soon succumbs to Madeleine's light-hearted worldliness and her friendship with Evelyn is threatened. When Evelyn refuses to stay for tea with Madeleine and Elizabeth pedals off in a rage, it is the first time they have been parted by an argument, and when Elizabeth begins to spend more time with Madeleine, 'it seemed to Evelyn as if the world had cracked about her into little bits'.[22] Evelyn asks Miss Fenton whether it is possible 'to get free of people and just work'. This is the sad route that Miss Fenton has taken and she replies, 'It's very difficult. And I'm not sure that it isn't a coward's way out of the hurts of life.'[23] Although for that year the three girls go around together both in and out of school, Evelyn has become an outsider and, like Miss Fenton, begins to bury herself in her studies. She sees that she has spent her life being true to Elizabeth; now she must find her own self and be true to that.

In the upper sixth, Evelyn and Elizabeth drift further apart. Evelyn supports and befriends Rachel, who has been made Head Girl instead of the more popular and assertive Madeleine. She is also enthused and entranced by the new Botany mistress, Miss Yeo, nicknamed the 'Gypsy' because of her appearance: 'a tawny head, wide and shaggy like a lion's . . . . a rosy, sunburnt face . . . . a handwoven jumper of bright blue'.[24] At last there is a teacher who encourages, challenges and empathises with her. Madeleine makes the mistake of accusing Evelyn of having a schoolgirl crush on the Gypsy while Elizabeth grins in the background, but although the argument is patched up, the rift between Evelyn and Elizabeth grows wider. Evelyn is interested in her work, the books the Gypsy gives her to read, and school matters; Elizabeth, on the other hand, is captivated by dancing and clothes, and sneers when Evelyn talks about school. They misunderstand the smallest thing they say to each other. To Evelyn's disgust, Elizabeth copies Madeleine in powdering her face – not just a physical affectation, but a metaphor for the disguising of her self. She remembers Jennifer's warning that they must each follow their own star, but, as the narrator comments, 'She was only dreadfully sorry that their stars should have divided them so suddenly and so completely.'[25]

---

21. *Evelyn Finds Herself*, chapter 6.
22. *Evelyn Finds Herself*, chapter 8.
23. *Evelyn Finds Herself*, chapter 8.
24. *Evelyn Finds Herself*, chapter 10. The Gypsy reminds of Olive Potter's own inspirational teacher at Croydon High, Miss Ashford.
25. *Evelyn Finds Herself*, chapter 13.

In their final year at Addington High, after Rachel and Madeleine have left, Evelyn is made head prefect and Elizabeth becomes games captain. It is an opportunity for reconciliation, but Amabel does her spiteful best to undermine Evelyn; and when Amabel leaves under a cloud, Elizabeth blames the whole business on Evelyn: 'It wouldn't have happened if you weren't such a rotten officious idiot. I suppose you can't help it. It's what you're like. I can't think why I ever thought I liked you!'[26] Worse for Elizabeth is that without Amabel in goal Addington High will have no chance of winning the Hockey cup. Evelyn is consumed with misery and self-doubt, but the Gypsy offers tactful and sensible advice: Evelyn should make every effort to rebuild her friendship with Elizabeth (who has been 'bewitched by the pretty one'), but, 'It must be on the basis of two people with separate individualities, not one person who happens to be divided into two parts.'[27] In fact, it is Elizabeth who comes forward with an apology; the team plays better without Amabel and the Hockey cup is won (as in boys' school stories, all the best things happen on the games field); and the once good friends are good friends again and 'silently joined little fingers and wished'.[28]

So the novel concludes with Evelyn (like Olive Potter) winning a scholarship to Girton and Elizabeth (like Janet Townshend) to Newnham, and they will stay friends, developing in their own way, but 'trusting each other. . . . And telling each other things. And being there if wanted.'[29] And Evelyn, having tried to follow Elizabeth, and failed; and tried to be like Miss Fenton and failed; and tried to lean on the Gypsy, who would not let her; at last, as the title of the novel predicts, 'finds herself'. As term ends, the two girls turn their gaze away from school to the world beyond, summer takes over from winter and new life is breathed into the friendship that had almost died: 'It was high summer now, with green instead of brown everywhere, and no acrid smell of dead leaves.'[30] They turn their bicycles 'in opposite directions' and go 'their different ways'; but, 'I'll come along tonight,' says Elizabeth.[31]

Evelyn Finds Herself is written for a slightly older age group than the other novels discussed in Part III. Unlike the novels by Meade, Brazil, Bruce and Blyton, its primary intention is not to provide readers with a school that

---

26. *Evelyn Finds Herself*, chapter 15.
27. *Evelyn Finds Herself*, chapter 15.
28. *Evelyn Finds Herself*, chapter 16.
29. *Evelyn Finds Herself*, chapter 17. Girton (founded in 1869) was the first residential college for women in Cambridge; it became coeducational in 1976. Newnham College, Cambridge, was founded in 1871 and remains a women's college. Students of both colleges had to wait until 1948 before they were admitted fully into the University of Cambridge.
30. *Evelyn Finds Herself*, chapter 17.
31. *Evelyn Finds Herself*, chapter 17.

they can attend in their imaginations and join in with the escapades of its
characters. Rather it offers a perceptive account of a schoolgirl growing
up, with all the joys and miseries, the extremes of confidence and self-
doubt, which are the lot of adolescents. In particular, it is the study of
the inevitably changing relationship between Evelyn and Elizabeth, when,
as people, they grow and diverge. It is a relief that it avoids or scorns the
soppiness that characterises so many girls' school stories (as head prefect,
Evelyn is grateful for the 'unsentimental' friendship of the younger pupils).[32]
'Squashes' are accepted as part of school life, but 'raves' and 'G.P.s' (grand
passions) are frowned on, while the closeness of teachers (of Miss Byng and
Miss Gillies, who will only accept employment as a pair, and of the Gypsy
and Miss Hewer) suggests no more than that great friendship makes one
independent of other people.

The novel also has much to say about teaching. When Evelyn and
Elizabeth arrive in the upper fifth, they see for the first time that teachers
are not just 'machines' who teach and punish, but real people with 'likes
and dislikes strong enough to need control' and who are capable of being
hurt.[33] As well as Miss Reeve and her need to be liked, there are uncertain
and unpredictable Miss Gillies, whom they are glad to escape; Miss
Byng, with her grim and twisted smile, who balances firmness and good
humour, brings Latin alive, and makes them realise they are growing up;
fiery Mademoiselle, just managing to keep up appearances, even if her
hair dye is growing out, critical and encouraging in equal measure; Miss
Fenton, 'so absent-minded and odd-looking',[34] who has withdrawn into
the profession after some personal hurt, who keeps her distance from her
pupils, but whose History lessons sparkle and who always succeeds in
turning the new sixth form girls into responsible young ladies; and Miss
Bennet ('Nothey', because of her lisp and long nose), who stands on a
dignity she does not possess and who discourages questions and creativity.
Above all, there is the Gypsy, who, in spite of her unconventional
appearance, is able to combine a sense of fun with a quiet authority. It is
she who, through her own example, is able to inspire in Evelyn a passion
for botany and a love of learning, and whose unspoken decision to step
back from Evelyn for a time forces her to discover her own strength and
her own self.

In 1936, the High Mistress of St Paul's Girls' School famously declared
in assembly that she would collect and burn Angela Brazil's books, and
all school stories were banned in a number of girls' schools. This is hardly

32. *Evelyn Finds Herself*, chapter 16.
33. *Evelyn Finds Herself*, chapter 4.
34. *Evelyn Finds Herself*, chapter 4.

surprising, since too often their soppiness does a disservice to the cause of girls' education and to the wider feminist movement (Brazil even managed to call two of her romantically attached girls Lesbia and Regina – at Kingfield High School, where 'Any time was kissing time').[35] But *Evelyn Finds Herself* rises above the other stories (even if the academically weak at Addington High are relegated to the Home Life Department). It is an inspiring novel about real people who live in the real world and it is a shame that it has been largely forgotten.

---

35. Angela Brazil, *Loyal to the School* (London: Blackie, 1921).

Chapter 11

The Sunny Story

Enid Blyton – *The Naughtiest Girl in the School* (1940), *The Twins at St Clare's* (1941) and *First Term at Malory Towers* (1946)

Enid Blyton's *The Naughtiest Girl in the School*, published by George Newnes in 1940, is the first of four novels in the *Naughtiest Girl* series (1940-45).[1] There were later to be two further school series: *The Twins at St Clare's* (1941-45) and, most popular of all, *Malory Towers* (1946-51). They are all in the moral tradition, with each series charting the journey of its young heroine(s) from a variety of character failings to ultimate redemption, and with each novel in the series describing a step along that journey. There is a predictable sameness about the three series, as there is about all Blyton's work, which is part of their attraction to the conservatism of young readers: the schools are 'worlds apart', deep in the countryside; the children are types – confident, timid, spoilt or lonely, untroubled by their adolescence; the 'nice' teachers and older pupils all have 'kind' or 'warm' eyes, and there is always an excitable French 'Mam'zelle' whose classes are out of control; and the headmistresses are understanding and wise, able to put things right in an instant.

Blyton is the best-selling children's writer of all time (to date more than 600 million copies of her more than 600 books have been sold worldwide) and inevitably had a huge influence on mid-twentieth-century culture. She is also one of the most controversial. Her prose is bare: places and people

---

1. A fourth novel, *Here's the Naughtiest Girl*, was originally serialised in *Sunny Stories*. It was then used in *Enid Blyton's Omnibus* (1952) and published separately in 1997.

are drawn with broad, clear brush strokes, without any challenge to the reader to look beneath the surface, and the few images are clichés. Her characters lack depth, and although they may be morally confused, the strong narrative voice always intrudes to direct the reader. In *Reading Series Fiction*, Victor Watson describes Blyton as 'the great Nanny-Narrator',[2] while Mary Cadogan and Patricia Craig write of a 'disembodied benevolence'.[3]

Originality does not enter into Blyton's work. Her adventure series – most famously the *Famous Five* and *Secret Seven* – are influenced by writers like Arthur Ransome and the subsequent 'camping and tramping' genre. Her school stories hark back to the novels of Angela Brazil and her successors. She wrote to a formula – not surprisingly for someone who would write a 60,000-word novel in a week – but there is nothing to support the suggestion that she employed ghost writers to sustain her prodigious output. She was simply a workaholic and almost mechanical in her approach.

Critics, teachers and librarians have, on the whole, either judged Blyton's work harshly or have ignored it. They complain of the over-simple language, and they worry about Blyton's racism (her golliwogs, for example), her classism (the characters are firmly middle class) and her sexism (in the *Famous Five*, Anne is 'a proper little housewife'), even though such attitudes were commonplace when the novels were written. But I was one of the myriad children who owe a lifetime of reading to her stories, even if their appeal was short-lived and other more substantial novels quickly took their place. Here was instant gratification with the minimum of effort: no time wasted on lengthy description, no invitations to the imagination, and no complexities of plot or character to slow the storytelling, which is usually achieved through stilted (and now dated) dialogue.[4] Although Blyton's novels remain popular with children in the twenty-first century, they must now be seen as at least partly historical in both content and language – something that children (who are used to moving in and out of fantasy) seem to accept willingly, if only subconsciously. Attempts to modernise them have proved predictably unwelcome, not least to adult readers for whom nostalgia is a driving force.[5]

---

2. Victor Watson, *Reading Series Fiction* (London: Routledge Falmer, 2000), chapter 5.
3. Mary Cadogan and Patricia Craig, *You're a Brick, Angela!* (London: Gollancz, 1976), p. 337.
4. In defence of Blyton's narrative skill in the *Famous Five* novels, Peter Cash discusses her use in dialogue of verbs, adverbs and adverbial phrases (as well as exclamation marks!), suggesting that the adventures are an 'auditory experience' and that each of them 'unfolds to a sound-track on which the author is continually adjusting the volume-control'. Peter Cash, 'Enid Blyton: The Famous Five Books' (English Association Primary Bookmarks 5, 2013).
5. In 2010, Hodder published a revised edition of the *Famous Five* novels that

The Naughtiest Girl in the School (1940)

Both the *Naughtiest Girl* and the *St Clare's* series were written during World War II, and although Blyton's regular column in *Teachers' World* talked to children about the War's hardships, in her fictional world it simply does not exist. As with many other children's writers of the time, her novels provided a refuge for children from their disrupted wartime lives.

The central character of *The Naughtiest Girl in the School* is eleven-year-old Elizabeth Allen, an impossible only child who is packed off to Whyteleafe School in the hope that she will mend her ways (there is a parallel with Hester in Meade's *A World of Girls*). The indulgent parents cannot escape Blyton's implied censure of the way they have brought up her daughter: ' "You'll have to go to school, Elizabeth," said Mrs Allen. . . . "You are spoilt and naughty. . . . We have given you too many lovely things, and allowed you too much freedom." '[6] The governess, Miss Scott, joins in, just in case we have somehow missed the point: Elizabeth needs the company of 'obedient, well-mannered, hard-working children' and 'It isn't enough to have a pretty face and a merry smile – you must have a good heart too'.[7] Elizabeth, realising her selfish existence is under threat, is determined to be sent back home, so she sets out to behave as badly as possible. Blyton is having none of this and soon Elizabeth begins to learn from her mistakes and to understand that kindness will be reciprocated and hard work brings achievement. By the end of term, to the astonishment of her parents, the better side of her nature is showing through, she is accepted by her peers and she can hardly wait to return to Whyteleafe after Christmas.

Whyteleafe is an 'old country house' and 'its deep red walls, green with creeper, glowed in the April sun', but after this promising introduction the description becomes anodyne and there is little further sense of the school's physical presence. The dining room is 'a great high room'; the classrooms are 'big, sunny rooms'; in the girls' bedroom 'The sun poured in and made the room look very pleasant indeed' and 'The chests of drawers looked very pretty'.[8] 'Old', 'high', 'big', 'pleasant' and 'pretty' are typical of the range of Blyton's vocabulary. But Whyteleafe is not without interest: it is remarkably progressive for its time and not what we might expect from an apparently conservative writer. As a teacher, Blyton had

---

attempted to update the language and make it more gender-neutral, but in 2016 the original text was largely restored.
6. Enid Blyton, *The Naughtiest Girl in the School* (London: George Newnes, 1940), chapter 1.
7. *The Naughtiest Girl in the School*, chapter 1.
8. *The Naughtiest Girl in the School*, chapter 2.

been trained in the Froebel tradition, a child-centred philosophy that encourages young pupils to learn through play and through their own observations, experiences and experiments, something that is reflected in her *Teachers' World* columns. The fact that Whyteleafe first appeared in Blyton's *Sunny Stories* magazine may explain why it is a co-educational school – it had to appeal to boys as well as girls; and Blyton, who remained a child at heart, was sympathetic to the idea that children usually know better than adults.

Whyteleafe is loosely based on Summerhill, established by A. S. Neill at Leiston in Suffolk in 1921, and is a children's democracy.[9] All pocket money is pooled and drawn out each week in equal shares, and there is an expectation that all 'tuck' sent from home will be shared too. Nora describes how the school's rules, rewards and punishments are decided at a weekly meeting of pupils:

> We hold a big meeting once a week – oftener if necessary – and we hear complaints and grumbles, and if anyone has been behaving badly we fine them. Miss Belle or Miss Best [the headmistresses] come to the meeting too, of course, but they don't decide anything much. They trust us to decide for ourselves.[10]

The trust in the pupils' good sense is certainly repaid. The meeting establishes that the boy caught cheating in Mathematics has fallen behind and cannot cope – so he is prescribed extra tuition to help him catch up; the boy who has scribbled on the cloakroom walls is told to clean and repaint them; Elizabeth's refusal to go to bed on time results in an earlier bedtime. But Blyton was at heart no Neill and Whyteleafe is in no way permissive. When Elizabeth arrives at the station for the conventional beginning of term railway journey, the children are smartly uniformed and the boys and girls stand in separate groups (and will travel in separate carriages). The teachers are called 'Miss' and are 'very strict', lessons are compulsory and there are Bible readings at morning assembly. And ironically, throughout *The Naughtiest Girl in the School*, Blyton is quick to hammer home to the reader her own moral judgements, either through her characters or through

9. Gillian Baverstock, Introduction to Enid Blyton, *The Naughtiest Girl in the School* (London: Hodder, 2007). Summerhill, now run by Neill's daughter, Zoë Readhead, has certainly had its ups and downs. A threat of closure from Ofsted in 1999 was overturned by a special educational tribunal and an Ofsted inspection in 2011 judged Summerhill to be a good school. It was deemed outstanding in the pupil's spiritual, moral and cultural development; their welfare, health and safety; and in the overall effectiveness of the boarding experience.

10. *The Naughtiest Girl in the School*, chapter 3.

the intrusive narrative voice. Neill made no such judgements: 'Parents and teachers make it a business to influence children because they think they know what children ought to have, ought to learn, ought to be. I disagree. I never attempt to get children to share my beliefs or prejudices. . . . I know that preaching cuts no ice with children.'[11]

Adult readers of Blyton's novels are likely to be irritated by the repeated pronouncements of how children should behave and life should be lived, but young readers do not seem to be bothered by her nagging. Perhaps they are simply caught up in the onrush of the plot. Perhaps they are untroubled by Blyton's reinforcing of the attitudes of their own parents and teachers. Or perhaps they are proof, as Neill would have it, that 'preaching cuts no ice with children'. (In *Last Term at Malory Towers*, one of the girls, quite without irony, will say to the matron, 'You're an awful preacher matron. I can't imagine why I like you!')[12]

The opening chapters of *The Naughtiest Girl in the School* are episodic and mainly concerned with Elizabeth's refusal to accept Whyteleafe's rules and its share-and-share-alike philosophy, and with incidents of the bad behaviour that she hopes will get her sent home. She will not share her cake and sweets; she will not hand in her pocket money; she will not do as she is asked by the older pupils; and she is rude and disruptive in class. To her astonishment and dismay, the headmistresses, Miss Belle and Miss Best ('Beauty and the Beast', Elizabeth calls them, in a rare flash of Blyton's wit) find her behaviour rather amusing and have no intention of sending her away, but in case the reader's moral compass goes awry, the narrative voice cannot help commenting, 'It was certainly not a very good beginning.'[13]

However, even in these early chapters Whyteleafe begins to work its magic on Elizabeth, although she is reluctant to admit it. Not only does she enjoy the host of activities – the riding, music, dancing, painting, tennis, gardening (lessons, where her intelligence shines through, are largely ignored) – but she also finds it hard to overlook the kindness that others show to her in spite of the way she treats them. As she says to Rita, the head girl, 'Thank you for being so nice. You make it rather difficult for me to be as horrid as I want to be.'[14] But the main thrust of the plot begins in chapter 9 after Rita asks Elizabeth to befriend Joan, who is miserable because her parents 'don't seem to want her or to love her'.[15] The reverse psychology

11. A.S. Neill, *Summerhill* (Harmondsworth: Pelican, 1968), p. 224.
12. Enid Blyton, *Last Term at Malory Towers* (London: George Newnes, 1946), chapter 19.
13. *The Naughtiest Girl in the School*, chapter 2.
14. *The Naughtiest Girl in the School*, chapter 9.
15. *The Naughtiest Girl in the School*, chapter 9.

works immediately (there is nothing slow-burning in Blyton's novels): 'It was good to have a friend. It was lovely to be thought very nice. No boy or girl had ever said that of Elizabeth before!'[16] For Blyton, Joan's misery appears to hold especial significance. Was she remembering the unhappy relationship with her own mother, and how her father, whom she adored, walked out on the family for another woman? Did she feel guilty about the way she sometimes neglected her daughters, Gillian and Imogen, because she was so immersed in her work? Or was it something to do with the miscarriage she had suffered in 1934 when she and her husband had so wanted a boy? Imogen, born in 1935, always thought Blyton was the worst of mothers: 'The truth is, Enid Blyton was arrogant, insecure, pretentious, very skilled at putting difficult or unpleasant things out of her mind and without a trace of maternal instinct.'[17]

Elizabeth is fierce in defending Joan against the teasing she endures because she receives no letters and on Joan's eleventh birthday she sends her cards in the post purporting to come from her mother and father, as well as the gift of a book from her mother, a card and a gift from herself, and a large cake with the message, 'A happy birthday for my darling Joan!' Joan is overjoyed, but when she writes to thank her mother for her new generosity, the truth comes out. Angry and upset, she walks off by herself, is caught in a thunderstorm, and becomes ill. Elizabeth writes to Joan's mother, apologising for her well-intentioned deceit but telling of Joan's unhappiness. Unbeknown to Joan, she once had a twin brother who died in infancy and her mother has been unable to forgive her for surviving. Now, as a result of Elizabeth's intervention, mother and daughter are reconciled.

Elizabeth's changed behaviour (which, reciprocally, owes much to Joan's friendship and calming influence) means that she becomes happy at Whyteleafe and would like to stay, but having declared her intention to leave she is too obdurate to give in: 'It's only feeble people that change their minds, and say one thing and then another.'[18] However, Blyton comes to the rescue. First, William, the head boy, tells her that 'Only the strongest people have the pluck to change their minds, and say so, if they see they have been wrong in their ideas';[19] then John tells her she's feeble because she's too proud to climb down. So, after fighting with herself, Elizabeth decides to stay; it is only left for Miss Best to conclude that 'One of these

16. *The Naughtiest Girl in the School*, chapter 14. Compare with Tom being asked to look after George Arthur in *Tom Brown's Schooldays*.
17. Interview with Giles Brandreth, 'Unhappy families', in *The Age*, 31 March 2002.
18. *The Naughtiest Girl in the School*, chapter 22.
19. *The Naughtiest Girl in the School*, chapter 22.

days she will be the best girl in the school'[20], and for Elizabeth and Joan to leave with their mothers for lunch in a hotel and strawberry ice creams all round.

The Twins at St Clare's (1941)

After the publication of *The Naughtiest Girl in the School*, Alan White of Methuen suggested that Blyton write a further series set in a conventional school. *The Twins at St Clare's* appeared in 1941 and is the first of six novels about the twins. It is for slightly older children and more accomplished than the *Naughtiest Girl* novels, but it lacks the spark of Whyteleafe's child-centred existence. The main theme is the same: the O'Sullivan twins are spoilt, like Elizabeth Allen. They are fourteen (though to the modern reader, at least, they appear to be much younger) and the time has come for them to move on from Redroofs, where they have been head girls and have thought too much of themselves. Their friends are all going on to Ringmere School – as one of the mothers says, 'It's such a nice exclusive school. . . . You know – only girls of rich parents, very well-bred, go there, and you make such nice friends.' But the twins' parents have decided that their girls will instead go to St Clare's, 'a very sensible sort of school'. Mrs O'Sullivan, who is also very sensible, says Ringmere is 'a very snobbish school, and I'm not going to have you two girls coming home and turning up your noses at everything and everybody.' So the twins are sent off to St Clare's protesting and (like Elizabeth Allen) 'determined to make the worst of things'. [21]

However, it is not long before the twins start enjoying life at St Clare's. There are successes in lacrosse, a pillow fight in the dormitory, high jinks and firecrackers in the classroom, a midnight feast, playing truant to go to the circus, rescuing an injured dog, and a near disaster in the Geography exam. It is all rounded off with a rousing end-of-term concert. 'What a lovely evening!' Pat whispers to Isabel. 'It beats Redroofs hollow, don't you think?'[22] But alongside the redemption of the twins ('They've got good stuff in them. One of these days St Clare's will be proud of them'),[23] there is the story of Sheila, the 'plain and ordinary girl, with rather bad manners, who didn't speak very well', who is shunned because of her 'airs and graces'.[24] Just as Rita in *The Naughtiest Girl in the School* explains Joan's unhappy home life, here Winifred, the head girl of St Clare's, reveals that Sheila comes from a once poor home, but her father

20. *The Naughtiest Girl in the School*, chapter 24.
21. Enid Blyton, *The Twins at St Clare's* (London: Methuen, 1941), chapter 1.
22. *The Twins at St Clare's*, chapter 20.
23. *The Twins at St Clare's*, chapter 21.
24. *The Twins at St Clare's*, chapter 15.

has made a fortune and sent her to St Clare's to be turned into a lady; her conceited manner is a mask to hide her roots and her insecurity. So instead of excluding her, the girls rally round. After Vera suffers a broken arm, Sheila takes on the main part in the play and triumphs. This time Blyton leaves it to Janet to draw the moral (though one hopes the smug tone is the author's): 'Who would have thought there was a hardworking, interesting little person like that underneath all those posings and boastings of hers?'[25]

And just as in *The Naughtiest Girl in the School* Joan is miserable because her parents don't appear to love her, here Kathleen turns to stealing because she hasn't a mother, her father is (conventionally) abroad, and her mean aunt only gives her a penny. The money she takes is not for herself but so she can be as generous to others as they are to her.[26] After Kathleen is caught, it is the twins' intervention with the headmistress that saves her from being expelled. So there are yet more morals to be drawn. 'You are kind and understanding', says Miss Theobald to the twins; and Pat says to Kathleen, 'That's just silly pride, to be afraid of saying when you can't afford something.'[27]

First Term at Malory Towers (1946)

First Term at Malory Towers was published in 1946 (again by Methuen), when both the previous series had been completed. Malory Towers has its roots in Benenden School, Kent, the public school attended by Blyton's daughters (founded in 1923, it was then more relaxed in atmosphere than the Victorian foundations and possibly more like St Clare's than Red Roofs). Benenden evacuated to Cornwall (the setting for *Malory Towers*) in 1940 for the duration of the war. Its temporary home was at the Bristol Hotel in Newquay, but the strange towered building of the novel is based on Lulworth Castle in Dorset, near to which Blyton and her family had spent their summer holidays at Swanage since 1942. Gillian and Imogen joined Benenden in September 1945, so spent only three months in Cornwall before the school returned to its Kent home, but nothing of the imminent real-life upheaval is allowed to intrude on the excitements of the novel's 'first term'. It is given to Miss Grayling, the archetypal headmistress, to set out Blyton's educational philosophy, typical of innumerable small girls' boarding schools of fact and fiction, patronising to women, but not

25. *The Twins at St Clare's*, chapter 20.
26. Neill believed compulsive stealing is 'a symbolic stealing of love, the staking out of a claim for love, based on, and justified by, the expectation that the real thing would be denied'. Robert Skidelski, *English Progressive Schools* (Harmondsworth: Penguin, 1969), p. 165.
27. *The Twins at St Clare's*, chapter 10.

dissimilar to Squire Brown's philosophy a century before: 'I do not count as our successes those who have won scholarships and passed exams, though these are good things to do. I count as our successes those who learn to be good-hearted and kind, sensible and trustable, good, sound women the world can lean on.'[28]

The central character, Darrell Rivers,[29] aged twelve, is more immediately attractive than Elizabeth Allen and the twins (she reminds of Dorita Fairlie Bruce's Dimsie). Unlike them, she is excited about going to boarding school and 'looked forward to many terms of fun and friendship, work and play', and this allows the reader to identify more closely with her.[30] The problem is that in spite of her good nature she has inherited a fiery temper from her father. It gets her into all sorts of trouble, but, as the narrator is quick to point out: 'Here was a person who had a fault, and who said so, and was sorry about it, and didn't attempt to excuse herself. Who could help warming to a person like that?'[31] She also falls under the influence of Alicia, a high-spirited but irresponsible classmate.

But the novel's chief interest lies in Darrell's interaction with three other girls, Gwendoline, Mary-Lou and Sally. Gwendoline is another of Blyton's spoiled children. At the station, her mother cries more than Gwendoline at their parting; on the train to Malory Towers she feigns unhappiness and sickness, but she is ignored by Alicia, who has been told to look after her. The no-nonsense narrator is quick to side with Alicia: 'Poor Gwendoline! If she had only known it, Alicia's lack of sympathy was the best thing for her. She had always had too much of it'.[32] When the girls go swimming, Gwendoline ducks Mary-Lou, the only girl who is weaker than she is. Darrell loses her temper and although she is quick to apologise, Gwendoline spends the rest of the novel trying to turn others against her. Timid Mary-Lou is desperate to be friends with Darrell and in the end she proves herself by jumping into the swimming pool to save Darrell when she pretends to be drowning, and by solving the mystery of the broken fountain pen that Gwendoline has blamed on Darrell.

Like Joan (in *The Naughtiest Girl*) and Kathleen (in *St Clare's*), Sally feels unloved. At the start of term, nobody sees her off at the station. On the first day she sits alone with 'no expression on her closed up face' and soon 'the girls let her live in her shell, and not come out of it at all'.[33] But at half-

28. Enid Blyton, *First Term at Malory Towers* (London: Methuen, 1946), chapter 3.
29. Darrell is named after her stepfather, Kenneth Darrell Rivers.
30. *First Term at Malory Towers*, chapter 1.
31. *First Term at Malory Towers*, chapter 8.
32. *First Term at Malory Towers*, chapter 1.
33. *First Term at Malory Towers*, chapter 5.

term Sally's mother does not visit her because she is too busy looking after her new baby sister – a sister Sally denies having. An argument in a music practice room results in Darrell losing her temper again and pushing Sally off her stool, after which Sally becomes seriously ill. Appalled at what she has done, Darrell writes to Sally's mother to apologise (the same device as Elizabeth's letter in *The Naughtiest Girl in the School*); Darrell's father carries out an emergency appendectomy on Sally (her illness was nothing to do with Darrell's push); and Sally's mother comes to visit. Darrell's letter has revealed Sally's jealousy of the new baby and how she has felt unwanted, but now, with the intervention of the headmistress, she is reassured. The novel ends with Darrell, Sally and Mary-Lou as firm friends, Alicia largely ignored, and Gwendoline despised by the other girls. Even the narrator still has no sympathy for Gwendoline: 'She was only reaping what she had sowed, so she could not grumble!'[34]

Although *First Term at Malory Towers* shares many of the banalities of the earlier series, it does capture the hero worship, the petty spitefulness and squabbles, and the shifting friendships of schoolgirls. Darrell is a likeable character and her night-time meeting with her father, though sentimental, just avoids mawkishness. The novel foregrounds again Blyton's preoccupation with the miseries of children who feel unloved by their parents: the problem is that in real life Sally's pathological jealousy of a baby sister that she denies having isn't going to disappear in an instant, any more than Joan's mistrust of her parents; and whatever the reason for Kathleen's stealing, her rehabilitation with the other girls is never going to be instant either. Headmistresses do not have magic powers, whatever they might like to believe.

*

Blyton's school stories are as unworldly as earlier girls' school novels. In *Too Marvellous for Words! – The Real Malory Towers Life* (2017), Julie Welch writes about the similarities between Malory Towers and her own time in the 1960s at the all-girls Felixstowe College, and recalls the same pranks, pillow fights, midnight feasts and trophies for houses. But she goes on:

> But then there were the goings-on that Enid Blyton didn't write about: the rather dodgy love-ins in the nine-dorm; the Drambuie kept in shampoo bottles; the smoking on the fire escape; the History and English teachers who lived together – were they or weren't they? And ooh, the scandals. The girl who

---

34. *First Term at Malory Towers*, chapter 22.

disappeared abruptly in mid-term (whisper: *she was pregnant*). The other girl who was *actually caught at it* with . . . was it a painter and decorator? An under-gardener? Anyway, they were doing the deed in the chapel garden. Round the back, in a nice secluded garden with a pond.[35]

It may be just possible that the pre-pubescent twelve-year-olds of *First Term at Malory Towers* are not yet concerned about such things, but five years later, in *Last Term at Malory Towers*, they have hardly changed, and Darrell, though shorn of her quick temper, goes out into the world utterly naïve and unprepared, and utterly unreal: ' "And what fun they were going to have! We'll have a good look backwards, today, then we'll set our eyes forward," said Sally. "College will be better fun still – everyone says so." ' (Darrell and Sally are bound for university at St Andrews – socially fashionable well before it boasted Prince William and the Duchess of Cambridge as alumni. Their less academic friends will follow suitably feminine careers – singer, dress designer, children's nurse, artist, riding school proprietors, and 'saintly little daughter'.)

To be fair to Blyton, her problem (which affects all three of her school series) is not an uncommon one for writers of children's series fiction: how is it possible to reconcile a cast that grows older year by year with a readership that remains the same age (one can hardly expect a seventeen-year-old reader to have an interest in a seventeen-year-old Darrell Rivers). The problem was made harder for Blyton and her contemporaries by the fact that until the 1960s things like puberty and adolescent emotion, let alone sex, were just not talked about (at least by adults). As we have seen, Frank Richards and Anthony Buckeridge avoided the difficulty by never allowing their characters to age. Blyton, on the other hand, in *Last Term at Malory Towers*, concentrates most of the action on younger girls (Darrell's sister, Felicity; Alicia's cousin, June; Jo, the impossible American and her timid sidekick, Deirdre) and on the arrogant new sixth-form pupil Amanda, who hopes 'to be chosen for the Olympics next year'[36] (here Blyton joins in the debate over the prominence still given to sport in many girls' as well as boys' schools – 'Malory Towers didn't make a religion of sport').[37] But she is only half successful, and Darrell and her contemporaries are no more than sanitised imitations of their younger selves.

In the end, however, it is the unreality of Blyton's world of amateur psychology and quick fixes that makes her novels potentially dangerous. Their language is careless and there is no invitation to or time for the

---

35. Julie Welch, *Too Marvellous for Words!* (London: Simon and Schuster, 2017).
36. *Last Term at Malory Towers*, chapter 5.
37. *Last Term at Malory Towers*, chapter 6.

imagination. The thoughts and feelings of the characters are imposed on them by the author. Every chapter has a closed ending, either through the dialogue, or through the ever-present narrative voice. Victor Watson suggested (in 2000) that in fifty years' time Blyton would be forgotten, or at best a footnote in the history of children's literature, but he may have been optimistic.[38] Well into the twenty-first century, Blyton's novels remain remarkably popular. Indeed, buoyed up by the Harry Potter/Hogwarts phenomenon, her publishers have commissioned writers to continue all three series of school stories in the same style as the originals.[39] Perhaps in an age when childhood innocence is fleeting, when morality is ambivalent, when everything moves at pace and there is little time or desire for reflection, and when fiction for the young is increasingly about issues rather than dreams, it is inevitable that unreality is sometimes preferable to reality, and that Whyteleafe, St Clare's and Malory Towers retain their fairytale attraction when real schools of their kind have just about disappeared.

---

38. Watson, p. 84.

39. Six new *Naughtiest Girl* novels written by Anne Digby (author of the *Trebizon* school series) were published in 1999-2000. Three new *St Clare's* novels written by Pamela Cox were published in 2000-2008 and six new *Malory Towers* novels, also by Pamela Cox, were published in 2009.

Chapter 12

The Twins' Story

Antonia Forest – *Autumn Term* (1948)

Antonia Forest's *Autumn Term* (1948) stands in total contrast with Blyton's novels. The pace is leisurely and there is time to linger over descriptions and emotions; the central characters are fully rounded and as readers we not only observe them but are given insight into how they feel and think; there is no controlling narrator to fix our moral compass; and there is a pervading gentle and ironic humour. Perhaps these strengths are explained by the fact that *Autumn Term* is in essence more than a girls' school story, and certainly not the sort of boarding-school fantasy that had predominated in the early century. It is, rather, the first in a ten-novel series about the changing fortunes of the Marlow children (there are eight of them in all, in a post-War naval family) and about growing up. Four of the novels are set at Kingscote, a girls' boarding school[1] – inevitably, because school is where so much of growing up is done – but the other six explore the children's experiences more widely and in a variety of different situations – a Cold War adventure; the training of a goshawk; a complex psychological novel in which personality is explored through play-acting, fantasy and literature; a tale of drug-running; a domestic drama in which family ties are stretched to breaking point; and a sea story in which a Swiss boy is sailed across the English Channel to his home.

---

1. The others are *End of Term* (1959), *The Attic Term* (1974) and *The Cricket Term* (1976). A fifth novel, *Spring Term*, was written by Sally Hayward as a sequel (Bath: Girls Gone By, 2011).

Autumn Term describes the first term of the twelve-year-old Marlow twins, Nicola and Lawrie, the youngest in the family, at Kingscote School. As if to distance them from the usual girlishness of schoolgirl novels, high-spirited Nicola (who keeps pictures of her brother's warship and Horatio Nelson beside her bed) is known as Nick, and Lawrie was christened Lawrence because she was expected to be a boy. Their four elder sisters are already at Kingscote, so there is much to live up to: Karen is Head Girl, Rowan is in the netball team ('an excellent person to have in a team because she always played best on the losing side'),[2] Ginty (the wild, popular one) is in the second XI hockey team, and Ann (the one with an annoyingly good nature) is a swot and a Patrol Leader in the Guides. Already they have their own paths to greatness mapped out. They will start in IIIA, as their sisters have done, be in the teams (captain and vice-captain, of course), and make their name as Guides. This, at least, is what Lawrie pours out to Tim, another new girl whom they meet on the school train:

> 'Do shut up, Lawrie,' said Nicola gruffly, interrupting her at last. It sounds so mad when you say it like that. It probably doesn't matter much with Tim, but you can't go round saying things like that to people.'
> ' "Vaulting Ambition," ' said Tim solemnly, shaking her head at Lawrie, ' "which o'er leaps itself, and falls on the other." '
> 'Gosh,' said Lawrie abashed. 'Whatever's that?'
> 'That's Macbeth,' said Tim, 'and look what happened to him.'
> Nicola and Lawrie were vague on this point, but they looked as intelligent as possible.[3]

Typically of Forest's writing, there is much going on here. Nicola is the more dominant of the twins (most of the Marlow series revolves around her) and feels the weight of expectation the most, but she has the emotional sense to see that Lawrie's outpouring of their intentions, oblivious to her 'warning frown', is doing them no favours. Notice the embarrassment of 'gruffly' as she sees Tim's disapproval of her sister, and her half apology (though she knows that inside she shares all Lawrie's ambitions and to her they are not mad at all). Notice Tim's lightly worn learning, the unspoken rebuke in 'shaking her head', and the intended warning in the quotation from *Macbeth*. And notice, in the playful final line of the extract, how the warning goes unheeded – the twins may manage to look intelligent, but Macbeth and his fate mean nothing to them at all. However, in spite of their very different characters, the twins strike up a friendship with Tim,

2. Antonia Forest, *Autumn Term* (London: Faber and Faber, 1948), chapter 1.
3. *Autumn Term*, chapter 1.

whose pleasant cynicism provides an alternative commentary throughout the novel. Tim (whose real name is Thalia, to rhyme with 'Failure', after the comic muse), is the niece of Miss Keith, the headmistress, and while the twins are determined to distance themselves from their illustrious sisters, Tim sees no reason why she should not play the situation to advantage. 'Tom, Dick and Harry,' she muses about their adopted masculine names.

It is on the school train that Nicola first makes her mark. As a parting present from her parents, she has chosen a sixteen-blade penknife that she has long admired in a shop; it means everything to her (and is another pointer to her practical nature). But as the girls examine it, it falls from the open window. For a while it jigs around on the carriage step, but when the train comes out of the tunnel it has disappeared. Nicola, following her father's dictum always to act at once in an emergency (and forgetting the bit about thinking clearly and sensibly), pulls the communication cord.

The interest is not so much in the event itself (Nicola jumps down from the train, runs into the tunnel, and retrieves the knife) but in Karen's reaction to it. Her usual air of authority vanishes and she gets into one of her flaps. Her voice shakes; she turns scarlet with embarrassment; she digs her hands into her pockets; if Nicola had been within reach, she would have smacked her. When Miss Cromwell, who disapproves of the whole idea of prefects, belittles her, she blushes and stammers, leaving it to Rowan to smooth over the situation with courtesy and good sense, and as the train starts moving again, she looks determinedly out of the window. As always with Forest, it is the small observations that say so much: Ironsides' tweed suit; the back of the train's guard that somehow expresses his anger; the sympathetic glances cast by the other girls at Karen; the flowers outside the station and the bulk of the cathedral making everything around seem small and flimsy; Nicola's legs dangling from the high stool in the tea shop where Rowan buys her a raspberryade and a peach melba to restore her spirits, and her astonishment that anyone should think she should have resigned herself to losing the knife instead of stopping the train; and Nicola's sudden apprehension and shyness when she arrives at Kingscote, which she has known for so long, as a pupil herself.

When the new girls sit the Form Examination it dawns on the twins for the first time that they may not be in IIIA after all. Outside a bee buzzes angrily and the sounds of tennis become a distraction. Nicola realises she can only answer bits of the questions, Lawrie looks as if she might cry, and Tim doesn't bother too much and has a relaxing afternoon. Then the results are posted and reveal the horrible truth that, for all the twins' hopes and boasts, 'vaulting ambition' has been punished and they will join Tim among the 'Dimwits' of the Third Remove. Worse, being in the Remove means they are not allowed to play netball, so their hopes of sporting glory are dashed as well.

After Lawrie has wept and Nicola has managed not to, the twins throw themselves into the Guides, where at least they can make their mark. They pass their Tenderfoot test and set about achieving their Second Class badge with added enthusiasm. Even Tim, who cannot think of much worse than something with Laws, Promises and Rallies, feels left out. By now they are in the Patrol led by Lois Sanger, who resents the popularity of the Marlows, but they resolve to support her on the hike that she needs for her First Class badge. After a time the twins become bored and suggest they take a short cut through a farmyard so they can collect driftwood on the beach ready to make a fire. Lois half agrees, and when she changes her mind they have gone, and Marie, who is sent after them, bottles out altogether. It is just unfortunate that a fire is started in the farmyard and Nicola and Lawrie are blamed. There will be a Court of Honour at which the case will be investigated and it is clear Lois will twist the truth to protect herself:

> 'I wanted to know,' she [Nicola] said with an effort at nonchalance, 'are you going to go on pretending that we just ran off and you don't know why?'
>
> They stared at one another, silent and furious.
>
> 'Yes, I am,' said Lois at last, her heart thudding. 'And it isn't particularly pretence. Lawrie gabbled something about a fire, but – '
>
> 'All right,' said Nicola. 'I only wanted to know.' She swung her haversack across her shoulder like a Dick Whittington bundle and went off up the stairs.[4]

Again, the conversation implies much more than is said. Nicola, who is 'furious' at Lois's dishonesty, tries to make it look as if she is unconcerned. There is her 'effort at nonchalance', her cutting off of Lois's stumbling half-justification with an 'All right', and her apparently casual exit up the stairs. As for Lois, her self-justification that 'it isn't particularly pretence' means (because of 'particularly') that it is, and her heart thuds as she consigns her supporters to their fate. At the Court of Honour, Lois is only 'fairly true' in her account and Marie tells the truth not as it was but as she has come to believe it, so the twins, who have been entirely truthful, are dismissed from the Guides.[5] Afterwards Lois is on the point of owning up to what actually happened, but her courage fails her and she misses the moment; after all,

4. *Autumn Term*, chapter 7.
5. *Autumn Term*, chapter 8.

she says to herself, 'what she'd said had been quite fairly true'. But instead of feeling relieved that she has escaped any sanction, 'she felt depressed and apprehensive and queerly humiliated'.[6]

Half-term comes and goes. The disasters of the first weeks are largely forgotten and two events stand out in the final chapters of the novel. The first is Nicola's attempt at running away. The second is the play that III Remove puts on at the Christmas bazaar.

After the various ignominies, the one thing that Nicola does well is her job as the form's Tidiness Monitor, so when Tim draws a picture of Pomona, their spoiled girly class-mate, on the blackboard, and Nicola rubs it off because the room is about to be inspected, an argument ensues. Nicola apologises, but Tim, who is dismissive of both tidiness and the twins' ambitions, is having none of it:

> 'Thank you,' said Tim elaborately. 'But one quite sees you know. Wrong form, wrong games, kicked out of Guides, so you must win something. One sees, absolutely. . . . It's a mistake to try to be distinguished when you haven't anything to be distinguished with. It makes you look foolish. People laugh.'[7]

Here there is scorn in 'elaborately' and 'absolutely', and in the pompous use of 'one', and spite in the curt final sentences. Worse for Nicola, Lawrie takes Tim's side against her sister. It has been a beastly term and she decides to catch the train to Port Wade where her brother's ship is in dock. On the train she feels a sense of relief. She enjoys the sunlight, the dust hanging in the air, being alone, the thought of her brother admiring her spirit. But at Port Wade reality closes in, with 'the pictured pleasures of the afternoon thinning into nothingness'.[8] She cannot find her brother and has no money for the return fair; and when she does by chance find him he is furious. There is a silent tea in the station café and on the train back everything has changed. It is cold and dark; the rain beats against the windows and she only wants to return to school – 'Nice, safe school.'[9] Nobody important has missed her, and the morning's argument is not mentioned. Then, as she sinks into a steaming bath, she thinks that there were nice bits to the afternoon after all. It is this true-to-life confusion of emotions that is characteristic of Forest's writing. As Nicola reflects, 'Life . . . was a very funny mixture. And there seemed to be nothing to be done about it.'[10]

6. *Autumn Term*, chapter 8.
7. *Autumn Term*, chapter 12.
8. *Autumn Term*, chapter 13.
9. *Autumn Term*, chapter 14.
10. *Autumn Term*, chapter 14.

The play is Tim's idea. When the Thirds' bazaar is arranged, III Remove is charged with running the Kitchen and Jumble stalls, while the A and B forms are given more exciting roles. Such shame cannot be tolerated and Tim makes use of his relationship to Miss Keith to gain permission to put on a play instead. She becomes the prime mover, writing the script of *The Prince and the Pauper* herself (with more than a little help from Mark Twain) and arranging the whole affair. The story is of Edward VI, who swaps places with Tom, a beggar boy, who nearly gets crowned by mistake, so the twins are ideal for the leading parts. Nicola throws herself into the enterprise, enjoying it all, particularly sloshing paint on the scenery, while Lawrie, up to now overshadowed by her more assertive sister, immerses herself in her part and discovers that she is a stunningly good actress.

It has always been planned that Tim will act as narrator, but she is hopeless at reading aloud, a fact that Lawrie, with newfound confidence, is ruthless in pointing out. She remembers how well Lois has read on the fateful hike, and Tim goes off to seek her advice. Lois offers to take over the reading herself: in a way she would be doing something for the Marlow twins, on whom she had brought such trouble, and anyway nothing seemed to have gone right for her since the disastrous Court of Honour. She finds it disconcerting how her own partly selfish motives accord with Tim's.

The performance is an unexpected triumph. Lawrie is physically sick with nerves, and unreliable Marie, always full of herself in rehearsal, becomes a shambling wreck, forgets her lines, and makes out that plays are silly anyway. But Pomona comes good as Henry VIII, Lois reads beautifully, and Lawrie is the undoubted star of the show. Moreover it is the relief and glow they all feel in the aftermath of the play that is caught so strikingly: the laughter in the dressing room at nothing at all; the need to put on unfelt modesty when they join the audience afterwards; the bashfulness when other pupils you hardly know suddenly take notice of you; Commander and Mrs Marlow being careful not to praise their daughters too much (and their daughters wishing they 'would say how frightfully good they'd been, instead of just looking calm and pleased'); and other parents coming up and praising them, and singling out Lawrie especially, until she is tactfully sent away to find more cakes. Miss Keith is pleased it was such a 'corporate form effort', which it was not, and hopes they will put on one or two scenes on Speech Day.[11] Says Lawrie, 'I say. It just occurred to me a while back. We really are good at something now. Quite like the other Marlows.'[12] The term has not turned out so badly after all.

11. *Autumn Term*, chapter 18.
12. *Autumn Term*, chapter 18.

Autumn Term is an accomplished novel, with a depth rare in school stories. Nothing much happens, but it is more a novel about people, their thoughts and emotions, than a novel about school itself. It is about identical twins who, aside from their looks, are not identical at all; about Nicola, who is both impulsive and reflective, and uncertain and weepy Lawrie, whose discovery of a real talent transforms her, not least in the eyes of her parents. It is about Tim, spiky and worldly-wise, who proves herself to be a great organiser (her name, her short hair, her practical approach, her mocking of sentimentality, her untidy curtain call, and her imploring of the twins 'to remain boyish and unspoilt' suggest that, even more than them, she is mocking the schoolgirl stereotype).[13] It is about Lois, who is selfish and weak but goes some way towards making amends. All this comes from the inside out, from what the characters think and do, more than from what we are told about them. The smallest details are remarked upon and have meaning; each word is carefully chosen. In all the conversations there are nuances that tell more than what is said, and people do not always mean what they say.

However, *Autumn Term* and the Kingscote novels have never achieved the popularity that they deserve. First, as we have seen in Part II, by 1948 tales of boarding school life were no longer of such interest to young readers. Secondly, unlike the plot-centric stories of authors like Enid Blyton, they demand close attention from the reader and a tuning-in to the way their language works. Thirdly, although the entire Marlow series covers just over two years in the life of the family, it was written over thirty-four years. So a twelve-year-old experiencing *Autumn Term* on its first publication would have been aged twenty-eight (and most probably no longer interested in children's fiction at all) when Forest's next school story, *End of Term*, was published (with Nicola and Lawrie still in their early teens), and forty by the time the series drew to a close; and by this time children's and young adult literature had taken an altogether different direction (see chapter 13). Fourthly, although *Autumn Term* can stand by itself, it is hard to read the later school stories without a knowledge of other titles in the series. So Puffin Books publication of the Kingscote novels in 1977 as a stand-alone quartet was never going to be wholly successful. In all these ways, it was time that beat the Marlows, and a writer who should have stood alongside the likes of Ransome, Garner, Mayne and Peyton as one of the outstanding children's writers of the twentieth century was very quickly overlooked.

---

13. *Autumn Term*, chapter 18. One is reminded of Arthur Ransome's she-pirate, Nancy Blackett, in the *Swallows and Amazons* novels and of George in Enid Blyton's *Famous Five*.

Part IV

The School Story Revived

Introductory: Magic and Mayhem

Butler's 1944 Education Act saw the brief flowering of the tri-partite system of secondary education, though as few technical schools were ever built, in most areas it remained a bi-partite system in all but name. To some extent, the grammar schools achieved the aim of encouraging social mobility by offering an academic education to children from every social class, and they enabled some to scale heights of which they could hardly have dreamed (especially since until 1998 university tuition in the United Kingdom was free and there were generous means-tested grants for living costs). But the downside was that too often the grammar schools creamed off the best teachers as well as the best pupils, leaving secondary modern schools struggling to offer an adequate curriculum to the 75-85% of secondary school age pupils for whom they had to provide (often they were too ill-equipped and ill-funded to provide the vocational courses that were crucial to the 1944 Act). Some secondary modern schools rose to the challenge, but some lacked ambition, and those they taught knew that they had 'failed' the 11-plus tests and regarded themselves as second-class citizens. As usual, the middle classes were at an advantage. They were educationally ambitious; their homes were likely to be filled with books; and they had the means to pay for extra tuition that would better prepare their children for the selection process. So a system that had the vision of at last offering equality of opportunity for all (which implies teaching by ability, and a method of matching pupils with schools and teachers appropriate to their needs, irrespective of their background or ability to pay), turned out to be somewhat different. Although there were many fortunate winners, there were many losers as well.

But the 1960s was an age of sweeping aside old hierarchies, including hierarchies in education, and ironically it was in part pressure from middle-class parents, whose children were failing to secure a grammar school place in spite of all their advantages, that helped bring to an end to the system they had originally supported. In 1965, less than twenty years after the 1944 Act, the then Labour government's Circular 10/65 heralded the end of secondary school selection in all but a few areas and the change to comprehensive schools. If the promise of the Prime Minister, Harold Wilson, that all children would now receive a grammar school education, had been kept, all would have been well. However, the reality was different. Some comprehensive schools decided to teach children with no setting or streaming according to ability and aptitude, so everyone was let down; other schools thrived or failed because of their location – in affluent middle-class areas, with motivated parents, the new comprehensive schools blossomed, while in deprived areas they were frequently no better than the secondary modern schools whose buildings they probably occupied. So now, inadvertently, selection was by 'neighbourhood' and those who could afford the soaring house prices near a good school won out again. Half a century on, education in the comprehensive system has never been better, perhaps because the 1988 Education Reform Act encouraged competition between schools by offering parents a degree of choice, thus moving away from the 'neighbourhood' model. Renewed calls for the return of grammar schools have come to nothing.

There was also a change in the approach to primary education. Learning became active instead of passive, tables replaced desks and in some schools teaching was in open plan areas instead of classrooms. Although some of this was impractical, the underlying principle of putting the child and not the teacher or school at the centre of education was long overdue. Today, the best primary schools have achieved a sensible blend of traditional and modern teaching methods, although the steady closing of village schools in favour of much larger establishments has done nothing to improve standards (especially in the basic skills and in behaviour) and has had an adverse effect on village communities.[1]

Thankfully, the zeitgeist of the 1960s brought change to independent schools as well. Although even in the 1970s and 1980s the colonial spirit of Sneath and his contemporaries lived on, and such practices as corporal

---

1. A delightful portrait of the English village school at its best is drawn by 'Miss Read' in *Village School* (London: Michael Joseph, 1955).

punishment and fagging continued, little by little boarding schools adapted to the new, more liberal era and have become happier and more tolerant as a result.[2] Most boys' public schools have embraced coeducation and accepted day pupils, and all have become less Spartan and gratuitously tough. Most girls' schools are no longer 'worlds apart', but actively preparing their pupils for challenging careers (though for cultural reasons, very few have attracted boys as pupils, and as their market has shrunk, a number have been forced to close). Importantly, both boys' and girls' independent schools now stand for excellence in teaching and learning above all else. But in the twenty-first century, the majority charge such high fees that they risk becoming an élite again, out of reach of even the middle classes who in Victorian times had championed their foundation.

As the public schools struggled to adapt, it was inevitable that the preparatory schools would be affected as well. By the 1960s, many of the smaller preparatory schools were closing down and those that survived became more tolerant and kind. Like the public schools, they admitted more day pupils and offered coeducation – policies driven as much by business considerations as by philosophical ones. Perhaps the preparatory schools felt the changes in society more than most: mothers as much as fathers now had a say in their children's education and were not so willing for them to leave home at an early age. In our own century, they have become flexible in their approach, not least to boarding, and with both parents often working, they have opened nurseries as well – running throughout the year and in some cases taking babies as young as 6-weeks-old.

The Stories: From Social Realism to Magic

It is not unreasonable to think that the introduction and improvement of compulsory secondary education for all, and the transformation of boarding schools into more civilised and humane places, would spell the end of the school story. However, that has turned out to be not quite the case, and in recent times what has undoubtedly been lost in quantity has more than been made up in quality. Far from being dead, the school story is enjoying a quiet but definite renaissance.

The Otterbury Incident (1948), by the poet and novelist C. Day-Lewis, begins and ends at the King's School in Otterbury, but the main action is the boys' exposing of a criminal gang. Geoffrey Trease, who more than anyone helped to establish children's literature as a serious discipline, was another established writer who saw the possibilities of novels set in post-

---

2. Corporal punishment in independent schools was not made illegal until 1999, but it had mainly died out long before then.

War maintained schools and his *Bannerdale* series is one of the subjects of chapter 13. However, like Day-Lewis, he involved his characters in adventures that take them outside the school gates (and even touring abroad with a production of *Romeo and Juliet*). Anthony Buckeridge, author of the *Jennings* novels, set his *Rex Milligan* stories (also discussed in chapter 13) in a traditional grammar school, but in spite of the huge appeal of his exaggerated humour at Linbury Court, in the real world it struggles to work. Then the 1960s made their inevitable mark in children's literature, with a new social realism that can be seen in such novels as John Rowe Townsend's *Gumble's Yard* (1961) and *The Intruder* (1969), and Sylvia Sherry's *A Pair of Jesus Boots* (1969).

It is in this context that K.M. Peyton's *Pennington's Seventeenth Summer* (1970), the final ingredient of chapter 13, brought the school story fiercely up to date. Set in a secondary modern school in a deprived area, its anti-hero, Pennington, is a troubled teenager from a dysfunctional working-class family; he has an extraordinary talent for music and a hatred of authority. So it moves out of the comfortable middle-class world that had previously dominated the school story and brings the reader up against problems that are very different from lost letters and schoolgirl squabbles. Peyton's *Flambards* and *Pennington* novels were instrumental in the move towards specifically young adult fiction, which became a new and profitable market for publishing houses, though it is predominantly centred on issues rather than schools and so has its own agenda: coping with bereavement, disability, divorce, step-families, underage sex, pregnancy, menstruation, birth control, masturbation, drugs, gang crime, racism, and the rest. The American writer Judy Blume was the first major writer in the field – provoking controversy among adults, many of whom continued to think these were subjects that should not be explored publically, if at all, but with tremendous appeal to her adolescent audience (typical of her own school stories are *Tales of a Fourth Grade Nothing*, 1972, and *Forever*, 1975). In England, Jacqueline Wilson has achieved similar success and notoriety, though her tone is less strident; she is best known for her *Tracy Beaker* series (1991-2006) and her *Hetty Feather* series (2009-2017). Critics have rightly remarked that the danger of issue-based fiction is that the issue can dominate to such an extent that the story itself becomes no more than a vehicle for highlighting and debating the problems encountered by young people.

In the same vein of social realism, and central to the school story at the end of the twentieth century, was the BBC television series *Grange Hill*, which ran from 1978 to 2008. Created by scriptwriter Phil Redmond, it followed the lives of working-class pupils at the fictional

Grange Hill comprehensive school, tackling such issues as bullying, knife crime, disability, drugs and rape, although, reacting to parental complaint, the BBC soon demanded a more comfortable approach. In the 1990s, the focus shifted to concentrate as much on the lives of the staff as the pupils; then in 2007 the BBC insisted that to fit into its CBBC channel *Grange Hill* should cater for an under-twelve audience and the action shifted to 'The Grange', a multi-media learning centre frequently used by primary school pupils. By now the series was far removed from its original hard-hitting vision and it finished its long run soon after its thirtieth birthday. When the series was enjoying its greatest popularity in the first ten years of its existence, there were also fourteen books (novels and collections of short stories), written mainly by Phil Redmond and children's author Robert Leeson, as well as eight *Grange Hill* annuals.

Another long-running BBC television series set in a comprehensive school was *Waterloo Road* (2006-15). However, this concentrated more and more on the problems of teachers and their various ill-advised relationships than on the children they taught; with the episodes scheduled in the late evening, it became as much a 'soap' for adults as for teenagers. In the eighth series (owing to the demolition in real life of its setting), *Waterloo Road* made an unlikely relocation to Greenock, Scotland, and briefly became an independent school, funded by a former pupil. It is not surprising that its ratings fell into decline.

In adult novels, a gritty Scottish realism is at the heart of Alan Warner's *The Sopranos* (1998), an excoriating account of the day the fifth-year choir of Our Lady of Perpetual Succour School for Girls in 'The Port' go to the big city for the singing competition and what they do instead (before rushing back to 'The Port' and its nightclub, The Mantrap, to throw themselves under the next shore party of sailors).[3] This is in sharp contrast to Muriel Spark's account of middle-class girls at Marcia Blaine in *The Prime of Miss Jean Brodie*.[4] At times it is outrageously funny; just as often it is unbearably sad, as the reader glimpses the backgrounds and insecurities that are disguised by bravado, bad language and drink. But the girls are survivors and, against all expectation, the lasting impression is not of despair but of the enduring energy and optimism of youth against insuperable odds. So, somehow avoiding a hangover, the novel concludes

---

3. The musical adaptation of *The Sopranos – Our Ladies of Perpetual Virtue –* has been critically acclaimed, but what happens when the girls hit the city is not for the faint-hearted.

4. Muriel Spark, *The Prime of Miss Jean Brodie* (London: Macmillan, 1961). See Introductory, Part III.

brightly and in almost poetic vein, as, at sunrise the next day, the girls look out over the bay and the back country hills 'already in full summer flush in this time of their lives'.[5]

For younger readers, Gene Kemp's *Cricklepit* novels, discussed in chapter 14, hover between being school stories and issue stories, but the subjects are largely handled with imagination and sensitivity. Also for younger children is Gillian Cross's *The Demon Headmaster* series (1982-2017): here, at last, is a school where the children are hard-working and impeccably behaved, but there is something unnerving about it. In the first novel of the series, *The Demon Headmaster* (1982), Dinah, just arrived as the foster-sister of Lloyd and Harvey, finds her new school strangely different. In the playground, instead of games and laughter, the children stand in neat groups rehearsing their twenty-one times-table. She discovers the Headmaster has, through the power of hypnotism, obtained total control, maintained by his prefects in a sinister corruption of Arnold's ideal (' "All pupils shall obey the prefects," chanted Rose, in the same stiff voice. "The prefects are the voice of the Headmaster." ').[6] Now he intends to obtain the same control over the country and the world. If only the school can win the televised Eddy Hair Quiz, he can use his headmaster's victory speech to hypnotise the nation. Dinah, the star of the quiz team, is able to answer the questions easily, but how can she answer the last mathematical puzzle if it will give the Headmaster the platform that he craves? As she wrestles with her conscience, Eddy Hair gives an unneeded clue – Winston Smith; but it is Lucy, unaware of the danger and of the irony, who shouts out the answer, 'I know it. Winston Smith's the name of the man in that funny book you told me about. Dinah! It's nineteen eighty-four!'[7] The Demon Headmaster begins his hypnotic address, but as her eyelids close, Dinah realises the red pepperpot in her hand is the weapon she needs and his plan disintegrates in a cacophony of sneezing and laughing.

The *Demon Headmaster* novels are too often underrated. There is a complexity and wit to the writing that is not immediately apparent, and, in this first novel in the series, a depth to the characterisation of Dinah (the sub-plot, which sees her winning acceptance in her foster family, adds a warmth that is otherwise missing). Importantly, the novels are about the power of education, for good and ill, and the danger of that power being misused; about the impotence of rote learning, which is creeping back into schools ('We're not learning to think. We're just learning to repeat things. Like robots. It looks good, but it's no use

5. Alan Warner, *The Sopranos* (London: Jonathan Cape, 1998).
6. *The Demon Headmaster*, chapter 3.
7. *The Demon Headmaster*, chapter 15.

at all.');[8] about the dreadfulness of Eddy Hair, fighting with a giant plate of spaghetti – meaningless entertainment, almost as appalling as the Headmaster himself; about loyalty, and friendship, and fairness, whatever Mr Venables may say ('Fairness is an illusion, designed to create disorder').[9]

However, after the 1950s the boarding school novel found little to excite children going to school every day, who needed far more magic in their fantasies than a boys' school dormitory or a girls' school adventure. The antics of the privileged minority were no longer of interest. Jennings struggled on in the fourth form, but, as I have suggested in chapter 7, the later novels lost their appeal, while the addition of boys to the usual girls'-school-story mix in Anne Digby's *Trebizon* novels fails to lift them above the mundane. That magic is provided for young readers by Jill Murphy's *The Worst Witch* books (1974-2018) and, famously, for slightly older readers by J.K. Rowling's *Harry Potter* novels (1997-2007). They are the subject of chapter 15.

Finally, the journey of *From Morality to Mayhem* ends in the chaos of Ribblestrop, more than 150 years after Tom Brown set out on the Tally-ho coach. It is, in its captivating anarchy, just the right counterbalance to *The Demon Headmaster*, and although it is fixed firmly in the Devon countryside, it is as magical a place as Miss Cackle's Academy or Hogwarts. All the tropes of the school story are there, though they glisten in an unfamiliar and satirical light and, like the best of school stories, it is life-affirming. Millie, the rebel, the arsonist, the thief, is changed by school, like so many other of the malcontents we have met. So she will be coming back to Ribblestrop when Christmas is over and for the moment the school story will survive. After all, 'There are worse places. . . . You've got to go somewhere',[10] and, 'Next term would be amazing.'[11]

---

8. *The Demon Headmaster*, chapter 9.
9. *The Demon Headmaster*, chapter 11.
10. Andy Mulligan, *Ribblestrop* (London: Simon and Schuster, 2009), Epilogue III.
11. *Ribblestrop*, Epilogue IV.

Chapter 13

The Secondary School Story

Geoffrey Trease – *No Boats on Bannermere* (1949)
Anthony Buckeridge – *Rex Milligan's Busy Term* (1953)
K. M. Peyton – *Pennington's Seventeenth Summer* (1970)

Geoffrey Trease – *No Boats on Bannermere* (1949)

Geoffrey Trease's *No Boats on Bannermere* and the ensuing *Bannerdale* series
are notable as an early attempt to shift the school story from boarding school
to day school. They follow the lives of Bill and Sue Melbury from their arrival
as young teenagers in the Lake District, where they become best friends with
Tim and Penny, until Bill goes off to Oxford with Penny, and Sue marries
a local farmer. The novels were prompted by two girls suggesting that
Trease write stories 'about real boys and girls, going to day-schools as nearly
everybody did'.[1] Bill, a would-be author who narrates the story and often
acts as Trease's voice, encapsulates the problem facing modern-day authors:

> People don't often put day-schools into stories. I don't know why.
> Life there is just as interesting as it is at boarding-schools. I've talked
> to chaps who've been away, and nothing much seems to happen
> to them. Midnight feasts hardly ever occur: they talk much more
> about the frightful meals that are served officially. I've never yet
> found anyone who really broke bounds by knotting sheets together,
> or dug up a secret passage, or socked a hooded figure and found it
> was the new housemaster who was really an international crook.[2]

1. Geoffrey Trease, *Laughter at the Door* (London: Macmillan, 1974), p.149.
2. Geoffrey Trease, *No Boats on Bannermere* (London: Heinemann, 1949), chapter 7.

Bill's summing up of the unlikely plots of school stories in the first half of the twentieth century is accurate enough, but the *Bannerdale* novels, while missing out on the midnight feasts and knotted sheets, relate their own unlikely adventures. Trease knew as well as anyone that in any era there is very little in the classroom of interest and so he moves the action to the surrounding countryside, the lake and even (in *Black Banner Abroad*, 1954) across the English Channel to Provence. Bill, who often reflects on the creative process, seems to be inspired by Trease's younger self. Trease (1909-98) was educated at Nottingham High School, where he already had ambitions to become a writer; then, like Bill, he won a Classics scholarship to Oxford. He wrote more than a 100 books, mainly for children – most notably *Cue for Treason* (1940), which recounts the adventures of two boys who are taken on as apprentices by William Shakespeare. His *Tales Out of School* (1948; rev. ed. 1964) was instrumental in children's literature being taken seriously as a critical genre.

In *No Boats on Bannermere*, Bill and Susan move with their mother to Bannerdale.[3] Bill goes to the Grammar School in the centre of nearby Winthwaite,[4] while Susan attends the more recently built Girls' County Secondary School farther out of town – 'Miss Florey's far-from-select academy for young ladies'.[5] In fact, so 'far-from-select', that on his first day Bill is in trouble for meeting Susan and Penny in the lunch hour, and the grammar school boys are prevented from attending the girls' school fête. But when the local landlord, Sir Alfred Askew, bans the children from his land and seems to be hiding skeletons, they set out to discover his secret and unearth buried treasure instead of murder as a result.

Thus although the *Bannerdale* novels have schools at their centre, school life remains in the background; in *No Boats on Bannermere* it serves only to get in the way of the action, with the young detectives 'hampered by bus-times and bed-times, not to mention Latin exercises and problems in arithmetic and compulsory cricket'.[6] So whatever Trease's intention, these are hardly school stories at all. They owe more to the 'camping and tramping' tradition of children's literature and evoke that other Lake District novelist, Arthur Ransome – at Bannerdale, there are a lake, a boat, a mountain, an island, a friendly local farmer and his wife (Tyler, not Tyson), and a cottage called Beckfoot (the same name as the Amazons' much grander home in

---

3. In 1940, while waiting to be called up, Trease taught at Gosforth in the Lake District and became enchanted by the area. Bannerdale and Bannermere are fictional, but borrow from different parts of the Lake District.
4. Winthwaite is based on Cockermouth.
5. *No Boats on Bannermere*, chapter 8.
6. *No Boats on Bannermere*, chapter 11.

Swallows and Amazons) – though Ransome would never have written about
Bill's and Penny's feelings for each other (something that Trease achieves
with the lightest touch) and never allowed his children to grow up.

In *No Boats on Bannermere*, the changes of the 1944 Education Act have
not quite reached the Lake District, where the Winthwaite Grammar School
was founded in 1630 and the Girls' County Secondary School was built in
1922 (later in the series the girls' school becomes the girls' 'High', presumably
because a secondary modern school was built locally as well). So Kingsford,
the headmaster of the Grammar School, still lives in the educational past,
where the academic is all-important and girls don't matter. He complains that
'The modern school-child spends half its time going round sausage factories
when it should have its nose to the grindstone';[7] and he finds it difficult to
come to terms with there being a girls' school at all.

Trease's *Bannerdale* novels move at a cracking pace, but his characters
lack something in substance and, in spite of Bill's and Sue's previously
straitened circumstances, are too middle class to be the 'real boys and
girls' that his starting point implies. He brings the Lake District to life,
but it never has the magic and mystery to inform his plots in the way that
Ransome achieves in the *Swallows and Amazons* novels. Similarly, although
Trease introduces tales of marauding Vikings, the past never intrudes on or
shapes the present as it does in, for example, the work of William Mayne
and Alan Garner.[8]

Anthony Buckeridge – *Rex Milligan's Busy Term* (1953)

Anthony Buckeridge, author of the Jennings series,[9] also attempted the
shift from boarding school to day school, with four novels set in a 1950s
grammar school, Sheldrake, in North London, and featuring Rex Milligan
as the central character and narrator. The series started life as individual
short stories in the *Eagle* comic (later collected in *Introducing Jennings*,
2002). Although Buckeridge rated it as 'just as good and just as funny as
Jennings',[10] it was never more than a modest success.

The first of the novels, *Rex Milligan's Busy Term* has two interlinked strands
to the plot: the threat to the Sheldrake playing fields, where it seems the
lease has expired and developers will move in, and the dodgy operations of
the Premier Garage, which is changing the identity of stolen cars and selling

7. *No Boats on Bannermere*, chapter 15.
8. In particular, William Mayne's *Earthfasts* (1966) – see also chapter 7 – and Alan
    Garner's *The Owl Service* (1967) and *Red Shift* (1973).
9. See chapter 7.
10. Anthony Buckeridge, *While I Remember*, revised edition (Petersfield: David
    Schutte, 1999), p.81.

them. Behind both is the shady Mr Lindgrun, and foiling his activities
are Milligan and his friend Jigger Johnson. There are obvious parallels
with the Jennings series: a fast-moving narrative; a duo of well-meaning
schoolboys whose good intentions land them in a variety of scrapes from
which they invariably come up smiling; a short-tempered schoolmaster, Mr
Birkinshaw, who is as explosive as Mr Wilkins of Linbury Court ('Doh!');
the same inimitable schoolboy slang – 'Fossilized fish-hooks' live again;
and, at its best, the same Wodehousean humour. There are incidents that
remind of the best of Jennings – the expedition in the Frizzer's car, when
it breaks down at the traffic lights; the auction, when Rex bids for a lot by
mistake; the test drive of Jiggers's bathtub amphibian, when it launches
itself into the lake and sinks because they have forgotten the bath plug; and
the tenser moment when Lindgrun discovers Rex and Jiggers spying in his
garage. But, in the end, the novel (and its successors) just does not work.

There are a number of reasons for this. First, the Jennings series is successful
because, as a boarding school, it can be a fantasy place where readers imagine
themselves and where reality does not matter unduly; but day schools are
more rooted in the real world, and the adventures of Rex Milligan demand
too much of our suspension of disbelief. Secondly, Jennings and Darbishire
are amusing because of their innocent take on life (Jennings is ten, and
sometimes has an eleventh birthday); but although Milligan and his chums
are fourteen-year-old boys, they behave in exactly the same uninhibited way
as Jennings and Darbishire, when we expect them to be moody adolescents,
with a couldn't-care-less attitude and broken voices, and with a dryer and
more cynical sense of humour; thirdly, the narrator in the Jennings novels
can look at the boys with a certain detached amusement, but in the Rex
Milligan novels Rex himself is the narrator and his exaggerated language
is too carefully crafted and too contrived when coming from a schoolboy.
Do grammar school boys 'trot' through the school gates and listen to a
'sizzling news-bulletin'? Do they verbalise 'Cutforth's cheeks wobbling with
woe and his eyes popping out like organ-stops'?[11] It might work for one of
Wodehouse's adult characters, with that faint air of self-mockery, but not
here, even as a period piece. Dialogue like this does not work either:

> 'You clumsy clodpoll, Boko!' stormed Scuttersthorp. 'You've
> bished up the game properly, doing a chronic boss-shot like that.
> We'll never get the ball down now.'
> 'Super sorrow – my foot slipped,' grinned the boss-shotter.[12]

11. Anthony Buckeridge, *Rex Milligan's Busy Term* (London: Lutterworth, 1953),
    'Grim News for the Grammar School'.
12. *Rex Milligan's Busy Term*, 'Bird's Eye View'.

In 1953-1957, when Buckeridge wrote the Milligan novels, Jennings was at the height of his popularity. One can only conclude that he was so immersed in the Jennings formula and in Linbury Court that he did not notice in the outside world boys had grown up and schools had moved on.

K. M. Peyton – *Pennington's Seventeenth Summer* (1970)

Both *No Boats on Bannermere* and *Rex Milligan's Busy Term* have more than a whiff of the past about them, and did so even when they were first published; as middle-class grammar and high school pupils, the Bannerdale children and Rex Milligan, were not at all the sort of 'real' characters that Trease's schoolgirls had in mind ('real' had somehow become synonymous with 'working class'). But Patrick Pennington, the anti-hero of K. M. Peyton's *Pennington's Seventeenth Summer* (1970), is altogether 'real' and inhabits a different world from every schoolboy and schoolgirl hero we have met so far. Peyton is best known for her award-winning *Flambards* series – about girls and their ponies, but controversial because of the romantic content ('It was quite sexy actually,' says Peyton);[13] in fact, Peyton wanted *Flambards* (1967) to be published for an adult audience, but her publisher disagreed and, without knowing it, she became a pioneer in young adult fiction.[14]

Pennington is significant for the development of the school story because he comes from a dysfunctional working-class family – 'a fourteen-stone hulk of a boy, with shoulders on him like an all-in wrestler, and long reddish-brown hair curling over his collar'.[15] His mother is 'flinty and unlovable' and his father, who settles all arguments 'by means of a good thumping', only supports him when he is in trouble with the law.[16] Since at school he has failed in everything apart from Music and Religious Knowledge, his mother has insisted that he stay on for another year at the Beehive Secondary Modern – to his disgust and to the despair of his long-suffering teachers. A rebellious malcontent, he is persecuted at every turn by his spiteful form master, Soggy Marsh, whose patience has long since expired. His only supporters on the staff are Matthews, the games master (because Pennington is at the centre of all the school teams, where his ruthless streak is an asset), and Crocker, the eccentric music master (because Pennington

13. Interview with Susanna Rustin, *The Guardian*, 15 February 2014. Peyton was awarded the Carnegie Medal in 1969 for the second novel in the *Flambards* trilogy, *Edge of the Cloud*. The trilogy won *The Guardian* Children's Fiction Prize in 1970.
14. The alternative though now less used term 'teen fiction' describes the target audience better.
15. K.M. Peyton, *Pennington's Seventeenth Summer* (Oxford: Oxford University Press, 1970), chapter 1.
16. *Pennington's Seventeenth Summer*, chapter 1.

is an outstanding pianist, though 'May God forgive this boy for abusing so unusual a talent').[17] His friend is Bates, 'a weedy specimen, a self-effacing, spotty-faced henchman', whose singing of downbeat songs punctuates the novel, while his arch-enemy is Smeeton, 'slight, sharp-witted, greasy, and mean', but afraid of Pennington's size and strength.[18] Two years before, Pennington and Smeeton, then friends, had been caught shoplifting; Smeeton was clever enough not to get caught, but Pennington got two years' probation and is now an outcast in the dead-end riverside village, unable to get a job and smarting at the injustice.

Pennington and Smeeton have jointly inherited a rotting fishing smack, the *Mathilda*. This evening, at the beginning of the Easter holiday, Pennington and Bates are on board when Smeeton and his party approach in their dinghy. Knowing he and Bates will be outnumbered in a fight, Pennington dives in and, as its crew panics, the dinghy capsizes. For good measure, Pennington all but drowns Smeeton and gets his own back on the protesting Major Harmsworth, who is rowing ashore from his smart yawl, by swimming underneath his rubber dinghy and rocking it. For good measure, he lets down the tyres on Harmsworth's Jaguar before he goes home. But the next morning a four-letter word has been painted in tar on the side of the car. It is Smeeton's handiwork, but, as he has calculated, it is Pennington who is blamed. A fight with Smeeton and his gang is broken up by the keen new police constable, Mitchell, though not before Smeeton has been thrown off the jetty into the mud.

In the detention room at the police station, Pennington thinks he will be sent to Oakhall, the detention centre, and, as the sounds, scents and tastes of the outside world drift in, we sense his despair at the hopelessness of his life and his fear of being locked up. This is Peyton at her evocative best:

> Outside he heard the boys going home from the playing-field, still punting the ball with hollow thuds across the road, and the sudden smell of soccer, the crushed grass and the sour leather, the sweat and salt of it on the tongue, made him suddenly feel as if he had been at it himself, out in the road. It gave him a twist of feeling that he could put no name to; it was like a pain, a great longing for something without identity; it made him feel sick for being where he was, and the thought of Oakhall. He didn't think his home was anything much, but, by God, he didn't want to be taken away and pushed around by blokes like Mitchell.[19]

---

17. *Pennington's Seventeenth Summer*, chapter 1.
18. *Pennington's Seventeenth Summer*, chapter 1.
19. *Pennington's Seventeenth Summer*, chapter 2.

Luckily for Pennington, the police sergeant is more sympathetic than his subordinate and he is freed. The holiday gets better when he is offered a part-time job at the local pub and, at a folk evening in the village hall, he listens to the singing of a girl with sad eyes, Sylvia, and is transfixed. Afterwards, 'Every time he recalled her he felt weak in his stomach, as if suffering from something physical' and 'could not understand why the little blond kept fluttering in his inside.'[20] However, back at school, the feeling of entrapment returns, summed up in an appropriate schoolboy image: 'His last term, true to form, stretched like grey, spent chewing-gum, tasteless, useless and tedious, into the hazy horizons of his seventeenth summer.'[21] Through the classroom window, the sight of the shimmering sea, and the freedom it symbolises, makes him feel physically unwell. Taking refuge on *Mathilda*, he and Bates are ambushed by Smeeton and friends and he has a broken glass thrust in his face. But when *Mathilda*'s engine fails in bad weather and the boat runs aground, Smeeton's bravado disappears and it is left to Pennington to sail them out of trouble. In spite of his fear, he finds something meaningful in the experience, an unaccustomed sense of achievement: 'He was pleased that he had kept his head. It made him feel strange, that he could enjoy what was happening at the same time as feeling scared to death. Not like Smeeton, giving in, like a jelly.'[22]

In the second half of the novel, other incidents crowd around Pennington: his continuing refusal to cut his hair (more out of contempt for Soggy than anything else) resulting in his being barred from games, with the time used for music practice instead; Mitchell trying wrongly to pin on him the theft of a motorbike from the quay; his jealousy at the folk club when Sylvia seems to be ignoring him; his almost drowning of Smeeton in a large dish of rice pudding in the school dining hall; his racing in the swimming gala in defiance of his ban and winning the cup for the Beehive; his having his hair cut in an attempt to keep Matthews, who asked him to swim, out of trouble.

At the beginning of *Pennington's Seventeenth Summer*, Pennington is hardly an attractive character: 'idle and destructive' at school; a shoplifter; a yob without manners, enjoying his physical superiority, and looking forward to 'mashing' Smeeton.[23] Refreshingly for a school story, Peyton makes no moral judgements, but as the novel progresses, Pennington is transformed from villain to hero. Every confrontation with Soggy, every altercation with Smeeton, and every attempt by Mitchell to bolster his own self-image by charging him, conspire to make us, as readers, take Pennington's side. It is

---

20. *Pennington's Seventeenth Summer*, chapter 3.
21. *Pennington's Seventeenth Summer*, chapter 3.
22. *Pennington's Seventeenth Summer*, chapter 4.
23. *Pennington's Seventeenth Summer*, chapter 1.

not, I think, that we approve of Pennington's behaviour, but that we feel he becomes increasingly more sinned against than sinning; we begin to despise the novel's figures of authority, because we see their malevolent pettiness through Pennington's eyes. At the same time, all the fears and uncertainties of adolescence, hidden just beneath the hulking exterior, are laid bare, not least in Pennington's confused and unfathomable love for Sylvia. Young readers in particular, male and female, understand and empathise with him completely.

As the novel reaches its climax, Crocker enters Pennington for a piano competition, but since it is on the same day as the Tolchester Folk Festival, where Sylvia will be performing, Pennington tells Croker that he will not be turning up. Then Mitchell discovers that Pennington has ridden his father's motorbike without insurance – something that Soggy is quick to corroborate. Without anything to lose now, Pennington douses Soggy in a bucket of water and for his pains is caned viciously on each hand – unaware that Pennington is refusing to compete in the piano competition, Soggy thinks he is ruining his chances. But, 'In that moment Penn, his satisfaction blasted, blind hate seizing him, vowed he would win that ruddy competition if it was the last thing he ever did in his life';[24] and, to avoid being locked up by Mitchell beforehand, he retires to *Mathilda*.

On the day of the piano competition, Crocker is found collapsed in his dinghy and Pennington and Bates have to rescue him. The delay means Pennington arrives late at the competition, but after some deliberation he is allowed to play. It is a winning performance and Sylvia, having also deserted the Tolchester Festival, is in the audience and takes Pennington home afterwards, where he is persuaded to play for her mother. Luckily for him, a Professor Hampton, staying next door, hears Pennington playing and when the next morning he has to report to the police station to answer for his motorbike escapade, Hampton negotiates his release on condition that he accepts a scholarship to study piano in London. Pennington is hardly thrilled by the proposal, but it is better than three months at Oakhill. So the novel ends on an upbeat note, with Crocker recovering in hospital and Pennington, playing in school assembly, enraging Soggy with his choice of music. What was going to happen afterwards, 'he neither knew nor cared'.[25]

Predictably, Pennington's subsequent career does not run smoothly, and in the sequel, *The Beethoven Medal* (1971), when he is working as a baker's boy, he is imprisoned for assault. He has fallen in love, not with Sylvia, but with Ruth Hollis, who wanders in from another of Peyton's novels, *Fly-by-Night* (1968), and who stands by him. In *Pennington's Heir* (1973),

---

24. *Pennington's Seventeenth Summer*, chapter 9.
25. *Pennington's Seventeenth Summer*, chapter 12.

Pennington and Ruth marry and have a son, while Pennington struggles to make his way as a concert pianist, but in a later novel, *Marion's Angel's* (1979),[26] he has at last achieved success.

For a time it had seemed there would be little room in the post-1945 world for the school story (even if Linbury Court, the Abbey School and the Chalet School were soldiering on), but *Pennington's Seventeenth Summer* contradicted that. Here is a novel set in a secondary modern school that has a strong plot and a central character who appeals to both boys and girls. It owes much to the 1950s and 1960s fashion for the 'angry young man', with an aggressive working-class anti-hero challenging authority, whether in the form of school (Soggy), police (Mitchell), or society at large (Major Harmsworth). Appealing to a neglected teenage audience, it points towards the 'issue-based' novel, but Pennington is created with such depth that the issues are never simplified and are shouldered aside. Above all, the realism and the poetry of *Pennington's Seventeenth Summer* are rare in the school story and have lost little with the passing of time.

---

26. In 1983, the title was changed to *Falling Angels*.

Chapter 14

The Combined School Story

Gene Kemp – *The Turbulent Term of Tyke Tiler* (1977), *Gowie Corby Plays Chicken* (1979) and five other novels

What *Pennington's Seventeenth Summer* did for secondary school pupils in bringing school into the everyday world, Gene Kemp's seven novels set in or around Cricklepit Combined School did for younger children. *The Turbulent Term of Tyke Tiler* (1977), the first novel in the series, is the only school story to have won the Library Association's Carnegie Medal. Narrated in the first person, and with a smattering of familiar school rhymes and corny jokes, it is Tyke's account of his last term at Cricklepit School. It is about the scrapes that Tyke gets into – usually to protect or placate the endearing Danny, who is intellectually challenged and suffers from a speech defect:

> 'He looks bright,' I've heard people say. 'There must be a block.'
> There is. I know that. I've known it for years. It's his head.'[1]

It is, above all, a story about the assumptions we make about identity and gender, and about the power of friendship.

The opening sentence plunges us into a wet Friday playtime and the first hint of trouble. The picture is painted in a few evocative strokes: 'the canteen that smelled of boiled swede and cabbage, enough to make you throw up'; 'a crowd of under-sized Chinamen streamed towards us,

---

1. Gene Kemp, *The Turbulent Term of Tyke Tiler* (London: Faber and Faber, 1977), chapter 1.

shouting, panting, kicking, the second year doing Aladdin again, I suppose';
Lorraine Fairchild and Linda Stoatway were dancing in a corner, 'all flying
skirts and hair, showing off to the boys who couldn't have cared less'.[2] This
is school life in all its mundane hilarity, expressed in the authentic voice of
childhood. Amid the chaos, Danny steals a ten-pound note from a teacher's
handbag, generously offering to share it with Tyke. To keep Danny out of
trouble, Tyke takes the note and hides it in an attic store until it can be
secretly returned. After school, Tyke takes his dog Crumble for a walk, and
from the bank he watches the weir in the river. The description of the river
in spate is woven seamlessly into the narrative, as is Tyke's inner relief at
saving Danny from the consequences of his thieving:

> All the murky feeling about the money washed away as I stood
> there. Nothing much mattered very much except the noise of
> the water and the wetness in the air and the willows blowing in
> the mind on the other side of the bank.[3]

But when on the following Monday Tyke returns to the store to recover the
stolen note, it has gone. To make matters worse, in assembly Danny puts
his pet mouse into Linda's hair. The resulting scene is carefully handled
farce, as children fall like ninepins, Mrs Somers climbs up the wall bars,
and Mr Merchant attempts a flying tackle. In due course, the matter of the
theft is sorted out by the headmaster ('Chief Sir'), with Tyler let off with a
cautionary letter home and Danny invited to tea by the guilt-ridden victim,
where he is entertained to 'ice-cream and jelly and cakes and sausages'. It is
an example, says Tyke, of 'the unfairness of things'.[4]

The middle chapters of the novel are laced with similar episodes: Tyke
retrieving a rotting sheep's carcase from the weir stream so Danny can
gain house points for bringing a 'skellinton' to school; Tyke accidentally
dropping his father's election leaflets into the river, then making amends
by removing a rival's leaflets from the town doorsteps; the setting up of
a hide-out in the derelict paper mill; and an account of Mr Merchant's
brilliant lesson on William the Conqueror (with a re-enactment of the
English fighting the Normans) to which even the tramp and the gardeners
in the park begin to listen; the love hearts scrawled on the front of the
school after Merchant's ill-advised assignation with the delectable student
teacher, Miss Honeywell ('Miss is so super star she could get anyone,' says
Tyke).[5]

---

2. *The Turbulent Term of Tyke Tiler*, chapter 1.
3. *The Turbulent Term of Tyke Tiler*, chapter 1.
4. *The Turbulent Term of Tyke Tiler*, chapter 2.
5. *The Turbulent Term of Tyke Tiler*, chapter 9.

But when Tyke overhears the teachers discussing the secondary school selection test, it seems Danny is destined to be sent to a boarding school for backward children unless he does well, and Tyke knows that Danny can't manage if they are separated. Desperate measures are called for and Tyke takes a test paper from the headmaster's office, works out the answers with the help of his bright seventeen-year-old sister Beryl, and persuades Danny to learn them. Not surprisingly, Danny does well enough in the test to go to the comprehensive school, but Tyke does too well and is offered a place at the school for gifted children. Luckily, Tyke and Danny's friendship is saved because Mr Tiler 'doesn't believe in privilege and that place is so privileged that even saints and millionaires have a hard time getting in'.[6]

Thus the novel moves to a series of climaxes. While Tyke is ill, a gold watch is stolen; Danny is accused of the theft and disappears. But Tyke knows that Danny would not steal a watch (' "Nasty staff time is", says Danny. "My Dad does time in the nick." ')[7] and that he has been framed by two class bullies. Somehow Tyke manages to 'strike a deal' with 'Chief Sir', Danny is rescued from the paper mill, and the real culprits are discovered.

The account of the last day of term captures all the familiar excitement and emotion: the school play; the prayer for the school and those leaving; the singing of 'Lord Dismiss Us With Thy Blessing' while Linda and Lorraine sob and wail in the back row; and, above all, the uncertainty and desolation of moving on to a different and unknown world suddenly overtaking the excitement of it all. Here, typically of the novel, the unmistakeable language of school is overlaid surreptitiously with the more reflective voice of the author:

> It was the last time I should be here. No more Sir, gloom. No more Mrs Somers, FANTASTIC. I'd come here, holding Berry's hand, when I was four, and now I was twelve. Eight years had gone somewhere. And I didn't want to go to a new school. And I didn't want to grow up. Growing up seemed a pretty grotty sort of thing to have to do. I felt empty, strange, restless.[8]

But when, far away, a clock strikes four, Tyke has an urge to ring the bell in the school's bell-tower – just as his ancestor Thomas Tiler had done long ago. Tyke shins up the drain pipe and straddles the roof. It is here that Mrs Somers, in shouting at Tyke to come down, reveals the novel's extraordinary secret, that rough and tough Tyke is a girl, not a boy, and we are brought face to face with our own often misguided assumptions about girls and boys.

6. *The Turbulent Term of Tyke Tiler*, chapter 12.
7. *The Turbulent Term of Tyke Tiler*, chapter 13.
8. *The Turbulent Term of Tyke Tiler*, chapter 14.

Defiantly Tyke tolls the bell 'as if summoning the whole city to come. And people came'.[9] But the bell tower is weak. Bell, tower and roof crash to the ground, and, with them, Tyke. In the Postscript, attributed to Will Merchant, Mr Merchant visits Tyke in hospital ('a broken arm, a broken ankle, bruises and concussion') and ties up the loose ends.[10] But in another, metafictional twist, he reveals himself as the teller, or at least the reteller, of the entire story: 'When I went again she was much recovered, and started to tell me all about the term, which I enjoyed. I began to try to put it down just as she told it to me. . . . Oh, Tyke wanted the jokes put in, because . . . there can't be too many jokes'.[11]

However, what mostly sets the novel apart is its original use of language, which starts with its alliterative title. Look, for example, at the sympathetic humour of 'Chief Sir' interviewing Danny and Tyke about the stolen money. Look at the way the shouts from the crowded playground are echoed in the way they are crowded together in two columns on the printed page,[12] and the neat juxtaposition as Tyke sees the route to the bell tower: 'Perfectly simple. Simply perfect.'[13] And look at the aptness of the imagery: 'Life, all clear and bright again, stretched before me like the first page of a fresh exercise book';[14] 'the cane, lying like a snake that had been turned to stone';[15] and 'Danny went as pink as school blancmange'.[16] And listen: Kemp has a sharp ear for language and the dialogue she creates is exactly the way that children speak. What is most striking, though, is the lack of any overt moralising. Although *The Turbulent Term of Tyke Tiler* is very much in the moral tradition of the mainstream of school stories, children hate being patronised, and not only does the novel's first-person narration preclude any direct authorial intervention, but the writing is so subtle that there is also little sense that the author is standing behind her characters, and directing their and our response. As readers, we are nearly left to reach our own conclusions.

Gowie Corby Plays Chicken (1979)

We have seen the not very satisfactory ways in which writers of series of school stories deal with the problem of their characters growing up. Some (for example, Frank Richards in the Greyfriars series and Anthony

---

9. *The Turbulent Term of Tyke Tiler*, chapter 14.
10. *The Turbulent Term of Tyke Tiler*, Postscript.
11. *The Turbulent Term of Tyke Tiler*, Postscript.
12. *The Turbulent Term of Tyke Tiler*, chapter 12.
13. *The Turbulent Term of Tyke Tiler*, chapter 14.
14. *The Turbulent Term of Tyke Tiler*, chapter 2.
15. *The Turbulent Term of Tyke Tiler*, chapter 9.
16. *The Turbulent Term of Tyke Tiler*, chapter 10.

Buckeridge in the Jennings series) lock their children in time, so they never age and never move up the school. Others (for example, Enid Blyton in all three of her series) follow their children through their school career, without ever allowing them properly to develop and change. Kemp, however, takes a different and more satisfactory route, which opens up a number of possibilities. It is Cricklepit Combined School that remains constant, while each year the eldest class of children moves on to secondary school and another class takes its place. So when school reassembles the term after Tyke's dramatic finale, the school building still lies in ruins, but it is Gowie Corby and his peers (more enemies than friends) who are being taught by Mr Merchant.

Gowie Corby Plays Chicken is an angrier and more challenging book than *Tyke Tiler*, with a less easy-to-like child narrator; perhaps for this reason it has proved less popular, especially with adult readers. It is again about the power of friendship, but also confronts the problem of the deprived and disturbed child. Always in trouble and unpopular at school, Gowie is in a downward spiral of despair. When term starts, isolated from the other children, he kicks a marble aimlessly in the playground – 'It goes down the drain, of course' (note Gowie's sarcastic resignation). So he kicks litter instead, and is told to pick it up: 'I pick it up, hate, hate. They've started already. Picking on me. Bossing me about. Telling me off. Gowie Corby, Gowie Corby, the theme for all that's wrong in this school.'[17] He hasn't brought any gym kit; he is branded a thief; he slices up a new rubber ('What is a new rubber for if not to be spoilt?'); he defaces his exercise books and scrawls over Heather's folder.[18] He steals JJ's silver pen and after a chase Stewart's elbow is broken when Gowie pushes him down the library steps. In class – 'the torture room' – nobody will sit next to him (apart from Heather, who throughout the novel makes unrequited attempts to befriend him – 'Given a straight choice, I'd rather sit by a slug'): 'It's always the same. No place for me. Other people have friends. I have enemies. Not that I care.'[19] Not caring is a jarring refrain, suggesting how, beneath the angry façade, Gowie does care, desperately.

The tensions explode when Gowie refuses to join the football TEAM and is subjected to a brutal attack. The violence and the fear are captured in a frightening stream of consciousness. This is Kemp at her best, inside Gowie's head, making us feel his pain and terror and loneliness and confusion, worth a thousand words of authorial comment:

---

17. Gene Kemp, *Gowie Corby Plays Chicken* (London: Faber and Faber, 1999), chapter 1.

18. *Gowie Corby Plays Chicken*, chapter 1.

19. *Gowie Corby Plays Chicken*, chapter 1.

I try to cover my head, my body. The pavement's hard, it tears my trousers, gashes my knees, scrunch, scrape, blood, warm and wet. Blood and salt in my mouth, tears pouring, I'm scared, I can't think, I can't fight, there are too many of them, help me, help me somebody, help me please, why won't somebody come, help, no one will, no one ever did, no one, there's only you and all of them . . . lie still . . . play dead . . . lie still . . . lie dead . . . perhaps I am dead . . . voices above the grunts.[20]

And help does come in the form of strange-looking Rosie Lee, another outsider, a black girl who has just moved in next door; and suddenly somebody cares about Gowie. As Rosie treats his wounds, he tells of his background, matter-of-factly, without any hint of self-pity or shame. His abusive father has left and is now in prison, and his mother works at a club every night. His eldest brother, Joe, 'the best of us', has been killed in a motorcycle accident, and his other brother, Mark, has been sent to reform school for stealing cigarettes.[21] Gowie trusts Rosie Lee sufficiently to introduce her to the creepy substitute family that he has assembled in the basement: the gerbils, Zombie and Voodoo; the mice, Terror, Ghoulie, Weird, Lurch and Witchie; and the rat, Boris Karloff, who is 'clever and smart and he loves me'.[22]

Bolstered by Rosie's unconditional friendship, Gowie's rehabilitation begins. In school he starts working and achieving; out of school, he is accepted into Rosie's family and is invited to go on holiday with them. But when JJ smashes the puppet that Gowie has made, he chases him into the cloakroom, where in his effort to escape JJ climbs onto the cistern and brings it crashing down. Retribution is inevitable and swift, described in the most searing passage in the novel:

> Don't let him cane me, don't let him cane me, DON'T LET HIM CANE ME. Then as in a nightmare I hold out my hand, the cane whooshes, it hurts, it hurts, I don't cry. He looks at me. Is he waiting for tears?
>   'Corby, did that hurt'
>   'Yes, Sir. On the outside, Sir.'
>   He puts down the cane.
>   'Not an inside hurt. Not like . . . ?' He watches me. . . . Not like with Joe. When he was dead, and my mother wouldn't stop

---

20. *Gowie Corby Plays Chicken*, chapter 4.
21. *Gowie Corby Plays Chicken*, chapter 5.
22. *Gowie Corby Plays Chicken*, chapter 5.

screaming. Or seeing my puppet broken. Sir. . . . Sir. Aren't you
going to cane me, any more?' . . .
   'You want to be caned."
   'No. But I don't want not to be.'
   The blows are sharp and swift. I cry as I leave the headmaster's
study. Only, I'm crying for a lot of things that have nothing to
do with hands that hurt.'[23]

There is no reflection here on the irony of JJ's revenge and Gowie's
reaction; no reflection on Gowie's fear of physical pain; no reflection on the
headmaster's continuing Gowie's punishment against his better judgement;
no reflection on the juxtaposition of Joe's death and the smashed puppet;
no reflection on Gowie's inside hurt. As readers, we are left to reflect for
ourselves. Victor Watson (*Reading Series Fiction*) suggests that 'because
Gene Kemp does not provide quotable and conclusive wisdom in an adult
authorial voice, her work can be regarded as slight . . . [her] ability to "do
the voices" of her child characters is both her greatness and her undoing'.[24]
I think children, who are constantly having to make sense of the world,
recognise and relate to the novel's ironies and to Gowie's confused emotions.
No other authorial comment is needed or wanted.

   In the final chapters of the novel, Gowie 'plays chicken' with JJ in front
of a car and 'playing chicken' becomes a Cricklepit craze. Having admitted
he's too 'chicken' to hide in the allegedly haunted school, he ends up there
at night as he tries to escape from the now-released Mark and his gang. He
is discovered by Rosie Lee and then by Mark and friends: they threaten
to set light to the place, but Rosie faces them down and, when the police
arrive, they all hide in the cellar together. The next day Gowie lets the
classroom mice escape and 'the pandemonium in the school grows louder
and louder and LOUDER'.[25]

   In the short Prologue to *Gowie Corby Plays Chicken*, as a family have
breakfast in 'a comfortable room', the father reads from a newspaper: 'Dr
Rosie Angela Lee has been nominated for the Nobel Peace Prize for her
work with children in need throughout the world. . . . If it hadn't been
for Rosie, you probably wouldn't be here now, and I would be in gaol, I
suspect.'[26]

   With no context, the Prologue makes little sense (it is nearly fifty
pages before Rosie Lee makes an appearance), but the first sentence of
the opening chapter may give us a clue: 'I didn't want to go back, but

23. *Gowie Corby Plays Chicken*, chapter 9.
24. Victor Watson, *Reading Series Fiction* (London: RoutledgeFalmer, 2000), p. 203.
25. *Gowie Corby Plays Chicken*, chapter 15.
26. *Gowie Corby Plays Chicken*, Postscript.

then I never do, anyway.'[27] This is the remembering of something that has happened in the past – 'didn't want' (and not 'hadn't wanted') and 'go' (and not 'come'). The father telling a story to his children, perhaps. But then the tense changes – 'but then I never do, anyway' – and the novel has switched to a present-tense, first-person narrative, the aggressive voice of a child 'baddie', the voice of Gowie.[28] At the end of the novel, the Epilogue continues the breakfast table dialogue ('Did they catch all the mice safely?'), so the father is identified as the grown-up Gowie made good, and in a way he has been telling the story; and in a way he hasn't, because everything has been told from the young Gowie's perspective, with almost no adult point of view.[29] And as we ponder the novel's narrative trick, we are treated to another surprise revelation – the unexpected fate of the hapless Heather.

Charlie Lewis Plays for Time (1984), *Juniper* (1986), *Just Ferret* (1990), *Zowey Corby's Story* (1995) and *Snaggletooth's Mystery* (2002)

For me, the third novel in the series, *Charlie Lewis Plays for Time*, is a disappointment. The hardly inspiring plot centres on the arrival of Mr Carter at Cricklepit as teacher of 4F, covering for Mr Merchant who has been injured falling from a ladder, and the main thrust is an unflattering comparison between Carter's 'traditional' teaching method ('Your trouble is you think you're different'; 'This is a language lesson so there should be no talking AT ALL'; 'I can't read this,' said Rocket. . . . 'I didn't ask you to read it. Just copy it for now.')[30] and Merchant's 'child-centred' approach. At the end of term, we are reminded again of the novel's political agenda, when Carter leaves to take up a post at a 'great Cathedral School' and Trish comes out with another joke: 'Listen, Charlie. Cut Education costs. Shoot the teachers.'[31] More interesting is the central character, Charlie Lewis, who suffers from a usually absent mother (a touring concert pianist, who on a visit home responds to Carter's fawning overtures) and an absent father in Australia, and is left in the charge of Hortense, an ineffectual Belgian au pair. Emotionally, rich children can be as deprived as poor children, and Charlie finds sanctuary with the chaotic and impoverished family next door. However, he is a brilliant musician (like Pennington) and much of the action is played out in the compositions that run through his mind

---

27. *Gowie Corby Plays Chicken*, chapter 1.
28. The novel is dedicated 'For All My Baddies'.
29. *Gowie Corby Plays Chicken*, Postscript.
30. Gene Kemp, *Charlie Lewis Plays for Time*, (London: Faber and Faber, 1984), chapter 5.
31. *Charlie Lewis Plays for Time*, chapter 16.

– and when in the final paragraph, true to school-story form, his father arrives from Australia and it seems that his problems may be over, 'The waiting melody crescendos into a mad finale as I run to open the door.'[32]

With *Juniper* (1986), Kemp is back on terrific form, though this is an intriguing mystery story and most of the action is played out away from school. Juniper's criminal father has disappeared, her mother Ellie is mentally ill, there's no money for food and rent, she has only 'one point five arms' (but no self-pity, 'no handicap-patting, thank you very much')[33] and she may be taken into care. Then Juniper senses that two shady men are stalking her and she has no-one to turn to for help except her school friend Ranjit. The cast is completed by old Nancy, who lives next door and doles out food and comfort; Mr Beamish, the sleazy debt collector; Jake, who makes Juniper go weak at the knees; Juniper's patronising cousins, aunt and uncle; and Tom, the vicious cat, who is a danger to more than birds and mice ('Lord Tom, King Tom, bow down, bow down and grovel, you wets').[34]

Juniper is a more complex novel than its predecessors, something made possible by the shift to an overarching narrator and by the way it can leave the trivia of school behind. There are small time shifts and breath-taking dream sequences that turn into nightmares, like the one about Juniper's cousins Marie and the spiteful Olga, in which Juniper's longing to be whole and beautiful collides with reality: 'She was seventeen and in a garden, full of flowers, sunshine, trees, lawns, fountains and white balconies and shining pools. . . . She was rich and scented and clever and confident and beautiful – and the Juniper that was still the other Juniper knew how clean she felt and was surprised.'[35]

There are allusions to other texts: Mr Beamish is 'straight out of a story by Dickens or Joan Aiken';[36] the previous winter 'had been just like *The Long Winter* in *The House on the Prairie* series';[37] Juniper's secret path, which runs behind the house, is likened to the road in Rudyard Kipling's poem ('And now you would never know / There was once a road through the woods.');[38] and the carol playing in the cathedral has a chill beneath the triumphant birth ('Now the holly bears a berry as black as the coal' and 'a berry as blood it is red').[39] There are also particular debts to folk

---

32. *Charlie Lewis Plays for Time*, chapter 16.
33. Gene Kemp, *Juniper* (London: Faber and Faber, 1986), chapter 1.
34. *Juniper*, chapter 1.
35. *Juniper*, chapter 2.
36. *Juniper*, chapter 1.
37. *Juniper*, chapter 2.
38. *Juniper*, chapter 7.
39. *Juniper*, chapter 9.

tales: Ellie's bedroom, with its 'snakes of beads, shawls and shoes, fans and shells' is 'Aladdin's cave' (Ellie herself, with her 'silver-gilt hair spread over the pillow', reminds of Snow White).[40] And later, Juniper wishes for Aladdin's lamp: 'But, Charlie, there isn't a lamp and I don't know what to do. I'm just so hungry.'[41] The frying pan in which Nancy cooks enormous breakfasts 'must have come from the Fee Fie Fo Fum Giant's Castle';[42] Jake calls Juniper 'Goldilocks' and she sees him as 'a huge, golden bear';[43] and her own name derives from Grimm's 'The Juniper Tree', where the Tree brings good fortune:

> But pretty Margery pitied me
> And laid me under the Juniper tree.

'But,' says Juniper to Ranjit, 'it wasn't like that. It was the other way round. Don't you understand? The song was the wrong way round. And we lived unhappily ever after. Ever after.'[44] And all the time, the mystery is working itself out, and Juniper is like a pawn in a chess game. But when the game ends in the violent dramatic finale, many of the characters turn out not to be what they seem, and as the cathedral bells ring out for Christmas, for Juniper, in spite of everything, it may just be that there will be a 'happy-ever-after' ending.

There are three further novels in the Cricklepit series. *Just Ferret* (1990) is about bullying, with another outsider, Owen Hardacre, or Ferret, at its centre. His mother has gone (Mrs Flint, the teacher, 'sighed crossly as if I'd deliberately lost her somewhere')[45] and his father, Joe Hardacre, an itinerant artist, is usually too busy painting or drinking to take much notice of him. Although bright and resourceful, he can't read or write, and he becomes a victim of Magnus and his gang. But with the help of two unlikely allies, Minty (whose mother is a wacky poet) and the sickly Beany, Ferret stands up to the bullies who steal money to fund their slot-machine gambling and are sly enough to have the teachers thinking they are angels. The novel also makes Kemp's familiar points about teachers and teaching, and although they remain a sub-text (efficient Mrs Flint examines Ferret like 'a small sliced-off bit of louse in a slide under a microscope' and 'Not being able to read doesn't always mean dyslexia. And people aren't quite sure what they mean by it.'), they are a rebuke to the old 'one size fits all' approach

---

40. *Juniper*, chapter 1.
41. *Juniper*, chapter 2.
42. *Juniper*, chapter 3.
43. *Juniper*, chapter 3.
44. *Juniper*, chapter 11.
45. Gene Kemp, *Just Ferret* (London: Faber and Faber, 1990), chapter 2.

to education.[46] In the end, Mr Hardacre confronts Magnus's father, and Magnus's aura and credibility are shattered; Ferret learns to read and write; and Ferret and Minty come to the rescue of a runaway teenage mother-to-be (this added-on sub-plot feels contrived: they are heroes enough without it). The concluding chapter is not in Ferret's voice, but is an extract from 'Minty's Private Book' and does not quite sum things up: 'I fancy Mr Hardacre no end, but so does Mum so that's no good. . . . I did think of Ferret as a boyfriend but he said don't be barmy and ran off as fast as he could. . . . You see it's the teacher, Miss, that makes the difference.'[47]

Zowey Corby and the Black Cat Tunnel (1995) is about the arrival at Cricklepit of posh Lucy and her struggle to fit in (as we have seen in Part III, this is a staple of the girls' school story). It transpires much later that her father has been caught embezzling and has killed himself, and her mother has run off with her father's best friend. So Lucy is left living next door to Zowey Corby in Black Cat Lane, with her grandmother who cannot accept coming down in the world either. The action of the novel is book-ended by two incidents on the railway that runs through Black Cat Tunnel. In the first, Zowey and Lucy manage to remove stones from the line, put there to derail a train; in the second, she and Lucy are attacked by a gang and are in danger of serious sexual assault. Between these, there are a campaign for Cricklepit School to opt out of local authority control (another example of Kemp's political agenda taking over), an attack on Rosie Lee by thugs from the National Front, and a vibrant description of adolescent girls electrified at the Saturday market – 'Lights switched on, music played, my feet zipped, go, go, go, girl, dance, dance as we weaved through the crowds, looking, searching, everybody's looking for something, dreams, adventure, danger.'[48] There is, I think, a sense that *Zowey Corby and the Black Cat Tunnel* might be the last of the Cricklepit series, with the reappearance of Gowie (Zowey's half-brother), with Lorraine, Ruth and Heather still in tow; Rosie Lee; and Mr Tiler (Tyke's father) as a city councillor. The end of the novel is elegiac in tone, with Rosie leaving to work as a volunteer in Africa, Gowie going out with the other girls, and Zowey's Gran lamenting the threat to the old tree: 'It's the end of an era. My Youth gone.'

In fact there was to be one more novel, but a largely disappointing one. In *Snaggletooth's Mystery* (2002), written twenty-five years after *Tyke Tiler*, 'Chief Sir' has retired, Mr Merchant has become deputy head, and

---

46. *Just Ferret*, chapter 3.
47. *Just Ferret*, chapter 17.
48. Gene Kemp, *Zowey Corby and the Black Cat Tunnel* (London: Puffin, 1997), chapter 12. First published in 1995 by Faber and Faber under the title *Zowey Corby's Story*.

Mrs Somers, Tyke's *bête-noir*, has become a hateful chair of governors. Snaggletooth is the editor of *The Cricklepit Chronicle*, which reports on the haunting of Cricklepit School and offers a possible explanation when a flash flood reveals the skeletons of two children who long ago have died from cholera. It is left for the reader to decide whether this 'SCOOP OF SCOOPS'[49] is fact or fiction: 'We tried to bring you the news. We tried to tell you the truth. It's up to you, kids, to decide if the school was haunted.'[50] But the real failure is not only that Snaggletooth comes across as a self-centred poseur ('I, me, moi, Snaggle'),[51] but that the first-person narration no longer has that sharp ear for children's language that characterises its predecessors.

It could be argued that the Cricklepit series is an example of the fashion for issue-based writing in children's literature. Learning difficulty, deprivation, disability, dyslexia, bullying, parenthood, and teachers and teaching: all these are subjects that Kemp views from a child's point of view. But it is when the issues and not the characters are foregrounded, and there is more than a hint of authorial intervention, that the novels are least successful. The triumph of the best of the Cricklepit novels lies in the way that they look at school life – its jokes and its disappointments, its successes and its pain – through a child's eyes and in a child's voice; in the way they stand up for 'the lonely, the lost and the damaged';[52] and in the way that the children manage to win through, often against almost impossible odds.

---

49. Gene Kemp, *Snaggletooth's Mystery* (London: Faber and Faber, 2002), Introduction.
50. *Snaggletooth's Mystery*, Postscript – 'The Last Cricklepit Chronicle'.
51. *Snaggletooth's Mystery*, chapter 13.
52. *Zowey Corby and the Black Cat Tunnel*, chapter 10.

Chapter 15

The Magic Story

Jill Murphy – *The Worst Witch* (1974)
J.K. Rowling – *Harry Potter and the Philosopher's Stone* (1997)

The boarding school made an unexpected but triumphant return in two series that literally imbue it with magic. First were Jill Murphy's eight beautifully illustrated *Worst Witch* stories (1974-2018) for younger readers (aged seven to nine, and mainly girls), which trace Mildred Hubble's career at Miss Cackle's Academy. Second were J.K. Rowling's seven *Harry Potter* novels (1997-2007) for teenage readers, but also read avidly by adults, for whom editions were produced with muted covers. Here I have chosen to discuss the first novel in each series. However, for all the success of these series, it would be misleading to argue that they signal a rebirth of the boarding-school story; rather they look back to the boarding-school story and use its setting, themes and images to provide the foundation for a different kind of fantasy.

Jill Murphy – *The Worst Witch*

The conventional school story, with its accounts of the triumphs and disasters of boarding-school life, offered little of appeal to the post-1960s reader. But a school for witches, which is the setting for Jill Murphy's *The Worst Witch*[1] (1974), could combine the traditional subjects of battles

---

1. Jill Murphy, *The Worst Witch* (London: Allison and Busby, 1974). Later editions published by Puffin.

with teachers and night-time escapades, of loyalty and friendship, with
an almost gothic fantasy of castles, witches and wizards. Miss Cackle's
Academy was inspired by Murphy's own school, the Ursuline Convent
in Wimbledon: 'I was being taught by nuns in long black robes, and you
couldn't see anything except their faces. The school had lots of creepy
corridors and we would be muttering about the teachers, something like,
"we can't stand Mother Joseph", and she would suddenly appear behind
you.'[2] It is just the sort of place for children to go in their imagination,
full of fun, laughter and apprentice witches, and just that little bit scary:
'It looked more like a prison than a school, with its gloomy grey walls and
turrets. . . . Everything about the school was dark and shadowy'.[3] Miss
Cackle is a kindly but very traditional headmistress; Miss Hardbroom
is the strictest of teachers with a habit of disappearing, but not without
a flicker of kindness; and Mildred Hubble, well-meaning but always in
trouble, is an endearingly scatty central character who in the final chapter
saves the Academy from disaster. Mildred is based on Murphy's younger
self: 'I was tall and thin with black plaits and golden freckles and I couldn't
do anything.'[4]

Instead of dreary lessons in physical education, the girls in form I have
to learn to ride broomsticks (Mildred's is held together by sticky tape after
a crash) and teach their kittens to ride as well. Mildred's kitten, Tabby, is
unreliable too and, unable to balance, ends up being carried in a school
bag. When Mildred is mocked for her incompetence by the snobbish
Ethel, Miss Hardbroom's favourite, Mildred turns her into a pig. There
is a lesson on the making of laughing potions, in which Mildred and
her friend Maud make themselves invisible by mistake. Then there is
the form I formation display, in which Ethel lends Mildred her spare
broomstick, but, as an act of revenge, puts a curse on it so that Mildred
loses control and the presentation is a disaster. Mildred is so upset that
she runs away, but she comes across twenty witches plotting to take over
the Academy and manages to turn them into snails. In an assembly in
the Great Hall, Miss Cackle congratulates her for her action, grants a
half-holiday in her honour, and calls for three rousing cheers. Even Miss
Hardbroom is impressed and Ethel gets her come-uppance when it leaks
out that it was she, not Mildred, who was responsible for the broomstick
chaos.

2. Jill Murphy, interviewed by Alice Vincent, 'An Oral History of The Worst Witch',
   The Telegraph, 31 October 2014.
3. *The Worst Witch*, chapter 1.
4. Jill Murphy, interviewed by Alice Vincent, 'An Oral History of The Worst Witch',
   The Telegraph, 31 October 2014.

Amidst all this excitement and for all her faults, Mildred is supported by her friends: 'Anyway, she had lots of friends, even if they did keep their distance in the potions laboratory, and her best friend Maud stayed loyally by her through everything'.[5] The girls, in their black uniforms and pointed witches' hats, sing the school song with gusto: 'It was the usual type of school song, full of pride, joy and striving.'[6] And when things go wrong, Mildred stays true to the schoolgirl code, taking the blame that should have been Ethel's. Miss Cackle's Academy is not that different from the Jane Willard Foundation or Malory Towers after all, and Mildred is perhaps Dimsie or Darrell in magical disguise.

J.K. Rowling –
Harry Potter and the Philosopher's Stone (1997)

But if Jill Murphy sprinkled magic dust over the boarding-school story, and a similar idea lay behind Anthony Horowitz's *Groosham Grange* (1988), J.K. Rowling's *Hogwarts* series cast an even stronger spell. Having poured all the traditional ingredients into a giant cauldron, she stirred in her own enchantments. Rowling's spell has not yet been broken: each of the novels has been published in a variety of new editions and languages, and has been turned into a block-buster film; there have also been a stage musical and a welter of marketing material ranging from articles of Hogwarts uniform to an array of different magic wands and the inevitable computer games.

The seven *Harry Potter* novels cover Harry's seven years (from the ages of eleven to eighteen) at Hogwarts School of Witchcraft and Wizardry, set somewhere in the wilds of Scotland. To start with, Harry is an irrepressible Tom-Brown-like boy, full of fun and trouble, but he grows up during his time at Hogwarts and in some ways the series as a whole is about adolescence and 'coming of age'. The later novels do not shy away from the characters' growing sexual awareness: in *Harry Potter and the Half-Blood Prince* (2005), Harry begins a relationship with Ginny Weasley (the younger sister of his friend Ron, and also a Hogwarts pupil), Ron falls for Lavender Brown, and Hermione Granger has strong and jealous feelings for Ron. Nineteen years later, in the Epilogue of the final novel in the series, *Harry Potter and the Deathly Hallows* (2007), Harry and Ginny and Ron and Hermione are both happily married.

The first of the novels, *Harry Potter and the Philosopher's Stone* (1997), tells how Harry, an orphan, arrives at Hogwarts.[7] There he confronts Lord Voldemort, the most evil magician in centuries, who seeks total power

---

5. *The Worst Witch*, chapter 1.
6. *The Worst Witch*, chapter 2.
7. J.K. Rowling, *Harry Potter and the Philosopher's Stone* (London: Bloomsbury, 1997).

and immortality. Voldemort murdered Harry's magician parents, but was unable to kill Harry, who still carries on his forehead a lightning-shaped scar from the attack, and instead was himself disembodied when his curse rebounded. Now he can only exist by inhabiting the body and soul of someone in thrall to him. Dumbledore, the headmaster of Hogwarts and the strong moral voice of the story, later explains to Harry: 'Your mother died to save you. If there is one thing Voldemort cannot understand, it is love . . . to have been loved so deeply, even though the person who loved us is gone, will give us some protection for ever'.[8] After a procession of adventures at Hogwarts, Harry comes literally face-to-face with Voldemort. He is able to prevent him from stealing the Philosopher's Stone, which offers not only the alchemist's ability to turn base metal into gold,[9] but also immortality and, for Voldemort, a way back into his own body and to power. However, although *Harry Potter and the Philosopher's Stone* contains obvious Christian echoes, it is much wider in scope than narrowly evangelical stories like *Tom Brown's Schooldays*, *Eric* and *A World of Girls*. It is, rather, an allegory of good and evil, hate and love, life and death; a story for all faiths and none. Moreover, the dark struggle between Harry and Voldemort is balanced by a lightness of touch and a quirky humour (with a clear debt to Roald Dahl in such delights as 'the Curse of the Bogies'[10] and the 'lumpy grey glue'[11] on Harry's wand after he has extracted it from the troll's nose), and there is a nice balance between the saving of humanity and the winning of the house cup.

At the start of the novel, in suburban Little Whinging, Harry lives in the under-stairs cupboard of his uncle and aunt, Vernon and Petunia Dursley. They have always been sceptical about the magical powers of Harry's parents and resent having to look after their son; at the same time they lavish their own offspring, Dudley, with an excess of gifts and unmerited attention. Dudley bullies Harry (much to his parents' delight), but Harry suffers in silence and his plight goes unnoticed. However, strange things happen around Harry (like the escape of a boa constrictor at the zoo when the glass of its tank simply vanishes) and as his eleventh birthday approaches even stranger things begin to happen. A letter arrives for him, but is intercepted by Mr Dursley. More and more letters arrive, until Mr Dursley is driven

---

8. *Harry Potter and the Philosopher's Stone*, chapter 17.
9. In medieval times alchemists were often known as philosophers. In the American and some other overseas editions of the story, the title was changed to *Harry Potter and the Sorcerer's Stone*, which risks missing an essential dimension. It was a change Rowling later regretted.
10. *Harry Potter and the Philosopher's Stone*, chapter 9.
11. *Harry Potter and the Philosopher's Stone*, chapter 10.

to hide the family at the nicely named Railview Hotel, Cokeworth (where there is another torrent of letters) and then in a shack on a rock out at sea. It is there that Hagrid, the half-giant from Hogwarts, at last manages to deliver Harry's missive, offering him a place at Hogwarts for the new school year. Mr Dursley does his best to stop Harry going, but Hagrid persuades him otherwise. Here is another reworking of the Cinderella myth, with evil foster parents, an ugly and unpleasant cousin, and a fairy godmother disguised as someone quite different.

New School

So begin Harry's preparations for Hogwarts. Hagrid takes him to buy his school uniform, though the list is hardly conventional – black robes, pointed hat, wand and cauldron. In London they enter a seedy pub, The Leaky Cauldron, part of the wizard world that ordinary people – 'muggles' – are unable to see. Inside, Harry is treated as a celebrity (his survival of Voldemort's attack is legendary), not least by the pale and stammering Professor Quirrell, Hogwarts's Professor of the Dark Arts ('They say he met vampires in the Black Forest and there was a nasty bit o' trouble with a hag – never been the same since').[12] Hagrid takes him through the courtyard, where the entrance to Diagon Alley opens up – a literally magical place, with shops selling cauldrons, owls, broomsticks, robes, spell books and potions. He buys his uniform in Madam Malkin's (where he meets Malfoy, an unpleasant snob and a bully, dismissive of servants and of the 'other sort' – class division seems to infect Hogwarts as much as any Victorian public school); then his books, his cauldron, a supply of ingredients, and a wand that chooses him, rather than the other way about.

A month later, at the beginning of September, Harry's journey to Hogwarts has all the hallmarks of the boarding-school story – though it is a journey to a world even more apart. It is like Alice going through the looking glass or the Pevensie children going through the wardrobe into Narnia (Rowling acknowledges C.S. Lewis's *Narnia* series as a particular influence). Confusingly, Harry is told to report to platform 9¾ at King's Cross station. After a moment of panic, he launches himself into the barrier between platforms 9 and 10, and somehow finds himself looking at a scarlet steam engine – the Hogwarts Express. Owls hoot, there are cats everywhere, and Neville Longbottom has lost his toad; but otherwise, with the banging of trunks, and pupils hanging out of windows and fighting over seats, it could be any conventional school train.

---

12. *Harry Potter and the Philosopher's Stone*, chapter 5.

When they arrive at Hogwarts, Harry suffers from the same nerves as any other new boy. Again, the tired school-story ingredients are transformed into something new and different. The first-years are greeted by Hagrid, who ferries them across a glistening lake to the gothic castle beyond, through the ivy into an underground tunnel and harbour, and then up to the great oak front door where they are greeted by a black-haired witch in green robes. They encounter a procession of ghosts and an annoying poltergeist called Peeves, the portraits on the walls whisper and point, and doorways are hidden behind sliding panels. As at other boarding schools, the pupils are divided into houses, each with its own history and culture, though here the allocation is decided by the 'sorting hat'. Harry is sorted to Gryffindor, which is known for its 'daring, nerve and chivalry'.[13] At the feast that follows, Dumbledore, addresses the assembly, parodying the worthy welcome offered by headmasters and headmistresses to their new charges: 'Before we begin our banquet, I would like to say a few words. And here they are: Nitwit! Blubber! Oddment! Tweak!'[14] The banquet ends with the singing of the school song, whose words fly out of Dumbledore's wand in a golden ribbon.

On one level, Harry feels out of place at Hogwarts. He is unsure of the identity of his parents and, having spent his life with 'muggles', does not have the experience of wizardry that his fellow pupils enjoy. To this extent, he can be compared to scholarship pupils in the conventional school story, always conscious that their background is different and they are somehow unworthy. On another level, however, Harry discovers his fame in the wizard world puts a different pressure on him: he will have to live up to the legend that surrounds him. As Professor McGonagall says with metafictional irony, 'There will be books written about Harry – every child in our world will know his name.'[15]

Friendship and Bravery

But, like so many school stories, *Harry Potter and the Philosopher's Stone* is, among other things, about friendship and bravery. Harry immediately makes friends with red-haired Ron Weasley, and on Hallowe'en, when they save Hermione Granger, the class swot, from the giant troll, and she unexpectedly lies to get them out of trouble, she becomes their friend too. Neville, clumsy and nervous, tags along with them. Set against them are the bully Malfoy and his bodyguards, Crabbe and Goyle. When, in their

---

13. *Harry Potter and the Philosopher's Stone*, chapter 7.
14. *Harry Potter and the Philosopher's Stone*, chapter 7.
15. *Harry Potter and the Philosopher's Stone*, chapter 1.

first lesson on riding broomsticks, Malfoy steals Neville's 'Remembrall' and refuses Harry's demand that he return it, Harry chases him into the sky ('No Crabbe and Goyle up here to save your neck, Malfoy')[16] and in a daring manoeuvre retrieves the glittering ball. Later Ron will turn on the taunting Malfoy, blackening his eye (while Neville attacks Crabbe and Goyle with rather less success), and Malfoy will show his essential cowardice when Hagrid leads them into the Forbidden Forest.

When the novel nears its climax, and Harry is in a race to reach the Philosopher's Stone before Voldemort, Hermione and Ron insist on accompanying him in spite of the danger. Neville tries to stop them – their adventures have lost enough house points for Gryffindor already – but Hermione casts a disabling spell on him. Having charmed Fluffy, a massive dog with three heads, with music, they drop through the trapdoor, where they encounter a succession of traps laid by their professors. After escaping the Devil's Snare (a plant that wraps its tendrils round them), they have to catch a flying key to unlock the door to the next chamber. Here they have to win a chess match to proceed further, only to discover a huge troll has been knocked out by someone who has arrived before them. Finally they have to solve a riddle that will tell them which one of seven bottles (some poisoned) they should drink to protect them from the black flames burning in the next doorway. It is Ron who sacrifices himself in the chess game to allow Harry to go on. He is prepared to demonstrate the greatest love, to die if necessary for his friends: ' "That's chess!" snapped Ron. "You've got to make sacrifices. I'll make my move and she'll take me – that leaves you free to checkmate the king, Harry!" '[17] And it is Hermione who creates the fire that releases the grip of the Devil's Snare and who solves the riddle of the bottles. She accepts that, for all her intelligence, there are more important things in life: 'Books! And cleverness: there are more important things – friendship and bravery and – oh Harry – be *careful*.'[18] It could be Squire Brown speaking.

Quidditch and Classroom

Harry's skill in the aerial duel with Malfoy leads to his selection for Gryffindor's Quidditch team. Quidditch is an important part of life at Hogwarts, replicating the centrality of sport in school stories. It is something like basketball on broomsticks, but played with a red ball called a 'Quaffle' and with three hoops at either end; it is complicated by large balls called

16. *Harry Potter and the Philosopher's Stone*, chapter 9.
17. *Harry Potter and the Philosopher's Stone*, chapter 16.
18. *Harry Potter and the Philosopher's Stone*, chapter 16.

'Bludgers', which fly around trying to knock the players off their sticks, and by the tiny 'Golden Snitch', whose catching brings the game to an end and is worth so many points that it usually results in victory. A whole chapter is devoted to the house match between Gryffindor and Slytherin, but it is a livelier affair than the cricket and rugby matches of earlier school stories, cleverly brought to life by a politically incorrect commentary. Harry is so nervous that he cannot eat before the match. He nearly catches the Snitch, but is thwarted by a foul block by a Slytherin player. Then he loses control of his broomstick and it is Hermione who appears to see what is happening. Snape has fixed his eyes on Harry and is muttering under his breath. With Ron in tow, she rushes towards Snape and sets his cape on fire, knocking over Quirrell in the process. The spell is broken and, like a *Boy's Own* hero, Harry recovers enough to catch the Snitch (in his mouth) and the game is won.

But lessons, which are usually and understandably neglected in school stories, also get their share of attention. At Hogwarts, as at Miss Cackle's Academy, the curriculum has its own fascination – casting spells with Professor Flitwick, riding broomsticks with Madam Hooch, and learning about the Dark Arts with Professor Quirrell, all hold more interest than construing Latin texts. In the cold dungeons, where Professor Snape teaches Potions, there are pickled animals floating in glass jars, and there is still more creepiness in Snape's mesmerising introduction to his new pupils, with its haunting alliterations: 'I don't expect you will really understand the beauty of the softly simmering cauldron with its shimmering fumes, the delicate power of liquids that creep through human veins, bewitching the mind, ensnaring the senses.'[19] There are a powerful sleeping potion, the Draught of Living Death, dried nettles, crushed snake fangs, and Malfoy stewing slugs; and the lesson comes to an end when Neville mistakenly adds porcupine quills before taking his cauldron off the heat, creating a liquid that covers him in boils.

Face to Face with Voldemort

But the suspense of the novel comes from the efforts of Harry and his friends to thwart the stealing of the Philosopher's Stone. From the moment that Hagrid picks up the Stone from Gringott's bank in Diagon Alley, it is clear something is amiss, and Snape's continual persecution of Harry suggests it is he who is trying to steal it. The warnings begin to add up: on a midnight expedition, when Harry is to meet Malfoy in a wizard's duel, the trio find themselves in the forbidden corridor on the

19. *Harry Potter and the Philosopher's Stone*, chapter 8.

third floor where Fluffy is guarding a trapdoor; Harry overhears Snape talking to Quirrell about the Stone in the Forbidden Forest, and Harry and Malfoy see a hooded figure drinking unicorn's blood – blood that will keep him alive long enough to capture the Stone; Hagrid reveals how in the local pub, in return for a dragon's egg, he told a hooded figure how to get past Fluffy; and Dumbledore, the one person who can protect the Stone, receives a message calling him away to the Ministry of Magic in London.

So, in the final expedition to thwart Snape, and after the snares have been avoided, Harry reaches the last chamber, which harbours the Philosopher's Stone and his adversary. To his astonishment, he comes face to face with Quirrell, not Snape:

> 'But Snape always seemed to hate me so much.'
>
> 'Oh, he does,' said Quirrell casually, 'heavens, yes. He was at Hogwarts with your father, didn't you know? They loathed each other. But he never wanted you *dead*.'[20]

Quirrell, on the other hand, has encountered Voldemort during his travels (rather than the vampires in the Black Forest) and has been suffering in his service ever since. Now Harry and Quirrell are in a fight to capture the Stone and the secret lies in the Mirror of Erised, which reveals what the person who looks into it most desires.[21] Harry can see the Stone in the Mirror, and Quirrell cannot, because Harry's desire is to find the Stone but not to use it. His reflection winks at him and he finds that the Stone has been moved magically from the Mirror into his pocket.

Quirrell unwraps his turban, and on the back of his head is a hideous face. It is Voldemort demanding the Stone. Urged on by Voldemort, Quirrell tries to stop Harry escaping, but Harry is still protected by his mother's love, and when Quirrell touches him it is he who burns and howls in agony. At the same time, Harry feels a searing pain in the scar inflicted by Voldemort in his infancy: 'the pain in Harry's head was building – he couldn't see – he could only hear Quirrell's terrible shrieks and Voldemort's yells of KILL HIM! KILL HIM! and other voices, maybe in Harry's own head, crying, "Harry! Harry!" '[22] The 'other voices' are, in fact, the voice of Dumbledore, who has returned just in time to rescue him.

After three days in hospital at Hogwarts, Harry wakes up and learns from Dumbledore all that has happened and that the Philosopher's Stone, with its promise of riches and eternal life, has been destroyed:

---

20. *Harry Potter and the Philosopher's Stone*, chapter 17.
21. 'Erised' is, of course, 'Desire' reversed.
22. *Harry Potter and the Philosopher's Stone*, chapter 17.

After all, to the well-organised mind, death is but the next great adventure. You know, the Stone was really not such a wonderful thing. As much money and life as you could want! The two things most humans would choose above all – the trouble is, humans do have a knack of choosing precisely those things that are worst for them.[23]

Here, in an echo of J. M. Barrie's *Peter Pan* ('To die will be an awfully big adventure'), is one of the conclusions to which the novel has been heading.[24] If captured, the Philosopher's Stone would have offered Voldemort a way back from his half-life, but for humankind money and immortality are gods not to be chased, and death, the gateway to 'the next great adventure', is nothing to be feared. When interviewed in 2006, as the *Harry Potter* series was drawing to a close, Rowling said, 'My books are largely about death. They open with the death of Harry's parents. There is Voldemort's obsession with conquering death and his quest for immortality at any price, the goal of anyone with magic. I so understand why Voldemort wants to conquer death. We're all frightened of it.'[25] Although *Harry Potter and the Philosopher's Stone* does not shy away from death, and there is no reference to a specifically Christian afterlife, there remains the reassuring suggestion that it may not be the last full-stop.

Harry is well enough to be allowed to attend the end-of-term feast, where all the punishments handed out to Harry and his friends for their various escapades mean Slytherin will win the cup for the seventh consecutive year and Gryffindor will come last. But Dumbledore is standing up and adding more points – to Ron, for the best-played chess game; to Hermione, for coolness in the face of fire; to Harry himself for outstanding courage. Thus the scores of Slytherin and Gryffindor are tied, and Dumbledore has one more announcement: ' "There are all kinds of courage," said Dumbledore, smiling. "It takes a great deal of bravery to stand up to our enemies, but just as much to stand up to our friends. I therefore award ten points to Mr Neville Longbottom." '[26] So Gryffindor is triumphant and, in another of the novel's conclusions, courage has triumphed after all and it is the best evening of Harry's life. The next day he is on the Hogwarts Express, heading back to the real world and the Dursleys for the summer holiday, buoyed by the thought of breaking one rule and using his magic on the dreadful Dudley. It will be fun, in spite of everything.

23. *Harry Potter and the Philosopher's Stone*, chapter 17.
24. J.M. Barrie, *Peter and Wendy* (1911), chapter 8.
25. J.K. Rowling, interviewed by Geordie Greig: 'There would be so much to tell her. . .', *The Telegraph*, 10 January 2006.
26. *Harry Potter and the Philosopher's Stone*, chapter 17.

*

Despite their huge popularity, the Harry Potter novels have had a mixed reception from critics (which seems to have much to do with their debt to school stories). For example, Deborah Loudon writes:

> Hogwarts is a creation of genius, allowing Joanne Rowling to combine her story about magic with all the classic ingredients of the best school stories, not least an inspired school game, Quidditch, which gives rise to some of her funniest and most exciting passages. . . . The ingredients of Rowling's success are traditional – strong plots, engaging characters, excellent jokes and a moral message which flows naturally from the story.[27]

However, Anthony Holden argues almost exactly the opposite:

> Essentially patronizing, very conservative, highly derivative, dispiritingly nostalgic for a bygone Britain which only ever existed at Greyfriars and St Trinian's. . . . Why, in the weariest tradition of English children's literature from *Tom Brown's Schooldays* on, did she [Rowling] have to send Harry to a neo-Dotheboys Hall, complete with such arcane rituals as weirdly named hierarchies and home grown sports with incomprehensible rules?[28]

My own judgement lies somewhere in between. For me, for all its magic, *Harry Potter and the Philosopher's Stone* is very much in the tradition of the conventional school story. The action bubbles along merrily or darkly, the suspense is maintained, and the identity of Harry's real adversary is a neat twist at the end. But it is a weakness that the action is so concentrated on Harry and his immediate friends and enemies that there is little sense of the wider life of the school (except for in the set-piece feasts at the beginning and end of the novel). Sometimes there is an excess of description and an overuse of cliché. The minor characters may border on caricature, but within the parameters of the story they are engaging and credible. Their personalities and places are summed up in their almost Dickensian names: Dumbledore and Voldemort; Snape and Quirrell; Hagrid and Filch; Weasley, Malfoy, Crabbe and Goyle; Dursley and Little Whinging (in Surrey); and throughout there is a delight in the sound of words and an endless procession of puns and onomatopoeia. Above all, I think it is a shame that, like all the *Harry Potter* novels, *Harry Potter and the Philosopher's*

27. Deborah Loudon, 'At Hogwarts', in *The Times Literary Supplement*, 18 September 1998.
28. Anthony Holden, 'Why Harry Potter doesn't cast a spell over me', in *The Observer*, 25 June 2000.

Stone has been castigated as anti-Christian and a celebration of witchcraft, since the reverse is nearer the truth. In this first novel, Harry may have his flaws, but he not only stars in sport, passes his exams, stands up to bullies, and is loyal to his friends, like the schoolboy heroes of old, but he is also brave enough to fight the powers of evil, nearly at the cost of his own life. In subsequent novels, there are greater battles and greater sacrifices (and perhaps too many complexities), though Harry's resolve always to follow the right path and not the easy path means that in the concluding volume, *Harry Potter and the Deathly Hallows* (2007), at the Battle of Hogwarts, Voldemort and the tyranny that he represents are finally overcome.

Chapter 16

The Subversive School Story
Andy Mulligan – *Ribblestrop* (2009)

Millie Roads, the hero of Andy Mulligan's *Ribblestrop* (2009), is one of the great characters of the school story. *Ribblestrop* has a different kind of magic from the Harry Potter novels and challenges as much as uses the model of the conventional boarding-school model. At a time when schools are too often in thrall to league-table success, it warns that excitement is being driven out of learning and, as educational fashion comes full circle, that the idea of character-building may have receded too far. It is both outrageously and wickedly funny, and darkly sinister, and it is remarkable that it has not achieved the recognition it deserves. There are two sequels: *Return to Ribblestrop* (2011 – winner of *The Guardian* Children's Fiction Prize) and *Ribblestrop Forever* (2013).

Although things are done very differently at Ribblestrop Towers, the novel begins conventionally on yet another school train. Twelve-year-old Sam Tack, in an oversized uniform (he'll grow into it), is about to embark on 'the biggest adventure of his life', though is so accident-prone that he will spend most of his first term suffering from concussion. It is just unfortunate that he seems to have been recruited under false pretences:

> 'It is a real school isn't it? We saw the brochure and we thought it looked quite posh.'
> 'Yes. I saw that. It's called "marketing", Sam.'[1]

1. Andy Mulligan, *Ribblestrop* (London: Simon and Schuster, 2009), chapter 1.

On the platform, Sam meets up with Jacob Ruskin (round, jolly and intelligent, he is a singing scholar even though he can't sing a note) and is concussed by Ruskin's knee as he is helped into the carriage; on the train, he meets another new pupil, Millie Roads (which is a surprise, since until now Ribblestrop has been a boys' school). Millie, aged thirteen, an arsonist and a thief, has been excluded from what remains of her previous school after she set fire to it (the pillow said it met fire safety standards, but it didn't) and her fees are being paid by the government. It is not surprising she is endlessly resourceful. We also learn of two more pupils who have left Ribblestrop the term before: Miles, another arsonist, who succeeded in burning much of it down, and Tomaz, an orphan, who has simply disappeared.

The fun begins at Reading station after Ruskin has spilled tea over Sam's shorts (' "Reading," said Millie. 'Can you imagine living here? . . . Set fire to the place, that's what I'd do" ').[2] When Ruskin attempts to dry the shorts by hanging them out of the toilet window, he succeeds only in dropping them onto the track. Millie, taking charge of the situation, pulls the emergency lever and, as the train shudders to a halt, the three pupils jump down (a reminder, perhaps, of the opening of Forest's *Autumn Term*). Dodging the 11.14 from Paddington, they disappear into shrub land and take a taxi into town. Sam is bought new shorts and Millie goes off on a spending spree, financed by the credit card she has taken from an old lady's handbag. To round off the afternoon, they take another taxi to Benders, a wine bar for the rich and famous – where a fourth Ribblestrop pupil, Sanchez, is enjoying a meal with his gangster father. As Ruskin runs towards his friend, he is mistaken for an assassin – tables are overturned, Ruskin is floored by a karate dive and a bodyguard rakes the room with his machine gun. The error is soon sorted out amid gales of laughter and, after drinking too much champagne, the children head for Ribblestrop in the Sanchez helicopter, with Sam reflecting on the day with delicious understatement: 'All in all, despite the bruises, the day had been rather good. . . . And he still hadn't cried.'[3] As they swoop downwards, he sees the school for the first time. The description of the half castle, half mansion, with its towers and battlements, and its fluttering flag in black and gold, is a satirical take on almost every school story and on all those real schools whose prospectuses do not exactly portray the truth. ' "My school," whispered Sam.'[4]

Beneath the helicopter, the headmaster of Ribblestrop, Dr Giles Norcross-Webb, is attempting to explain to Lady Vyner, who lives in the south tower in a junkyard of antiques, why the rent has not been paid. Her grandson

---

2. *Ribblestrop*, chapter 2.
3. *Ribblestrop*, chapter 4.
4. *Ribblestrop*, chapter 4.

Caspar, an occasional pupil at the school, sits beside her, aiming a flintlock pistol at the headmaster's head. Ribblestrop Towers has been the seat of the Vyner family since the time of William the Conqueror and Lady Vyner is still clinging to it 'with nicotine-stained fingernails'.[5] During the War, Churchill worked there in a bunker, with an underground train to take him to and from Downing Street, and in the maze of tunnels plans of national importance were hatched and robots developed. Attempts to sell the place have proved futile because Lady Vyner has insisted on keeping rooms there; a donkey sanctuary moved in, failed to pay its debts, and moved out again, leaving behind two donkeys grazing on the tennis courts; the west wing was leased to the monks of the Brethren-of-the-Lost and they too reneged and have moved into a bunker beneath the ruined chapel; so Dr Norcross-Webb has started his school and he has not paid rent either. He once ran a small school in Suffolk, where at a parents' meeting he declared that children learn best underwater – a claim that prompted a vote of no confidence and the flight of his wife and son.[6] Incidentally, if Lady Vyner is to be believed (and why should she be?), he is a former jailbird and his degree is bogus.

Now Dr Norcross-Webb is standing on the terrace welcoming his pupils: Millie – 'I know you from a newspaper cutting'; Sam – 'We're building a dream here, Sam. Are you a dreamer, or a builder?'; a dozen or so orphans, led by Anjoli, formed up in height order, the result of a deal with an orphanage in the Himalayas; and massive Henry, with hairy legs and wrists.[7] And from the highest tower window, Lady Vyner is bombarding the pupils with her tea service and Caspar lobs equally dangerous scones: ' "Pay me my money," wailed a voice.' The tea service lands in the centre of the terrace; a milk jug explodes at the headmaster's feet; and Sam is knocked out again, this time by a Staffordshire teapot that lands on his capless head: 'Blood oozed and formed a puddle. The puddle became a pool. Sam was smiling but his eyes were closed.'[8] With Millie's help, Captain Routon, Geography teacher and chef, sews up Sam's head while cooking a pie. The headmaster, in gown and wellingtons, takes the opportunity to give a lecture on anatomy: ' "Gather round, have a look – can you see the blood congealing?" He sat Sam upright and pointed with a pencil.'[9] With the operation over, and because the heating system does not work, he hands out a tot of rum all round. Then things begin to go wrong.

5. *Ribblestrop*, chapter 5.
6. Summerhill, the progressive school founded by A. S. Neill, is situated in Suffolk. See chapter 11.
7. *Ribblestrop*, chapter 5.
8. *Ribblestrop*, chapter 5.
9. *Ribblestrop*, chapter 6.

The following morning, Captain Routon organises a geography expedition to chart the school grounds. The children get lost and end up in a railway tunnel in the path of an express train. Later there will be other, more successful lessons in which the children learn by doing: ' "When I was at school", said Dr Norcross-Webb . . . , "you had to keep your hands off. . . . I vowed that if ever I was in charge, the children would put their hands on. You can only learn by doing." '[10] The roof for the new dining room is designed by Ruskin, who has made a model of the structure, and when the children mark out their football pitch, 'Pythagoras's theorem was invoked and suddenly the antique words *hypotenuse, perimeter, circumference* transformed themselves to boundaries, centre-spots and penalty areas.'[11]

Meanwhile Millie has wandered off and finds herself in a sinister laboratory in the out-of-bounds cellars, surrounded by animals whose skulls have been broken open and who are victims of the most gruesome experiments. Two men enter – one a policeman – and set up a dentist's chair. Millie hides in a freezer, whose lid is slammed shut and, as the air runs out, she loses consciousness. Somehow she is freed; somehow, in trying to escape from the cellars, she pulls a lever, and her schoolmates tumble on top of her from the railway tunnel at the moment the express thunders past. The next day the policeman – Inspector Cuthbertson – visits Ribblestrop Towers, extracting hush money from the headmaster and warning Millie to stay above ground in the future. Predictably, she ignores his threats, and the cellars (which have secret entrances via a lift in the headmaster's study, a statue in the grounds, and a telephone box in the road outside) become the main focus of the action.

Two new members of staff arrive, representing, in their respective wacky and sinister ways, all that is good and bad in education, though that is not immediately apparent. Professor Clarissa Worthington, Zoologist, Astrologist and Meta-physicist, and an old friend of the headmaster, arrives with a truck piled high with equipment and, with the help of the well-drilled army of orphans, constructs her laboratory in the north tower, intent on harnessing the power of the universe. For Millie, the equation of animal experiments and a crackpot scientist, spells danger. 'This isn't right. . . . This isn't a school,' she thinks, as Professor Worthington's fireworks explode across the night sky, and the headmaster shows her to the girls' dormitory, which turns out to be a garden shed, with a small bed among the spades, the pitchforks and the lawnmower.[12]

---

10. *Ribblestrop*, chapter 15.
11. *Ribblestrop*, chapter 17.
12. *Ribblestrop*, chapter 15.

It is immediately obvious to Millie that Miss Hazlitt, the new deputy head – white face, black dress, shifting dentures, wig, rasping voice, and 'lipstick as red as a wound' – is the old lady whose credit card she stole on the train.[13] Miss Hazlitt is some kind of government agent, installed because Ribblestrop has lost its licence as a school, and she represents everything that is the school's antithesis: health and safety, dress-code, timetable, no make-up or jewellery, rule books (three), administration, discipline, bells, punctuality, surveillance, diet, even appropriate medication. 'Wow,' says Millie. 'What a cow.'[14] But she does not yet recognise the threat, the danger and the madness.

From here, both the plot and the humour become more threatening. Millie and Sanchez go back into the cellars and discover a child's body in the dentist's chair – 'the top of the skull had been removed and, sitting there ripe and raw, like a brightly coloured dessert, was the child's brain'.[15] It is a model of the disappeared Tomaz, but why? An underground train arrives and Cuthbertson alights with an elderly white-coated scientist called Jarman and others who seem to be government representatives. Jarman explains his chilling project, apparently financed by the government, that also, it seems, has arranged the Himalayan orphans as guinea pigs, and doubtless Tomaz before them. It is all about control; about intervening in the brain with corrosives; about destroying the instinct to challenge, question and rebel; about burning out *ego* and turning children into robots. However, the government has run out of patience and Jarman must operate on a real child without further delay. With Tomaz gone, Anjoli is to be the victim.

Back above ground, Millie is trying to figure things out. Who, exactly, is Jarman? And where does Professor Worthington fit in? In her escape from the laboratory she has left her tie behind; she knows too much and must be silenced. She is locked in her dormitory, which is set alight – Captain Crouton is horribly burned trying to rescue her, but inexplicably she is not inside. She fights with Inspector Cuthbertson in the lake and runs to the telephone box to call for help. Cuthbertson gives chase, fixing her in his headlights, watching her dialling desperately and knowing she won't get through. Then there are more twists and turns: Miss Hazlitt's stolen briefcase; Tomaz's enchanting underground home; the orphans welding the gates of Ribblestrop Towers so no-one can escape; Anjoli strapped in the dentist's chair ('Everyone ready,' says Jarman. . . . 'I'll create perfection with just five little holes')[16] and Millie

---

13. *Ribblestrop*, chapter 18.
14. *Ribblestrop*, chapter 19.
15. *Ribblestrop*, chapter 30.
16. *Ribblestrop*, chapter 45.

captured to be the next victim; mad car chases; another train crash in the tunnel; and Hazlitt turning out to be Jarman himself (' "It's her," said Millie. "She's him!" ').[17] The suspense never falters for a moment.

There are, as well, a rich vein of comedy that runs in parallel and numerous comic high points. One of the novel's most memorable episodes is the celebratory meal after Ribblestrop has lost its first football match against the High School (this being a school story, a football match is essential, and in fact there are two of them). Millie and Anjoli are unrestrained in their attack on the dreadful Miss Hazlitt (though the repeated 'woman' turns out to be nicely ironic): 'Millie flicked, and a line of gunk sprayed over the woman's chest all the way up to her cheek. Anjoli up-ended the bucket and the woman was drenched. A cheer went up, and the hammering of feet and cutlery became a roll of thunder.'[18]

A little later, Ruskin, warming himself with rum and wine while keeping watch for Millie, becomes hopelessly drunk, sees four of everything instead of one, and cannot help himself when Miss Hazlitt hauls him to his feet: 'It came from deep inside, a whole bucketful of rum, pie, vegetables and red wine. Ruskin vomited noisily and the geyser emptied itself over the deputy headmistress's sensible shoes. She danced backwards, slipped in the muck, and ended on her backside.'[19] Such are the moments of vengeance against authority that children instinctively enjoy.

Of course most things end happily. Ribblestrop Towers is allowed to continue trading and, to compensate for all the inconvenience, a mysterious government official hands over a cheque sufficient to pay off all its debts and to cover rent, staff and furniture in the future. It only requires the headmaster to confine any press statements to expressions of relief and to accept that the matter of 'deceased persons heretofore employed' remains under investigation.[20] Inspector Cuthbertson, on leave in the Caribbean, is commended for his exemplary handling of the whole situation. Aided by half-time coaching from Mr Tack, the return football match with the High School produces a heroic victory greeted by a roll of thunder (*Roy of the Rovers* stuff, but this time it is Sam and Anjoli). In the ensuing storm, pupils and staff gather in Professor Worthington's 'Tower of Science' and are literally electrified by the lightning, sparking, buzzing, and glowing as, metaphorically, they should and 'Life is Dangerous' is accepted as the new school motto. The end-of-term newsletter, which is as disingenuous as the prospectus, reports on an 'eventful term' of 'spectacular achievements',

---

17. *Ribblestrop*, chapter 47.
18. *Ribblestrop*, chapter 25.
19. *Ribblestrop*, chapter 32.
20. *Ribblestrop*, Epilogue I.

boasts that the children 'have developed their skills as drivers, welders and marksmen', and reminds them of the need of a flower-press for the Spring curriculum.[21]

Of course it is Millie who has led Ribblestrop Towers to victory over the dark plots (as well as in the football), but in the Epilogue she cuts a more fragile figure, and the depth of her characterisation is among the novel's chief strengths. Beneath the tough exterior, she is a frightened and lost thirteen-year-old: 'I was scared in the wood, Sanchez. I was scared when Tomaz got me, I thought he was going to kill me. I was so scared looking for Anjoli. . . . I was really scared when they were getting ready to drill him. . . . I'm scared now.'[22] As Sanchez talks excitedly about his Christmas holiday, she has nowhere to go. Her father is in Germany; her mother is away; she has been told to check into a hotel. Isn't that why she is an arsonist and a thief? And isn't it because at Ribblestrop she has found friends and at last belongs that she wants to come back after all? (The novel does not explicitly ask or answer the questions and does not need to.) Finally Millie asks Sanchez whether she can go with him – 'I was hoping you would ask.' In spite of their various fights and disagreements, it is as if there is a special bond between them. When he responds by formally inviting her to fly with him to Columbia, her reply is drowned out by the thunder.

Ribblestrop Towers is an impossible, zany place, staffed by the insane, yet the novel also has a serious intent. Without ever overtly saying as much, Ribblestrop challenges the idea of one-of-a-kind schools, ruled more and more by a nationally imposed curriculum. For all the diversification of the education system, there are still independent schools that fail to take proper advantage of their independence, and academies and free schools that are certainly not free. There are national examinations in which the ability to reproduce the 'correct' response has become more important than creativity and the unconventional answer risks failure.

What Jarman is all about is controlling children and turning them into robots, and he has a shady government machine behind him. He is the vengeful God in *Eric* and the cane-wielding Victorian schoolmasters. He is Blyton's 'nanny-narrator' and Cross's hypnotising 'Demon Headmaster'. He is the horror world of Huxley's *Brave New World* (1932) and Orwell's *1984* (1949), and a trope for the way that education is going. So all power to Norcross-Webb and Millie in their subversion of his agenda. The children's author, Salley Vickers, declares that 'If I had my time again, I would without hesitation send my children to Ribblestrop.'[23] I would hesitate to

---

21. *Ribblestrop*, Appendix I.
22. *Ribblestrop*, Epilogue III.
23. www.andymulliganbooks.com

go that far: there are too many guns, fires and madmen, but the point she is making is clear. Children should not have their spark obliterated, or their desire to rebel and their sense of self taken away. 'Life is Dangerous', but children need to learn how to cope, and too much mollycoddling makes it even more dangerous. It is their right to live life to the full, to learn from success and failure, and above all to have fun.

Afterword

This appreciation of school stories has inevitably been a personal one and I have been fascinated to find out how the stories speak to me after most of a lifetime, from the age of five to sixty-five, spent in education. What can we learn from them about the business of teaching and learning? What (if anything) has been lost over the years, and what warnings and lessons can we take away? How true are these stories, and how far do they reflect (and did they influence) the society in which they were written? Are they still relevant at all? And then, of course, there is nostalgia. How do the stories bring back memories of our own schooldays, whether or not we attended schools like those described in the novels, or perhaps colour our memories so that we only recall the good times of our youth?

Throughout my life I have enjoyed going to school. First I attended a tiny kindergarten, Gay Bowers, run by Miss Brown and her sister, Miss Vera, where I learnt to read and write, add and subtract, and where I fell blissfully in love with another five-year-old called Joanna. When I was seven, I caught the bus each day to Clyde House, a privately owned day school in St Leonard's-on-Sea, Sussex, where the Headmistress also ran the local launderette and smoked with a flashy cigarette holder. Her husband, whom we rarely saw, drove an equally flashy Austin Metropolitan and we thought he was a gun-runner.

At the age of nine, I became a weekly boarder at Westerleigh, a traditional prep school for about eighty boys, also in St. Leonards-on-Sea (until the 1960s, the south coast was awash with such schools). Westerleigh was a large tile-hung house, and its grounds swept down the hill towards the sea that glistened invitingly in the distance. The front hall, with its honours board and fresh flowers, smelt of polish, the dining room vaguely of stale cabbage, and the changing room of wet socks. The kitchen had a large AGA stove, where in winter the porridge cooked overnight, and it was always warm. According to its prospectus, the school fostered 'manliness, self-reliance and individuality' and prepared us boys for 'a life of happiness which is a life qualified and ready to give service to the community'. St Leonards, claims the prospectus, was 'much recommended by the medical profession' (nevertheless, our health was boosted further by large spoonfuls of Virol and Scott's Emulsion, and at breakfast there were halibut oil capsules as well).[1] Westerleigh was run by Mr Jim Wheeler (who had a qualification in Swedish drill and for whom everything was 'very braced up'). My school number, bradded into the soles of my shoes with small brass nails, was 52. The names of the dormitories said much about prep schools: Cornwall, Montgomery, Churchill, Edinburgh and Windsor. The fees were 50 guineas a term. Was it that different from Jennings's Linbury Court?

In September 1963, aged thirteen, stiff-collared and black-jacketed, I moved on to Sutton Valence School in Kent. Looking back, Sutton Valence was the best sort of public school. Its pupils were firmly middle class, many from farming families, and there was a cohort of dayboys, often with scholarships from the Kent County Council. The school had been founded in 1576 and its sense of history and tradition was important: we were going where so many others had gone before, over centuries and not years. There were, for example, the memorials in the chapel, the varnished honours boards in 'centre block', and the annual ceremony when the village paid the school a single red rose as rent for the village green. Status was shown by how many buttons (and in what order) were done up on our jackets and there came the day when we were at last allowed to walk on 'Prefects' Lawn'. Studies were called 'shows', washrooms were 'labs', and bread and butter was 'chuck and grease'. And on special occasions we sang the school song with gusto and pride:

> Nearly four hundred years ago
> An excellent gentleman, Lambe by name,
> Founded a school we all of us know,
> Sure to rise to honour and fame....

---

1. Virol was a malt extract. Scott's Emulsion was a foul tasting, orange-flavoured cod liver oil.

Somehow, unobtrusively, the past mattered and it challenged us. The photograph on our 'dayroom' wall of an Old Suttonian, Sidney Wooderson, small and bespectacled, who for nearly five years from 1937 held the world mile record, suggested just what we might achieve (and now there is a Sports Hall named in his honour).

If it is true (and unfortunately I think it is) that most success in life is still the result of 'connections', we didn't make many connections at Sutton Valence. There was not too much pressure either in those before-league-table days, but we were generally taught well and had countless opportunities outside the classroom. We made friends, learned about tolerance and good manners, and most of us enjoyed ourselves a great deal. It is a sadness that in reinventing themselves over the past fifty years, and reacting to market forces, public schools have embarked on a race to provide the finest of Olympic swimming pools, state-of-the-art theatres, concert halls, and the like, putting fees beyond the reach of all but the very rich.

After university (East Anglia and Southampton), I began my teaching career at Dulwich College Preparatory School (the country branch, in Kent), followed by an unforgettable three years in the palatial surroundings of Stowe School, Buckingham. Then, at the precocious age of twenty-nine, inexperienced and unprepared, I became headmaster of Akeley Wood, at that time an ailing proprietorial prep school of about 150 pupils, adjacent to Stowe. It was just clawing its way into a more enlightened world. It had already started an infant section and become coeducational, and very quickly we said goodbye to the remaining boarders. I stayed at Akeley Wood for twenty-seven years, during which time it developed both a thriving senior department and a sixth form, and expanded onto three sites to accommodate a roll of over 900. It was a relaxed environment, we had a lot of fun, and the academic results were good. We were competitive, but not too much so, and although sport was never an object of worship, we were hugely enthusiastic and a number of pupils went on to represent their country. As Mrs Marshall came to realise after Philippa collapses in *The Fortunes of Philippa*, a hot-house atmosphere benefits no-one in the long run.

Akeley Wood found its own niche. Most of our parents had not been to an independent school themselves, but were dismayed by what the maintained system was offering in their particular locality. We couldn't offer state-of-the-art buildings, but we could offer small classes, good teaching and time. At secondary level, our numbers benefited from the inadequacy of Buckingham's grammar school system, so many eleven-year-olds who just missed out on a grammar school place could still benefit from the academic curriculum which we offered. Our difficulties were in persuading them that they weren't failures and restoring their morale. It is a shame that the current government is still attempting to expand a divisive system, especially since most parents simply cannot afford an independent school alternative.

At Akeley Wood, we had experienced and dedicated teachers who hardly ever left, except to retire. We did not have prefects or hierarchies, remnants of a colonial age, but we believed in a high standard of behaviour and respect one for another. We nurtured talent beyond the classroom, especially in music and art. Two small examples may give more of a flavour of the School. On one occasion, a visiting prospective parent said, 'I'm so glad to see that you care about uniform and smartness,' and after a pause, 'but you don't care too much.' On another occasion, the former Chief Inspector of Schools, Sir Christopher Woodhead, visited Akeley Wood, and discovering that our 'middle school' had an especially efficient headmistress, declared, 'I see that your woolly liberalism hasn't spread everywhere yet.' The only better compliment he could have paid was to say that our 'liberalism' had spread everywhere – but it was a proud moment nonetheless.

I left Akeley Wood when it was bought by the Cognita group of schools, chaired by Sir Christopher. It was time for a change and I could not agree with a philosophy of education that appeared to be more about methods, outcomes and profits than about individual children; nor did I think that the short-term aims of venture capitalism and the long-term aims of schools could enjoy a happy marriage (though how I would have loved the improved facilities that Cognita has since brought).

Serendipity led to an unexpected ten years as a lecturer (and ultimately as a Dean and Pro Vice-Chancellor) at the University of Buckingham. It was a relief not to have to worry about untucked shirts and missing ties, but excuses about late essays were the same as those for not-done homework, and equally unbelievable.

*

I digress, but not, I think, too far. In *From Morality to Mayhem*, I have focused on a selection of stories that over these sixty years have spoken loudest to me. Some themes are never far away (though I have tried not to be too nannyish in pointing them out): the school story as *bildungsroman* and moral tale; its nostalgia and its humour; the relationship between schools and the school story with the wider world, and in particular the effect of Empire and the World Wars; the school story as satire and warning; above all, perhaps, the power of the teacher for good (from Arnold and the young Master in *Tom Brown's Schooldays* to Dumbledore in the *Harry Potter* novels) and ill (Buller in *The Loom of Youth*, Soggy Marsh in *Pennington's Seventeenth Summer*, and the Demon Headmaster, for example).

Looking back on school stories from a twenty-first century standpoint, it is clear that Victorian novels like *Tom Brown's Schooldays* and *Eric*, and their male successors in the first part of the twentieth century, do little more than romanticise an authoritarian and often cruel educational system that thankfully has had its day, and that most girls' school stories are sentimentalised and clichéd accounts of 'jolly hockey sticks', and education for domesticity and social climbing (though in reality the major girls' schools played an important role in women's emancipation). If school stories from before the 1960s are still read, it is usually by adults wanting to relive their own schooldays (but were they really like that?) or because of their value as socio-historical documents.

David Turner's history *The Old Boys* is sub-titled *The Decline and Rise of the Public School* and ironically school stories were inspired by the decline of the public school and were victims of its renaissance.[2] There are some who still view the nineteenth-century public school or the early girls' school as splendid places, but for all their moralising, the novels discussed in Parts I and III mainly paint a different and disturbing picture. In fact, as Turner argues, it is only in the last fifty years that public schools have become centres of excellence – and once they had been changed into civilised, efficient and happy places, they were of less interest to the novelist and school stories nearly died out. Thus P.W. Musgrave's *From Brown to Bunter* is understandably sub-titled *The Life and Death of the School Story*, but his ignoring of the post-Bunter novels misleads him and it is my argument that his announcement of the demise of the school story is premature.[3]

For the moment, then, school stories remain alive, if much less plentiful, and the best of those published recently are well written, lively and relevant. Although some borrow their form and, to an extent, their moral compass from their predecessors, they challenge the status quo in much the same way as more enlightened stories like *Stalky & Co.*, *The Loom of Youth*, and *Evelyn Finds Herself* once did. They believe that children have rights, and celebrate them as 'dreamers' and 'builders'. Pennington, Tyke, Zowey, Juniper and Millie are heroes for our time. *Lord of the Flies* remains as a warning to Norcross-Webb and his ilk of the dangers of a school without rules (though it is ambivalent about whether it is the rules that have created the dangers), but in many ways *Ribblestrop*, with its compromised heroine and for all its eccentricity, stands out as a celebration of individuality and childhood, and as the most enlightened school story of them all.

2. David Turner, *The Old Boys: The Decline and Rise of the Public School* (New Haven and London: Yale University Press, 2015).
3. P. W. Musgrave, *From Brown to Bunter: The Life and Death of the School Story* (London and Boston: Routledge and Kegan Paul, 1985).

When, not too long ago, I edited a book of contributions from headteachers of secondary schools, both state and independent, I was disappointed that so many of the articles turned out to be about management rather than vision:[4] although schools have to be managed, I believe it is only vision that will inspire the next generation. While it is certain that the quality of education in both state and independent sectors has improved immeasurably over the past half-century, I hope that the current drive for league-table success does not take the enjoyment out of learning. I hope that village schools, like Miss Read's, survive and that large schools, with all their wonderful buildings, are able to maintain a real sense of care and community.[5] I hope that independent schools will use their independence to offer an alternative to the juggernaut of conformity and short-term goals that the government continues to drive through the educational system, even as it careers from one new initiative to another. Above all, I hope there is still room for creativity and adventure, and for the young to remain young and be themselves. Of course we can rejoice that schools like Roslyn and Greyfriars no longer exist, but when the mental health of today's young people causes such concern, we should perhaps not rejoice too loudly.

---

4. Julian Lovelock (ed.), *The Head Speaks* (Buckingham: University of Buckingham Press, 2007).
5. Miss Read, *Village School* (London: Michael Joseph, 1955).

Select Bibliography

School Stories

Anstey, F., *Vice Versa* (1882)

Avery, Harold, *The Triple Alliance* (1897)

------ *The Dormitory Flag* (1899)

Bennett, Alan, *Forty Years On* (Leicester: F.A. Thorpe, 1985)

------ *The History Boys* (London: Faber and Faber, 2004)

Berkeley, Humphry, *The Life and Death of Rochester Sneath* (London: Harriman House, 1993)

Blume, Judy, *Tales of a Fourth Grade Nothing* (New York: E.P. Dutton, 1972)

------ *Forever* (Scarsdale, N.Y.: Bradbury Press, 1975)

Blyton, Enid, *The Naughtiest Girl in the School (London: Newnes, 1940)*

------ *The Twins at St Clare's* (London: Methuen, 1941)

------ *First Term at Malory Towers* (London: Methuen, 1946)

------ *Last Term at Malory Towers* (London: Methuen, 1951)

Booth, James (ed.), *Philip Larkin: Trouble at Willow Gables and Other Fictions* (London: Faber and Faber, 2002)

Bradby, G.F., *The Lanchester Tradition* (London: John Murray, 1913)

Braithwaite, E. R., *To Sir With Love* (London: The Bodley Head, 1959)

Brazil, Angela, *The Fortunes of Philippa* (London: Blackie, 1906)

------ *A Patriotic Schoolgirl* (London: Blackie, 1918)

------ *Loyal to the School* (London: Blackie, 1921)

Brent-Dyer, Elinor M., *The School at the Chalet* (London: W. and R. Chambers, 1925)

------ *Jo of the Chalet School* (London: W. and R. Chambers, 1926)

------ *Rivals of the Chalet School* (London: W. and R. Chambers, 1929)

------ *The Chalet School in Exile* (London: W. and R. Chambers, 1940)

------ *The Chalet School Goes to It* (London: W. and R. Chambers, 1941)

Buckeridge, Anthony, *Jennings Goes to School* (London: Collins, 1953)

------ *Jennings Again!* (London: Macmillan Children's Books, 1991)

------ *Jennings at Large* (London: Collins, 1971)

------ *Rex Milligan's Busy Term* (London: The Lutterworth Press, 1953)

------ *That's Jennings* (London: Macmillan Children's Books, 1994)

Chaundler, Christine, *The Fourth Form Detectives* (London: Nisbet and Co., 1920)

Cross, Gillian, *The Demon Headmaster* (Oxford: Oxford University Press, 1982)

Coleman, Brunette, *Trouble at Willow Gables* – see Booth, James, above

Cooper, Giles, *Unman, Wittering and Zigo* (1958). References are to Nelson's
      Dramascript series (London: Thomas Nelson, 1971)

Darch, Winifred, *The New School and Hilary* (Oxford: Oxford University Press, 1926)

Day-Lewis, C., *The Otterbury Incident* (London: Puttnam, 1948)

Delderfield, R.F., *To Serve Them All My Days* (London: Hodder and Stoughton, 1972)

Digby, Anne, *Trebizon* (London: W.H. Allen, 1978) and series (1978-1994)

Ellis, H.F., *The Papers of A.J. Wentworth, B.A.* (London: Evans Brothers, 1949)

------ *The Papers of A.J. Wentworth, B.A. (Ret'd)* (London: Geoffrey Bles, 1962)

------ *The Swan Song of A. J. Wentworth* (London: Hutchinson – Arrow, 1982)

Elder, Josephine, *Evelyn Finds Herself* (Oxford: Oxford University Press, 1929)

Erskine, Rosalind, *The Passion Flower Hotel* (London: Jonathan Cape, 1962)

Fairlie Bruce, Dorita, *Dimsie Moves Up* (Oxford: Oxford University Press, 1921)

Farmer, Penelope, *Charlotte Sometimes* (London: Chatto and Windus, 1969)

Farrar, F.W., *Eric, or, Little by Little* (1852)

------ *St Winifred's, or, The World of School* (1862)

Fielding, Sarah, *The Governess, or The Little Female Academy* (1749)

Finnemore, John, *Three School Chums* (London: W. and R. Chambers, 1907)

------ *His First Term: A Story of Slapton School* (London: W. and R. Chambers, 1909)

------ *Teddy Lester's Chums* (London: W. and R. Chambers, 1910)

------ *Teddy Lester's Schooldays* (London: W. and R. Chambers, 1914)

------ *Teddy Lester Captain of Cricket* (London: W. and R. Chambers, 1916)

------ *Teddy Lester in the Fifth* (London: W. and R. Chambers, 1921)

Forest, Antonia, *Autumn Term* (London: Faber and Faber, 1948)

------ *End of Term* (London: Faber and Faber, 1959)

------ *The Cricket Term* (London: Faber and Faber, 1974)

------ *The Attic Term* (London: Faber and Faber, 1976)

Forster, E.M., *The Longest Journey* (Edinburgh and London: Blackwood, 1907)

Francis, Joy, *Biddy at Greystones* (London: Blackie, 1928)

Golding, *William, Lord of the Flies* (London: Faber and Faber, 1954)

Grant, Mrs G. Forsyth, *The Boys of Penrohn* (1893)

------ *The Beresford Boys* (1906)

Hilton, James, *Goodbye Mr Chips* (London: Hodder and Stoughton, 1934)

Horowitz, Anthony, *Groosham Grange* (London: Walker Books, 1988)

------ *Return to Groosham Grange* (London: Walker Books, 2003). First published as
      The Unholy Grail (London: Walker Books, 1999)

Hughes, Thomas, *Tom Brown's Schooldays* (1857)

------ *Tom Brown at Oxford* (1861)

Kemp, Gene, *The Turbulent Term of Tyke Tiler* (London: Faber and Faber, 1977)

------ *Gowie Corby Plays Chicken* (London: Faber and Faber, 1979)

------ *Charlie Lewis Plays for Time* (London: Faber and Faber, 1984)

------ *Juniper* (London: Faber and Faber, 1986)

------ *Just Ferret* (London: Faber and Faber, 1990)

------ *Zowey Corby and the Black Cat Tunnel* (London: Puffin, 1997). First published
      in 1995 by Faber and Faber under the title, *Zowey Corby's Story*.

------ *Snaggletooth's Mystery* (London: Faber and Faber, 2002)

Kipling, Rudyard, *The Brushwood Boy* (1895)

------ *Stalky & Co.*, (1899)

------ *The Complete Stalky & Co.*, 1929)

Larkin, Philip, *Trouble at Willow Gables* – see Booth, James, above

Leslie, Shane, *The Oppidan* (London: Chatto and Windus, 1922)

Lunn, Arnold, *The Harrovians* (London: Methuen, 1913)

Martineau, Harriet, *The Crofton Boys* (1844)

Martyn, Harriet, *Balcombe Hall* trilogy (1982-1984)

------ *Jenny and the Syndicate* (London: Andre Deutsch, 1984)

------ *Jenny and the New Headmistress* (London: Andre Deutsch, 1984)

------ *Jenny and the New Girls* (London: Andre Deutsch, 1985)

Mayne, William, *A Swarm in May* (Oxford: Oxford University Press, 1955)

------ *Choristers' Cake* (Oxford: Oxford University Press, 1956)

------ *Cathedral Wednesday* (Oxford: Oxford University Press, 1960)

------ *Words and Music* (Oxford: Oxford University Press, 1963)

------ *No More School* (London: Hamish Hamilton, 1965)

Meade, L. T., *A World of Girls* (1886)

'Miss Read', *Village School* (London: Michael Joseph, 1955)

Moore, Dorothea, *The Only Day Girl* (London: Nisbet and Co., 1923)

Mulligan, Andy, *Ribblestrop* (London: Simon and Schuster, 2009)

------ *Return to Ribblestrop* (London: Simon and Schuster, 2011)

------ *Ribblestrop Forever!* (London: Simon and Schuster, 2012)

Murphy, Jill, *The Worst Witch* (London: Allison and Busby, 1974)

O'Connell, Tyne, *Pulling Princes* (London: Bloomsbury, 2003)

------ *Stealing Princes* (London: Bloomsbury, 2004)

------ *Duelling Princes* (London: Bloomsbury, 2005)

------ *Dumping Princes* (London: Bloomsbury, 2006)

Orwell, George, *1984* (London: Secker and Warburg, 1949)

Oxenham, Elsie, *Girls of the Hamlet Club* (London: W. and R. Chambers, 1914)

------ *The Abbey Girls* (London: W. and R. Chambers, 1920)

Peyton, K.M., *Pennington's Seventeenth Summer* (Oxford: Oxford University Press, 1970)

Rattigan, Terence, *The Browning Version* (1948)

Raymond, Ernest, *Tell England* (London: Cassell, 1922)

Reed, Talbot Baines, *The Fifth Form at St Dominic's* (The Religious Tract Society, 1887)

------ *The Adventures of a Three Guinea Watch* (The Religious Tract Society, 1883)

------ *The Willoughby Captains* (The Religious Tract Society, 1887)

------ *The Cock-House at Fellsgarth* (The Religious Tract Society, 1893)

------ *The Master of the Shell* (The Religious Tract Society, 1894)

------ *Tom, Dick and Harry* (The Religious Tract Society, 1894)

Rhoades, Walter C., *A Boy from Cuba* (London: S.G. Partridge, 1900)

Richards, Frank, 'The Making of Harry Wharton' in The Magnet, 15 February 1908

------ *Billy Bunter of Greyfriars School* (London: Charles Skilton, 1947)

Rowling, J.K., *Harry Potter and the Philosopher's Stone* (London: Bloomsbury, 1997)

------ *Harry Potter and the Chamber of Secrets* (London: Bloomsbury, 1998)

------ *Harry Potter and the Prisoner of Azkaban* (London: Bloomsbury, 1999)

------ *Harry Potter and the Goblet of Fire* (London: Bloomsbury, 2000)

------ *Harry Potter and the Order of the Phoenix* (London: Bloomsbury, 2003)
------ *Harry Potter and the Half-Blood Prince* (London: Bloomsbury, 2005)
------ *Harry Potter and the Deathly Hallows* ((London: Bloomsbury, 2007)
Searle, Ronald, *Hurrah for St Trinian's* (London: Macdonald, 1948)
------ *The Female Approach* (London: Macdonald, 1949)
------ *Back to the Slaughterhouse* (London: Macdonald, 1951)
------ *The Terror of St Trinian's* (London: Max Parrish, 1952)
------ *Souls in Torment* (London: Perpetua, 1953)
Seymour, A.E., *A Schoolgirl's Secret* (London: Sampson Low, Marston and Co., 1930)
Smith, Evelyn, *Marie Macleod, Schoolgirl* (Cassell and Co., 1925)
Spark, Muriel, *The Prime of Miss Jean Brodie* (London: Macmillan, 1961)
Trease, Geoffrey, *No Boats on Bannermere* (Heinemann, 1949)
------ *Under Black Banner* (Heinemann, 1951)
------ *Black Banner Players* (Heinemann, 1952)
------ *Black Banner Abroad* (Heinemann, 1954)
------ *The Gates of Bannerdale* (Heinemann, 1956)
Vachell, Horace Annesley, *The Hill: A Romance of Friendship* (1905)
Walpole, Hugh, *Mr Perrin and Mr Traill* (1907)
Waugh, Alec, *The Loom of Youth* (1917)
Waugh, Evelyn, *Decline and Fall* (1925)
Warner, Alan, *The Sopranos* (London: Jonathan Cape, 1998)
White, Antonia *Frost in May* (London: Harmsworth, 1933)
Wodehouse, P.G., 'Some Aspects of Captaincy', in *The Public School Magazine* (1900)
------ *The Pothunters* (London: A. and C. Black, 1902)
------ *A Prefect's Uncle* (London: A. and C. Black, 1903)
------ *The Gold Bat* London: (A. and C. Black, 1904)
------ *The Head of Kay's* (London: A. and C. Black, 1905)
------ *The White Feather* (London: A. and C. Black, 1907)
------ *Mike* (London: A. and C. Black, 1909)

Other Novels, Poems and Plays

Ballantyne, R.M., *Coral Island* (1857)
J.M. Barrie, *Peter and Wendy* (1911)
Brontë, Charlotte, *Jane Eyre* (1847)
Rupert Brooke, 'Peace', in *The Works of Rupert Brooke* (Ware: Wordsworth, 1994).
Burnett, Frances Hodgson, *A Little Princess* (1905)
Carroll, Lewis, *Alice's Adventures in Wonderland* (1865)
Coleridge, Samuel Taylor, *The Ancient Mariner* (1798)
Defoe, Daniel, *Robinson Crusoe* (1719)
Dickens, Charles, *Nicholas Nickleby* (1838)
------ *David Copperfield* (1850)
------ *Hard Times* (1854)
------ *Great Expectations* (1880)
Charles Dickens and Wilkie Collins *The Lazy Tour of Two Idle Apprentices* in *Household Words*, 1857.
Garner, Alan, *The Owl Service* (London: Collins, 1967)

------ *Red Shift* (London: Collins, 1973)

Houghton, Stanley, *The Younger Generation* (London: Sidgwick and Jackson, 1910)

Hughes, Thomas, *The Scouring of the White Horse* (1861)

Huxley, Aldous, *Brave New World* (London: Chatto and Windus, 1932)

Lewis, C.S., *The Chronicles of Narnia* (The Bodley Head, 1949-54)

Mayne, William, *Earthfasts* (London: Hamilton, 1966)

Peyton, K.M., *Flambards* (Oxford: Oxford University Press, 1967)

------ *Marion's Angel's* (Oxford: Oxford University Press, 1979). Republished as *Falling Angels* (London: Methuen, 1983)

Ransome, Arthur, *Swallows and Amazons* (London: Jonathan Cape, 1940)

Shelley, Percy Bysshe, 'Ode to the West Wind' (1819)

Sherriff, R.C., *Journey's End* (London: Victor Gollancz, 1929)

Sherry, Sylvia, *A Pair of Jesus Boots* (London: Heinemann, 1969)

Stevenson, Robert Louis, *Treasure Island* (1883)

Tolkien, J.R.R., *The Lord of the Rings* (London: Allen and Unwin, 1968)

Townsend, John Rowe, *Gumble's Yard* (London: Hutchinson, 1961)

------ *The Intruder* (Oxford: Oxford University Press, 1969)

Trease, Geoffrey, *Cue for Treason* (Oxford: Blackwell, 1940)

Wilson, Jacqueline, *Tracy Beaker* series (1991-2006)

------ *Hetty Feather* series (2009-2017)

Wyss, Johann David, *Swiss Family Robinson* (1812)

Biography, Criticism and History

Annan, Noel, *Roxburgh of Stowe* (London: Longmans, Green and Co., 1965)

Arnold, Matthew, *Culture and Anarchy* (1869), ed. J. Dover Wilson (Cambridge: Cambridge University Press, 1961)

------ 'An Eton Boy', in *Fortnightly Review*, June 1881

Avery, Gillian, *The Best Type of Girl* (London: André Deutsch, 1991)

Baverstock, Gillian, Introduction to Enid Blyton, *The Naughtiest Girl in the School* (London: Hodder, 2007)

Berg, Leila, *Risinghill: Death of a Comprehensive School* (Harmondsworth: Penguin Books, 1968)

Browne, Martin, *A Dream of Youth* (London: Longmans, Green and Co., 1918).

Buckeridge, Anthony, *While I Remember: An Autobiography* (London: David Schutte, 2nd revised edition, 1999)

Cadogan, Mary and Craig, Patricia, *You're a Brick, Angela!* (London: Gollancz, 1976)

Carey, John, *William Golding: The Man Who wrote 'Lord of the Flies'* (London: Simon and Schuster, 2009)

Carlyle, Thomas, *On Heroes, Hero-Worship, and The Heroic in History* (1841)

Cash, Peter, 'Enid Blyton: The Famous Five Books' (English Association Primary Bookmarks 5, 2013)

Davies, Russell, *Ronald Searle: A Biography* (London: Sinclair-Stevenson, 1990)

Dyson, A.E., *The Crazy Fabric* (London: Macmillan, 1965)

Dyson, A.E. and Lovelock, Julian (eds), *Education and Democracy* (London: Routledge and Kegan Paul, 1975)

Hawlin, Stefan, 'The Savages in the Forest: Decolonising William Golding', in Harold Bloom, ed., *Lord of the Flies: William Golding*, Modern Critical

Interpretations series (London: Chelsea House, 2008)

Holden, Anthony, 'Why Harry Potter doesn't cast a spell over me', in *The Observer*, 25 June, 2000.

Hood, Jack, *Heart of a Schoolboy* (London: Longmans, Green and Co., 1919)

Lawson, Harry Sackville, *Letters from a Headmaster Soldier* (London: H.R. Allenson, 1918)

Locke, John, *Some Thoughts Concerning Education* (1693)

Loudon, Deborah,' At Hogwarts', in *The Times Literary Supplement*, 18 September, 1998

Maxtone Graham, Ysenda, *Terms & Conditions – Life in Girls' Boarding Schools, 1939-1979* (London: Abacus, 2017)

Musgrave, P.W., *From Brown to Bunter* (London: Routledge and Kegan Paul, 1985)

Neill, A.S.,*Summerhill* (Harmondsworth: Pelican, 1968)

Orwell, George, 'Boys Weeklies' in *Horizon* (London: March 1940). Reprinted in Orwell, George, *Inside the Whale and Other Essays* (London: Victor Gollancz, 1940)

Parker, Peter, *The Old Lie: The Great War and the Public School Ethos* (London: Constable, 1987)

Quigly, Isabel, *The Heirs of Tom Brown: The English School Story* (Oxford: Oxford University Press, 1982)

Reimer, Mavis, 'Traditions of the School Story', in Grenby, M.O. and Immel, Andrea (eds), *The Cambridge Companion to Children's Literature* (Cambridge: Cambridge University Press, 2009)

Richards, Frank, 'Frank Richards Replies to George Orwell' in *Horizon* (London, May 1940)

Richards, Jeffrey, *Happiest Days; The Public Schools in English Fiction* (Manchester: Manchester University Press, 1988)

Roxburgh, J.F., 'The Public Schools and the Future' in *The Headmaster Speaks* (London: Kegan Paul, Trench, Trubner and Co., 1936)

Seldon, Anthony and Walsh, David, *Public Schools and the Great War* (Barnsley: Pen and Sword Military, 2013)

Trease, Geoffrey, *Laughter at the Door* (London: Macmillan, 1974)

------ *Tales Out of School* (London: Heinemann, 1948; rev. ed. 1964)

Watson, Victor, *Reading Series Fiction* (London: Routledge Falmer, 2000)

Tucker, Nicholas (ed.), *From Bunter to Buckeridge*, 2nd rev. edn. (Lichfield: Pied Piper Publishing, 2003)

Turner, David, *The Old Boys* (New Haven and London: Yale University Press, 2015)

Waugh, Alec, 'The Public Schools: the Difficulties of Reform' in *English Review*, 28 (January-June 1919)

------ *Public School Life* (London: Collins, 1982)

------ *The Early Years of Alec Waugh* (London: Cassell and Co., 1962)

Welch, Julie, *Too Marvellous for Words! – The Real Malory Towers Life* (London: Simon and Schuster, 2017)

Wodehouse, P.G., 'The Tom Brown Question', in *The Public School Magazine*, December 1901

Index

You might also be interested in:

Swallows, Amazons and Coots:
A Reading of Arthur Ransome

By Julian Lovelock

Paperback ISBN: 9780718894368
ePub eBook ISBN: 9780718844653
Kindle eBook: 9780718844660
PDF ISBN: 9780718842789

In 1929, Arthur Ransome (1884–1967), a journalist and war correspondent who was on the books of MI6, turned his hand to writing adventure stories for children. The result was *Swallows and Amazons* and eleven more wonderful books followed, spanning in publication the turbulent years from 1930 to 1947. They changed the course of children's literature and have never been out of print since. In them, Ransome creates a world of escape so close to reality that it is utterly believable, a world in which things always turn out right in the end.

Yet *Swallows, Amazons and Coots* shows that, to be properly appreciated today, the novels must be read as products of their era, inextricably bound up with Ransome's life and times as he bore witness to the end of Empire and the dark days of the Second World War. In the first critical book devoted wholly to the series, Julian Lovelock explores each novel in turn, offering an erudite assessment of Ransome's creative process and narrative technique, and highlighting his contradictory politics, his defence of rural England, and his reflections on colonialism and the place of women in society. Thus Lovelock demonstrates convincingly that, despite first appearances, the novels challenge as much as reinforce the pervading attitudes of their time.

You might also be interested in:

The Making of
Swallows and Amazons (1974)

By Sophie Neville

Paperback ISBN: 9780718894962
PDF ISBN: 9780718845896

In 1973 Sophie Neville was cast as Titty alongside Virginia McKenna, Ronald Fraser and Suzanna Hamilton in the film *Swallows & Amazons*. Made before the advent of digital technology, the child stars lived out Arthur Ransome's epic adventure in the great outdoors without ever seeing a script.

Encouraged by her mother, Sophie Neville kept a diary about her time filming on location in the lakes and mountains of Cumbria. Bouncy and effervescent, extracts from her childhood diary are interspersed among her memories of the cast and crew as well as photographs, maps and newspaper articles, offering a child's eye view of the making of the film from development to premiere – and the aftermath.

You might also be interested in:

From the Dairyman's Daughter to Worrals of the WAAF: *The RTS, Lutterworth Press and Children's Literature*

By Dennis Butts and Pat Garrett (editors)

Paperback ISBN: 9780718830557

A collection of essays based on the Children's Books History Society study conference marking the bicentenary of the Religious Tract Society and the Lutterworth Press. The book analyses the children's literature it produced, charting the development of the genre from the evangelical tract through to the popular school story, spanning the period from the late eighteenth to the mid-twentieth centuries. It shows how publishing worked within the context of a missionary society with a global reach.

The book details the nature and development of the tract genre both in Britain and America, before looking at the range of RTS and Lutterworth output of children's titles, including its movement into magazine publishing. The work studies the two great magazines for which the RTS and Lutterworth were known to generations of children, the *Boy's Own Paper* and the *Girl's Own Paper*, as well as other magazines, such the *The Child's Companion*. There are also chapters on popular tracts, such as *The Dairyman's Daughter*, and successful authors, from Hesba Stretton and Mrs Walton to W.E. Johns and Laura Ingalls Wilder.

You might also be interested in:

Children's Literature and Social Change:
Some Case Studies from Barbara Hofland to Philip Pullman
By Dennis Butts

Paperback ISBN: 9780718892081

While there are many books about children's literature, few discuss it within its social context or investigate the ways writers reflect or react to change in society. Dennis Butts explores how shifting attitudes and historical upheavals from the 1840s onwards affected and continue to affect books written for younger audiences. Spanning the period of the industrial revolution to the sexual revolution, this book reveals the impact that these external events have had on writers as diverse as moral storyteller Barbara Hofland and the controversial Melvin Burgess.

G.A. Henty, Robert Louis Stevenson and Philip Pullman are included in the discussion, as Butts identifies commonalities between books of the past and present, arguing that trends shown in most of the early children's literature are being displayed again now, albeit in a more subtle manner.

This book will appeal to undergraduate students attending complementary courses in children's literature during their degree in English Literature or Cultural Studies. It will also be of use to postgraduate research students working in the field of Children's Literature.

You might also be interested in:

How Did Long John Silver Lose his Leg?:
and Twenty-Six Other Mysteries of Children's Literature

By Dennis Butts

Paperback ISBN: 9780718893101
ePub eBook ISBN: 9780718841942
Kindle eBook: 9780718841959
PDF ISBN: 9780718841935

How did Long John Silver Lose His Leg? is a wonderfully diverting tour through some of the best-loved classics of children's literature, addressing many of the unanswered questions that inspire intense speculation when the books are laid down.

Could Bobbie's train really have stopped in time (*The Railway Children*)? Did Beatrix Potter have the 'flu in 1909, and did this lead to a certain darkness in her work (*The Tale of Mr Tod*)? Would the 'rugby football' played by Tom Brown be recognised by sportsmen today (*Tom Brown's Schooldays*)? Having established the cultural importance of children's books in the modern age, the authors also consider the more serious issues posed by the genre. Why are we so defensive of the idyllic worlds presented in children's books? Why have some of our best-loved authors been outed as neglectful parents to their own children? Should we ever separate the book from its creator and appreciate the works of writers convicted of crimes against children?

A treat for any enthusiast of children's literature, this entertaining book provides rich detail, witty explication, and serious food for thought.